THE ULTIMATE HONDA

Motorcycles

Doug Mitchel

EVERYTHING YOU NEED TO KNOW ABOUT EVERY HONDA STREET BIKE EVER BUILT

©2005 Doug Mitchel
Published by

kp books
An Imprint of F+W Publications

700 East State Street • Iola, WI 54990-0001
715-445-2214 • 888-457-2873

Our toll-free number to place an order or to obtain a free catalog is (800) 258-0929.

All information in this book is complete and true to the best of our knowledge. We recognize that some words, names, model and character designations belong to the holder of the trademark. These are used for identification only. This is not an official publication.

Library of Congress Catalog Number: 2005922949
ISBN: 0-87349-966-2

Edited by Brian Earnest
Designed by Sandy Kent

Printed in the United Sates of America

In memory of Keith C. Paul.

Those who knew him, loved him

CONTENTS

1980-1989

1990-1999

2000-2005

ACKNOWLEDGMENTS

- As always, a project like this could not be completed without the assistance of many patient, talented and willing individuals. They have provided me with not only terrific examples of Honda motorcycles, but reference materials and data that allowed me to create the work you are now reading.

- Harry Boatman at DGY Motorsports, Downers Grove, Illinois

- Mark Pawelski and Michelle Wagner at Fox Valley Cycles, Aurora, Illionois

- John Parham at J&P Cycles, Anamosa, Iowa

- Matt Jonas and his amazing collection of low mileage machines

- Gary Mares and Bob Roche at M&R Cycle Specialist, Inc. Downers Grove, Illinois

- Jeff Carstensen at the National Motorcycle Museum, Anamosa, Iowa

- Brad Niehaus and Bill Burke of Niehaus Cycle Sales, Litchfield, Illinois

- Pete Boody, President of VJMC, North America

- Buzz and Pixie Walneck, founders of Walneck's Cycle Trader

INTRODUCTION

The name "Honda" has become a household word whenever people speak of almost anything that provides convenience and efficiency to a motorized contrivance. The humble beginnings of one man have expanded into a worldwide empire that is embraced by anyone desiring technically advanced vehicles and household products.

Born near the city of Hamamatsu City Japan, Soichiro Honda discovered his interest in mechanical devices at an early age. His youthful imagination saw him creating a car of his own design, and he soon began to put his plans into action. Once grade school was complete he moved to Tokyo to begin work in a small automobile repair facility.

In 1946 he began what would become the precursor of the Honda Motor Company. Using the $2,700 he had saved over the years, Soichiro set up a business to create and develop his own line of motorcycles. His Honda

By utilizing war surplus frames and motors, Soichiro Honda built his first "production" cycles in 1946.
American Honda

*The 1949 Honda
Dream was
one of Honda's
early successes,
and pushed
him to produce
many more
motorcycles in
the following
years.*
American Honda

Technical Research Institute proved to be fertile ground for his technical abilities, and allowed him to expand his reach in the market.

As soon as the pall of World War II had ended, he was able to acquire 500 small motors that he fitted to bicycle frames, thus creating his first two-wheeled machines. This event took place only 1 year after he founded the Honda Technical Research Institute.

His success with the institute and his first motorized cycles paved the way for the formation of the Honda Motor Company, Ltd. Mr. Honda was 41 years of age when he formed the company, but held the dreams of a younger man in his heart. With starting capital of a million yen

A corporate portrait shows a smiling Soichiro Honda, the man who was responsible for the creation of the firm bearing his name.
American Honda

in 1948, he set out to produce his first real motorcycle. By joining forces with a financial guru named Takeo Fujisawa, his two-wheeled company was off and running.

The 1949 D-Type Dream was the child of these labors. The E-Type Cub would soon follow. It was powered by a four-stroke motor, and was the first of its type from Honda. In 1952, only 5 years of being an actual corporate entity, he began exporting his machines to other markets. The new F-Type Cub was a great success and allowed many overseas customers to experience the joy and economy of Mr. Honda's diminutive creation.

By 1959, the name Honda was common-

ly seen in overseas markets, as well as in the winner's circle at races across the globe. The dominance of his machines was growing with every passing year, and the United States had become was of his biggest export destinations. It was June 4, 1959 when the doors were first opened at 4077 Pico Boulevard in Los Angeles. The unassuming building at that address would be the first home for American Honda Motor Company, Inc., where 12 employees began their trek deep into the U.S. marketplace. With a newly minted ad campaign that claimed, "You meet the nicest people on a Honda," the company forever changed the world of mo-

torcycling in America. The management team at Honda believed that the current U.S. manufacturers were not in touch with what American riders wanted in a motorcycle. In the space of less than a year, Honda was outselling all other brands except two. One year later Honda were the top seller in the country, and determined to stay there.

While the roots of the company reach back to 1948, the creation of the American Honda Motor Company, Inc. in 1959 is where our journey will begin.

The C was another 1949 model. Not quite as elegant as the Dream, it still played a key role in the development of future Honda motorcycles.
American Honda

The two-stroke D-type Dream of 1949 is recognized as the Honda's first true production motorcycle. Within two years the company had shifted focus to 4-stroke engines, which were to become indelibly associated with the Honda brand.

The familiar Honda "wing" motif evolved from this early version on the 1949 Dream "D-type".

COLLECTOR BIKE VALUES

This book contains collector values for vintage or antique motorcycles 25 years old or older. These values are estimates based on recent auction prices realized and are strictly "ballpark" figures based on secondary market activity.

The values are taken from *Vintage Motorcycle Price Guide* published by F&W Publications. The six different condition grades are explained in the accompanying scale.

MOTORCYCLE CONDITION SCALE

6 PARTS BIKE: May or may not be running, but is weathered, wrecked and/or stripped to the point of being useful primarily for parts.

5 RESTORABLE: Needs complete restoration. May or may not be running, but isn't weathered, wrecked or stripped to the point of being useful only for parts.

4 GOOD: A drivable motorcycle needing no or only minor work to be functional. Also, a deteriorated restoration or a very poor amateur restoration. All components may need restoration to be "excellent," but the motorcycle is mostly useable "as is."

3 VERY GOOD: Complete operable original or older restoration. Also, a very good amateur restoration, all presentable and serviceable. Plus, a combination of well-done restoration and good operable components or a partially restored motorcycle with all parts necessary to compete and/or valuable NOS parts.

2 FINE: Well-restored or a combination of superior restoration and excellent original parts. Also, extremely well-maintained original motorcycle showing minimal wear.

1 EXCELLENT: Restored to current maximum professional standards of quality in every area, or perfect original with components operating and appearing as new.

EXAMPLE

1959 PRICE GUIDE	6	5	4	3	2	1
C100 Super Cub (49cc single)	600	900	1,350	1,800	2,400	3,000
CB92 Benly Super Sport (124cc twin)	2,400	3,600	5,400	7,200	9,600	12,000
CA95 Benly Touring "early" (154cc twin)	800	1,200	1,800	2,400	3,200	4,000
C71 Dream Touring (247cc twin)	1,300	1,950	2,930	3,900	5,200	6,500
CE71 Dream Sport (247cc twin)	2,400	3,600	5,400	7,200	9,600	12,000
C76 Dream Touring (305cc twin)	1,300	1,950	2,930	3,900	5,200	6,500
CA76 Dream Touring (305cc twin)	1,280	1,920	2,880	3,840	5,120	6,400

1959

Unlike many of the motorcycle builders at the turn of the 20th century in the U.S., Soichiro Honda entered the American market with a bevy of new machines. Of course he began his dream with a single model in 1946, but by the time his company reached the American shores he was armed with a well-stocked catalog of two-wheeled fun. By pitching his wares to a different audience than Harley-Davidson and the other major builders of the day, he hoped to put America on two wheels.

Two different models were released on June 4, 1959, and they would soon be followed by six more before the first year of U.S. operations was complete.

The CA92/C92 Benly Touring model featured 124cc of displacement in a parallel-twin cylinder configuration. The overhead-cam design was a radical departure from most approaches, but proved Honda's urgency to deliv-

The CB92 Benly Super Sport displaced 124ccs, and was a stable platform for those seeking performance from a small machine. American Honda

er machines that met with the public's desires. A single carburetor fed the power plant, which was brought to life at the touch of a button. The electric start was only a part of the complete electrical system found on the fledgling model.

A kick-start lever was also included to allow the rider to be on his way when the battery wouldn't cooperate. A four-speed transmission gave the rider plenty of options when riding on the diverse American roadways. Drum brakes mounted on both wheels provided adequate stopping power. The pressed steel backbone of the frame design allowed for a high degree of stiffness while staying fairly light. The high-tech alloys used on today's machines were not even a theory at this point in history.

1959 would be the only year for the CA92 Benly, but improved versions were soon to follow. As with many of the early Honda models, a "C" prefix was used on a Japanese specification machine that was sold in the U.S. and other markets. The "CA" designation pertained to U.S./North American specification cycles that were also sold in markets outside of America.

The second model to be released on June 4, 1959 was the CA71/C71 Dream Touring 250. This model was powered by a 247cc, parallel twin, overhead cam (OHC) dry sump motor. The CA71 featured tubular chrome handlebars, while the C71 had bars formed from pressed steel. The C71 had a slightly larger fuel tank, but both models had chrome insets on each side of the tank.

Available in White, Black, Blue or Scarlet Red, they were both stylish and highly functional over a variety of riding conditions.

First released on August 1 of the same year, the C100 Super Cub pounced onto the sales floor. These step-through chassis bikes were designed to entice new riders into the world of motorcycling, and were the models featured in Honda's ultra-successful "You meet the nicest people on a Honda" ad campaign. These mild bikes were less intimidating than other big machines of the day, and riders of all ages embraced these new offerings with open arms.

Powered by 49cc, single-cylinder motors, their power was nothing to be afraid of, but

Aggressively sporty despite its pressed-steel frame, the 125cc Benly CB92 of 1959 was the first of Honda's long line of CB Super Sports models. A genuine benchmark in Honda history, this taut little machine is immensely appealing and highly collectible.

The RC160 of 1959 was Honda's first dual overhead-cam four-cylinder 250cc road racer. Raced successfully in Japan in 1959, this precurser to the better-known RC161 was the beginning of a line of four-cylinder DOHC 250cc racers that eventually proved dominant. Surviving examples of vintage Honda racers are exceptionally rare and desirable.

was adequate to get you and a friend around town. Although most of the C100s featured a two-person saddle, some early examples were fitted with shorter solo pillions. Three speeds were available through an automatic clutch, and a kick-starter was the only way to bring the tiny machine to life. A complete set of lights permitted riding during the day and evening hours.

Trimmed in your choice of Scarlet Red and White, Blue and White, Black and White or an all black option, the Super Cub offered plenty of style, too. Returning a claimed 200 mpg, the newly minted C100 was also an efficient way to have fun.

The CA95 Benly Touring 150 bowed on September 1, 1959. With a 154cc parallel

twin motor, and four speeds on tap, this Benly looked and rode more like a real motorcycle than the smaller models. The center of the fuel tank was matched in the color chosen by the buyer, and the sides were trimmed with large chrome panels and small rubber knee pads. A square headlight was wrapped in an enclosure that included the integrated speedometer.

The final drive chain was fully enclosed, and the muffler was delivered with flat sides, but finished in chrome. Blackwall tires and the short rear fender brace help to set the 1959 Benly models apart.

Three additional Dream models also entered the fray on September 1 of 1959. The CE71 Dream Sport 250 featured a 247cc, OHC, dry sump, parallel twin motor, a four-speed transmission and a single carburetor. The fuel tank on the CE71 Dream Sport was always finished in silver, and was fitted with rubber knee pads but no chrome panels. The rest of the sheet metal was painted black or maroon, depending on which color was ordered.

Early examples of this model rolled on 18-inch wheels. Later entries had 16-inch hoops at each end.

Two more entrants for the 1959-year also arrived on September 1. The CA76/C76 Dream Touring 300 models were the biggest kids in the Honda sandbox. Motivation came from a 305cc, OHC, dry sump parallel twin motor that rowed through a four-speed transmission. A single carburetor fed the twin cylinders in efficient fashion. Available in your choice of White, Black, Blue or Scarlet Red, the fuel tanks were all mated with chrome panels inset on each side of the receptacle.

The CA76 featured high-rise tubular handlebars, while the C76 had a set of low-rise, pressed steel bars. Both models featured the square headlights found on other Hondas. The smooth nacelle that was fitted to the lights also held the speedometer.

Last, but not least, the CB92 Benly Super Sport arrived on November 1, 1959. This model met with the needs of quasi-racers everywhere. The 124cc, OHC parallel twin motor stirred a four-speed transmission and sipped fuel through a single carburetor.

A small, clear windscreen was fitted just above the square headlight, adding to the boy racer image. The fuel tank, front fender and side covers were all finished in silver, with a choice of red or blue accent hardware. The red version was mounted to a black saddle while the blue option came with a red pillion. Alloy was used to form the fuel tank, fenders and side covers of the early iterations.

1959 Price Guide	6	5	4	3	2	1
C100 Super Cub (49cc single)	600	900	1,350	1,800	2,400	3,000
CB92 Benly Super Sport (124cc twin)	2,400	3,600	5,400	7,200	9,600	12,000
CA95 Benly Touring "early" (154cc twin)	800	1,200	1,800	2,400	3,200	4,000
C71 Dream Touring (247cc twin)	1,300	1,950	2,930	3,900	5,200	6,500
CE71 Dream Sport (247cc twin)	2,400	3,600	5,400	7,200	9,600	12,000
C76 Dream Touring (305cc twin)	1,300	1,950	2,930	3,900	5,200	6,500
CA76 Dream Touring (305cc twin)	1,280	1,920	2,880	3,840	5,120	6,400

1959 MODELS

Model	Product Code	Engine Type/ Displacement	Transmission	Year(s) Available
C100 Super Cub	001	OHV Single/49cc	3-Speed	1959-62
CA92/C92 Benly Touring 125	203	OHC Parallel Twin/124cc	4-Speed	1959
CB92 Benly Super Sport 125	205	OHC Parallel Twin/124cc	4-Speed	1959-62
CA95 Benly Touring 150	206	OHC Parallel Twin/154cc	4-Speed	1959-63
CA71/C71 Dream Touring 250	255	OHC Parallel Twin/247cc	4-Speed	1959-60
CE71 Dream Sport 250	257	OHC Parallel Twin/247cc	4-Speed	1959-1960
CA76/C76 Dream Touring 300	260	OHC Parallel Twin/305cc	4-Speed	1959-60

1960

It was only Honda's second year of operations in the U.S., but model changes were abundant. With the exception of the CA92/C92 Benly Touring 125 model, the remaining 1959 team was carried over into the new year. 1960 would be the first year for numerous additions and the last year for many more. This trend of short product cycles would continue for many years as Honda wrestled with the product mix to meet with changing market demands.

First in the new model lineup was the CSA76/CS76 Dream Sport 300, which arrived in dealer showrooms January 1 of 1960. Only available for 1 year, these bikes had many features not seen before on a Honda.

Driven by a 305cc, OHC, parallel twin motor, both versions featured a pair of upswept exhaust pipes, one on each side of the chassis. The CSA76 steered with a set of high-rise tubular handle-

December 1, 1960, saw the introduction of the C110 Super Sports Cub into the Honda lineup. A 49cc motor motivated the sporty machine and helped to propel Honda toward a future of superior performance at every level.
American Honda

bars dipped in chrome. The CS76 had a set of painted, pressed steel, low-rise bars to control the cycle.

Both editions shifted through four-speed transmissions and were offered in the usual hues of White, Black, Blue and Scarlet red. Chrome side panels adorned the fuel tanks as well as a set of rubber knee pads.

Another new face for 1960, released on July 1, was the C102 Super Cub. It was identical to the still-available C100 Super Cub, except for the addition of an electric starter. The kickstart C100 was still sold at Honda retailers.

For 1960, the CA71 Dream Touring 250 was joined by the CA72 version on August 1. The CA72 was built with high-rise tubular handlebars and, although the fuel tank was the same shape, it was fitted with chrome panels and rubber knee pads.

A new addition to the family was the CA77 Dream Touring 305, which was released to the dealers on August 1, 1960. Featuring a 305cc, OHC parallel twin motor, and a fuel tank that was larger than the early CA72, the CA77 was ready for the open road. A pair of low-mounted exhaust pipes set the CA77 apart from the CSA77/CS77 models.

Since the CSA76/CS76 was only a single year model, the CSA77/CS77 would step in on September 1 and would run until 1963. The 77 versions were identical to the 76s they were scheduled to replace, but were often shown with whitewall tires.

A late entry in the 1960 lineup was the C110 Super Sports Cub. First available in December of 1960, the C110 was fitted with the same 49cc motor of the C100 and C102, but featured a more traditional motorcycle chassis. The Super Sports Cub did not have a step-through design. It had a standard solo saddle that was devoid of a rear hand strap. The three-speed transmission was also manually shifted, unlike the automatic boxes mounted in the C100 and C102. Color options were all based on a white tank and side covers. Contrasting frame and fender colors were Scarlet Red, Blue and Black.

1960 would be the final year for the CA71 Dream Touring 250, CE71 Dream Sport 250, and the CA76/C76 Dream Touring 300 models. All four had been introduced in 1959.

1960 PRICE GUIDE	6	5	4	3	2	1
C100 Super Cub (49cc single)	600	900	1,350	1,800	2,400	3,000
C102 Super Cub (49cc single)	600	900	1,350	1,800	2,400	3,000
C110 Super Sports Cub (49cc single)	600	900	1,350	1,800	2,400	3,000
CB92 Benly Super Sport (124cc twin)	2,400	3,600	5,400	7,200	9,600	12,000
CA95 Benly Touring "early" (154cc twin)	800	1,200	1,800	2,400	3,200	4,000
C71 Dream Touring (247cc twin)	1,300	1,950	2,930	3,900	5,200	6,500
CA71 Dream Touring (247cc twin)	1,300	1,950	2,930	3,900	5,200	6,500
CA72 Dream Touring "early" (247cc twin)	1,000	1,500	2,250	3,000	4,000	5,000
CE71 Dream Sport (247cc twin)	2,200	3,300	4,950	6,600	8,800	11,000
C76 Dream Touring (305cc twin)	1,300	1,950	2,930	3,900	5,200	6,500
CA76 Dream Touring (305cc twin)	1,200	1,800	2,700	3,600	4,800	6,000
CA77 Dream Touring "early" (305cc twin)	900	1,350	2,030	2,700	3,600	4,500
CS76 Dream Sport (305cc twin)	2,200	3,300	4,950	6,600	8,800	11,000
CS77 Dream Sport (305cc twin)	1,200	1,800	2,700	3,600	4,800	6,000
CSA76 Dream Sport (305cc twin)	1,800	2,700	4,050	5,400	7,200	9,000
CSA77 Dream Sport (305cc twin)	1,000	1,500	2,250	3,000	4,000	5,000

1960 MODELS

Model	Product Code	Engine Type/ Displacement	Transmission	Year(s) Available
C100 Super Cub	001	OHV Single/49cc	3-Speed, Auto	1959-62
C102 Super Cub	003	OHV Single/49cc	3-Speed, Auto	1960-62
C110 Super Sports Cub	011	OHV Single/49cc	3-Speed, Manual	1960-62
CB92 Benly Super Sport 125	205	OHC Parallel Twin/124cc	4-Speed	1959-62
CA95 Benly Touring 150	206	OHC Parallel Twin/154cc	4-Speed	1959-63
CA71/C71 Dream Touring 250	255	OHC Parallel Twin/247cc	4-Speed	1959-60
CE71 Dream Sport 250	257	OHC Parallel Twin/247cc	4-Speed	1959-60
CA72 Dream Touring 250	262	OHC Parallel Twin/247cc	4-Speed	1960-63
CA76/C76 Dream Touring 300	260	OHC Parallel Twin/305cc	4-Speed	1959-60
CSA76/CS76 Dream Sport 300	261	OHC Parallel Twin/305cc	4-Speed	1960
CA77 Dream Touring 305	267	OHC Parallel Twin/305cc	4-Speed	1960-63
CSA77/CS77 Dream Sport 305	267	OHC Parallel Twin/305cc	4-Speed	1960-63

1961

Honda's 1961 lineup was comprised of several carry-over models, but also added six new entrants to the mix. Missing from the 1961 offerings were the CA71/C71 Dream Touring 250, CE71 Dream Sport 250, CA76/C76 Dream Touring 300 and CSA76/CS76 Dream Sport 300.

February saw the CB72 Hawk 250 make its entrance. This sportier model featured the same 247cc OHC motor used on other Hondas, but took in fuel through a pair of carburetors. The chassis of the CB72 was formed of tubular

steel instead of the pressed steel used on other Hondas. Improved telescopic front forks were on hand to assist in the ride and handling department. Early models were fitted with flat handlebars while later entries had low-rise style bars. Your choice of Blue, Scarlet Red or Black was all accented with silver hardware.

March saw four new models roll into the showrooms. Smallest of the new models were the CA100T Trail 50/C100T Trail Cub variants. Designed more for use off-road, these 49cc machines came devoid of front fenders, and could be had with optional skid plates and rear mounted luggage racks. A small black plastic engine guard was standard.

The step-through layout was mated to a solo saddle and was sold in your choice of Scarlet Red or an all-chrome version. The chrome model came with accents of red plastic and a black seat.

The second March release was the CB92R Benly Super Sports Racer 125. Based on the CB92 Benly, the "R" version was equipped as a mini racing machine. The solo racing saddle, chrome megaphone exhaust pipes and a boost

1961 PRICE GUIDE	6	5	4	3	2	1
C100 Super Cub (49cc single)	600	900	1,350	1,800	2,400	3,000
C102 Super Cub (49cc single)	600	900	1,350	1,800	2,400	3,000
C110 Super Sports Cub (49cc single)	600	900	1,350	1,800	2,400	3,000
CB92 Benly Super Sport (124cc twin)	2,000	3,000	4,500	6,000	8,000	10,000
CB92R (124cc twin)	4,400	6,600	9,900	13,200	17,600	22,000
CA95 Benly Touring "early" (154cc twin)	800	1,200	1,800	2,400	3,200	4,000
C72 Dream Touring (247cc twin)	1,180	1,770	2,660	3,540	4,720	5,900
CA72 Dream Touring "early" (247cc twin)	940	1,410	2,120	2,820	3,760	4,700
CB72 Hawk (247cc twin)	960	1,440	2,160	2,880	3,840	4,800
CB72 Hawk Sport (247cc twin)	1,000	1,500	2,250	3,000	4,000	5,000
C77 Dream Touring (305cc twin)	820	1,230	1,850	2,460	3,280	4,100
CA77 Dream Touring "early" (305cc twin)	850	1,280	1,910	2,550	3,400	4,250
CB77 Super Hawk (305cc twin)	900	1,350	2,030	2,700	3,600	4,500
CS77 Dream Sport (305cc twin)	1,200	1,800	2,700	3,600	4,800	6,000
CSA77 Dream Sport (305cc twin)	1,000	1,500	2,250	3,000	4,000	5,000

1961 MODELS

Model	Product Code	Engine Type/ Displacement	Transmission	Year(s) Available
C100 Super Cub	001	OHV Single/49cc	3-Speed, Auto	1959-62
CA100T Trail 50/C100T Trail Cub	001	OHV Single/49cc	3-Speed, Auto	1961-62
C102 Super Cub	003	OHV Single/49cc	3-Speed, Auto	1960-62
C110 Super Sports Cub	011	OHV Single/49cc	3-Speed, Manual	1960-62
CB92 Benly Super Sport 125	205	OHC Parallel Twin/124cc	4-Speed	1959-62
CB92R Benly S.S. Racer 125	205	OHC Parallel Twin/124cc	4-Speed	1961-62
CA95 Benly Touring 150	206	OHC Parallel Twin/154cc	4-Speed	1959-63
C72 Dream Touring 250	259	OHC Parallel Twin/247cc	4-Speed	1961
CA72 Dream Touring 250	262	OHC Parallel Twin/247cc	4-Speed	1960-63
CB72 Hawk 250	268	OHC Parallel Twin/247cc	4-Speed	1961-66
C77 Dream Touring 305	266	OHC Parallel Twin/305cc	4-Speed	1961-64
CA77 Dream Touring 305	267	OHC Parallel Twin/305cc	4-Speed	1960-1963
CSA77/CS77 Dream Sport 305	267	OHC Parallel Twin/305cc	4-Speed	1960-1963
CB77 Super Hawk 305	275	OHC Parallel Twin/305cc	4-Speed	1961-68

in horsepower provided the added feel of a real race machine. Behind a small windscreen, the speedometer of the CB92 was replaced with a tachometer in the headlight nacelle.

The C72 Dream Touring 250 was a 1961 only model, and was built mainly for the domestic Japanese market.

The final March entry was the C77 Dream Touring 305. A virtual twin to the CA77 introduced in 1960, the C77 wore low-rise handlebars that were formed of pressed steel and painted, versus the tubular high-rise bars on the CA77. A small tire pump was also added to the C77 and was located under the seat.

April of 1961 saw the last new model introduced for the year. The CB77 Super Hawk 305 wore a pair of telescopic front forks in place of the pressed-steel affairs used on most other Hondas at the time.

Early Super Hawks wore flat bars with lower fork legs to match the chosen unit color. Later versions used low-rise bars and all silver fork lowers. The 305cc parallel twin motor was also fitted with a pair of carburetors to enhance performance. A four-speed transmission was still the standard application.

1962

nother year of model changes was on
tap for 1962. It would be the final year
for the C100 Super Cub, CA100T Trail50/
C100T Trail Cub, C102 Super Cub, C110
Super Sports Cub and both the CB92 Benly
Super Sport 125 and CB92R Benly Super
Sports Racer 125. In their wake, six new mod-
els would take up the slack.

To fill the void left by the departing C100
and C102 Super Cub models, the CA100 and
CA102 Honda 50s were installed in the catalog. Changes between the old and the new were
minor.

A "Honda 50" logo was placed on the front
cowl and a seat base emblem also helped to
identify the latest versions. The taillight was

also enlarged and was mounted with a bracket.

For the rider who still needed a small machine for off-
road adventures, the C105T
Trail 55 took the spot left by the CA100T and
C100T. The C105T Trail 55 now came with
the chrome luggage rack as standard equipment and had a larger saddle. An engine with
6 additional cc's of displacement was also installed on the 1962 model.

The departing C110 Super Sports Cub
would barely be missed with the rollout of the
CA110 Sport 50 model. Similar in most ways,
the new version did claim a few improvements.
Chrome panels on the sides of the fuel tank

*The C105T, also known as the Trail
55, was easy to identify by its low-
mounted exhaust.*
Owner: Stuart Covington

Displacing 54cc's, the single-cylinder motor delivered adequate power, but nothing to set any records.

dressed up the latest version and an aluminum cylinder head helped with cooling on the 49cc motor. The CA110 Sport 50 was fitted with a three-speed manual transmission up to serial no. "C110-218191", but another gear was added, starting with the subsequent serial number. The new tank badge read "Honda 50" to assist in differentiating one model from another.

A brand-new model was offered up in 1962 in the form of the CL72 Scrambler 250. An upswept, baffled straight pipe exhaust suggested off-road use, but the chrome front fender identified it as a road machine. The 247cc motor was fed with a pair of carburetors, and four-speeds were on duty.

Looking more like a musical instrument than an exhaust, the C105's chrome tube vented spent fumes through the vertical slots.

A pair of rear sprockets gave the C105 owner an option of final gear ratios to meet with changing conditions. By adding the supplied length of chain, the larger sprocket could then be used for a lower gear.

A rarely seen C105 option was the cushioned buddy seat that mounted to the rear luggage rack.

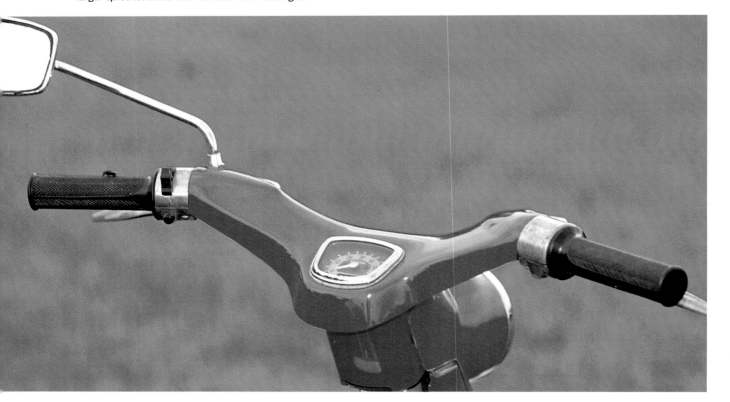

A single instrument was housed in the center of the pressed steel handlebars.

Featuring Grand Prix technology, the CR72 production racer of 1962 was developed for clubman racing, and made an impressive showing in the 1963 Isle of Man TT.
Rick Darke photo

1962 PRICE GUIDE	6	5	4	3	2	1
C100 Super Cub (49cc single)	600	900	1,350	1,800	2,400	3,000
C102 Super Cub (49cc single)	600	900	1,350	1,800	2,400	3,000
C110 Super Sports Cub (49cc single)	600	900	1,350	1,800	2,400	3,000
CA100 (49cc single)	600	900	1,350	1,800	2,400	3,000
CA100T (49cc single)	600	900	1,350	1,800	2,400	3,000
CA102 (49cc single)	600	900	1,350	1,800	2,400	3,000
CB92 Benly Super Sport (124cc twin)	2,000	3,000	4,500	6,000	8,000	10,000
CB92R (124cc twin)	4,400	6,600	9,900	13,200	17,600	22,000
CA95 Benly Touring "early" (154cc twin)	800	1,200	1,800	2,400	3,200	4,000
CA72 Dream Touring "early" (247cc twin)	940	1,410	2,120	2,820	3,760	4,700
CB72 Hawk (247cc twin)	1,000	1,500	2,250	3,000	4,000	5,000
CL72 Scrambler (247cc twin)	700	1,050	1,580	2,100	2,800	3,500
C77 Dream Touring (305cc twin)	820	1,230	1,850	2,460	3,280	4,100
CA77 Dream Touring "early" (305cc twin)	850	1,280	1,910	2,550	3,400	4,250
CB77 Super Hawk (305cc twin)	900	1,350	2,030	2,700	3,600	4,500
CS77 Dream Sport (305cc twin)	1,200	1,800	2,700	3,600	4,800	6,000
CSA77 Dream Sport (305cc twin)	1,000	1,500	2,250	3,000	4,000	5,000

1962 MODELS

Model	Product Code	Engine Type/ Displacement	Transmission	Year(s) Available
C100 Super Cub	001	OHV Single/49cc	3-Speed, Auto	1959-1962
CA100 Honda 50	005	OHV Single/49cc	3-Speed, Auto	1962-1970
CA100T Trail 50/C100T Trail Cub	001	OHV Single/49cc	3-Speed, Auto	1961-1962
C102 Super Cub	003	OHV Single/49cc	3-Speed, Auto	1960-62
CA102 Honda 50	006	OHV Single/49cc	3-Speed, Auto	1962-69
C105T Trail 55	002	OHV Single/54cc	3-Speed, Auto	1962-63
C110 Super Sports Cub	011	OHV Single/49cc	3-Speed, Manual	1960-62
CA110 Sport 50	022	OHV Single/49cc	3-Speed/4-Speed, Manual	1962-69
CB92 Benly Super Sport 125	205	OHC Parallel Twin/124cc	4-Speed	1959-62
CB92R Benly S.S. Racer 125	205	OHC Parallel Twin/124cc	4-Speed	1961-62
CA95 Benly Touring 150	206	OHC Parallel Twin/154cc	4-Speed	1959-63
CA72 Dream Touring 250	262	OHC Parallel Twin/247cc	4-Speed	1960-63
CB72 Hawk 250	268	OHC Parallel Twin/247cc	4-Speed	1961-66
CL72 Scrambler 250	273	OHC Parallel Twin/247cc	4-Speed	1962-65
C77 Dream Touring 305	266	OHC Parallel Twin/305cc	4-Speed	1961-64
CA77 Dream Touring 305	267	OHC Parallel Twin/305cc	4-Speed	1960-63
CSA77/CS77 Dream Sport 305	267	OHC Parallel Twin/305cc	4-Speed	1960-63
CB77 Super Hawk 305	275	OHC Parallel Twin/305cc	4-Speed	1961-68

1963

For those keeping score, the 1963 lineup included one brand-new model, lost another, and had four older versions being replaced by fresher metal.

With the release of the CA105T Trail 55, Honda filled the void left by the departed C105T Trail 55. The new version featured an upswept exhaust, and later models would include a chrome front fender.

The CA95 Benly Touring 150, first seen in 1959 was supplanted by a newer version of the same machine. The new version featured larger rubber knee pads on the tank, but smaller chrome panels. A larger taillight, white wall tires and a round section exhaust set the newer version apart from the old.

The April 1963 release of the latest CA72 Dream Touring 250 would only see the shape of the fuel tank change from the model sold between 1960 and 1963.

Another changing of the guard was applied to the CA77 Dream Touring 305. Released in April of 1963, the latest iteration featured a differently shaped fuel tank than the previous model. No other variations were made.

1963 would mark the final year for the CSA77 Dream Sport 305, and no replacement model was waiting in the wings.

A completely new machine was released to dealers in September of 1963. The CA200

1963 PRICE GUIDE	6	5	4	3	2	1
CA100 (49cc single)	500	750	1,130	1,500	2,000	2,500
CA102 (49cc single)	500	750	1,130	1,500	2,000	2,500
CA200 (89cc single)	480	720	1,080	1,440	1,920	2,400
CA95 Benly Touring "early" (154cc twin)	800	1,200	1,800	2,400	3,200	4,000
CA72 Dream Touring "early" (247cc twin)	940	1,410	2,120	2,820	3,760	4,700
CA72 Dream Touring "late" (247cc twin)	940	1,410	2,120	2,820	3,760	4,700
CB72 Hawk (247cc twin)	800	1,200	1,800	2,400	3,200	4,000
CL72 Scrambler (247cc twin)	700	1,050	1,580	2,100	2,800	3,500
C77 Dream Touring (305cc twin)	820	1,230	1,850	2,460	3,280	4,100
CA77 Dream Touring "early" (305cc twin)	850	1,280	1,910	2,550	3,400	4,250
CA77 Dream Touring "late" (305cc twin)	850	1,280	1,910	2,550	3,400	4,250
CB77 Super Hawk (305cc twin)	800	1,200	1,800	2,400	3,200	4,000
CS77 Dream Sport (305cc twin)	1,200	1,800	2,700	3,600	4,800	6,000
CSA77 Dream Sport (305cc twin)	1,000	1,500	2,250	3,000	4,000	5,000

Honda 90/C200 Touring 90 was moved by an 87cc single-cylinder motor, and shifted through the four speeds with a manual clutch. Turning the motor over was accomplished via kickstart pedal only. Sold in your choice of White, Black or Scarlet Red, the fuel tank was adorned with chrome panels and rubber knee pads. A "Honda 90" badge was also seen on the tank.

Advertising used in 1963 touted Honda's racing victories in all three major divisions of racing's events. Honda-built machines had dominated 125, 250 and now the 350cc divisions. This on-track supremacy did not go unnoticed at the retail level as people clamored to get their own world-class machines for their daily commute.

1963 MODELS

Model	Product Code	Engine Type/ Displacement	Transmission	Year(s) Available
CA100 Honda 50	005	OHV Single/49cc	3-Speed, Auto	1962-70
CA102 Honda 50	006	OHV Single/49cc	3-Speed, Auto	1962-69
C105T Trail 55	002	OHV Single/54cc	3-Speed, Auto	1962-63
CA105T Trail 55	007	OHV Single/54cc	3-Speed, Auto	1963-65
CA110 Sport 50	022	OHV Single/49cc	3-Speed/4-Speed, Manual	1962-69
CA200 Honda 90/C200 Touring 90	030	OHV Single/87cc	4-Speed	1963-66
CA95 Benly Touring 150	206	OHC Parallel Twin/154cc	4-Speed	1959-63
CA95 Benly Touring 150	206	OHC Parallel Twin/154cc	4-Speed	1963-66
CA72 Dream Touring 250	262	OHC Parallel Twin/247cc	4-Speed	1960-63
CA72 Dream Touring 250	262	OHC Parallel Twin/247cc	4-Speed	1963-66
CB72 Hawk 250	268	OHC Parallel Twin/247cc	4-Speed	1961-66
CL72 Scrambler 250	273	OHC Parallel Twin/247cc	4-Speed	1962-65
C77 Dream Touring 305	266	OHC Parallel Twin/305cc	4-Speed	1961-64
CA77 Dream Touring 305	267	OHC Parallel Twin/305cc	4-Speed	1960-63
CA77 Dream Touring 305	267	OHC Parallel Twin/305cc	4-Speed	1963-69
CB77 Super Hawk 305	275	OHC Parallel Twin/305cc	4-Speed	1961-68

1964

A bit of stability crept into the 1964 models as one machine was in its final year, and two more new additions were made. The rest of the lineup was carried over from 1963.

Although similar in layout to the CA105T Trail 55, the new CT200 Trail 90 was enhanced in many ways. The larger-displacement motor delivered more bang for the buck, and an extra gear was installed for versatility. The front suspension on the new 90 was of the bottom link variety, and a pair of dual overlay rear sprockets were installed on the rear wheel. The CT200 Trail 90 was released in May of 1964.

October of 1964 saw the entry of the next new model from Honda. The S90 Super 90 had the looks of a real motorcycle along with many common features of its bigger brethren. The 89cc single-cylinder motor shifted through four speeds manually. S90s built between October 1964 and March of 1968 wore silver painted fenders and could only be had in solid White, Black or Scarlet Red colors. Those built after March of 1968 featured chrome fenders and your choice of Candy Blue or Candy Red paint, as well as White and Black solids.

1964 would be the last year for the C77 Dream Touring 305 model, but the CA77 Dream Touring 305 would live on until 1969.

The tiny 49cc OHV motor on the Honda 50 resided mostly beneath the molded cowling that also provided some protection from the elements.

Both the swingarm and exhaust were constructed using pressed steel, which was then welded into its final form.

The one-piece molded cowling added a sleek touch of style to the simple Honda 50 models.

The two-person saddle made for a fairly comfortable perch, although the Honda only had 49cc's of displacement to haul 2 riders around.

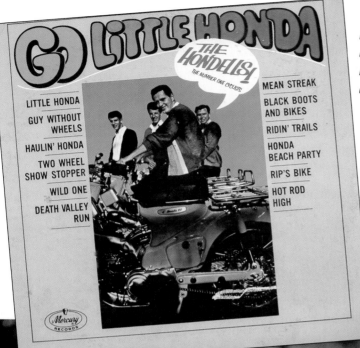

Honda's recent introduction in the states did not go unnoticed by the music industry in 1962, and "The Hondells" borrowed from the name of Honda and even used one of their machines on their LP cover.

Released in April of 1963, the CA95 Benly Touring 150 returned for another year in 1964. There were several minor alterations between the early and late models. Owner: Stuart Covington

The Benly Touring's parallel twin motor still displaced 154ccs in 1964 and delivered plenty of power for two riders.

1964 MODELS

Model	Product Code	Engine Type/ Displacement	Transmission	Year(s) Available
CA100 Honda 50	005	OHV Single/49cc	3-Speed, Auto	1962-70
CA102 Honda 50	006	OHV Single/49cc	3-Speed, Auto	1962-69
CA105T Trail 55	007	OHV Single/54cc	3-Speed, Auto	1963-65
CA110 Sport 50	022	OHV Single/49cc	3-Speed/4-Speed, Manual	1962-69
CA200 Honda 90/C200 Touring 90	030	OHV Single/87cc	4-Speed	1963-66
CT200 Trail 90	033	OHV Single/87cc	4-Speed, Auto	1964-66
S90 Super 90	028	OHV Single/89cc	4-Speed, Manual	1964-69
CA95 Benly Touring 150	206	OHC Parallel Twin/154cc	4-Speed	1963-66
CA72 Dream Touring 250	262	OHC Parallel Twin/247cc	4-Speed	1963-66
CB72 Hawk 250	268	OHC Parallel Twin/247cc	4-Speed	1961-66
CL72 Scrambler 250	273	OHC Parallel Twin/247cc	4-Speed	1962-65
C77 Dream Touring 305	266	OHC Parallel Twin/305cc	4-Speed	1961-64
CA77 Dream Touring 305	267	OHC Parallel Twin/305cc	4-Speed	1963-69
CB77 Super Hawk 305	275	OHC Parallel Twin/305cc	4-Speed	1961-68

Whitewall tires were another new addition to the late-1963 versions of the Benly Touring 150.

Late-edition CA95s wore larger rubber pads on the sides of the smaller chrome panels.

1964 PRICE GUIDE	6	5	4	3	2	1
CA100 (49cc single)	500	750	1,130	1,500	2,000	2,500
CA102 (49cc single)	500	750	1,130	1,500	2,000	2,500
CA200 (89cc single)	480	720	1,080	1,440	1,920	2,400
S90 (90cc single)	420	630	950	1,260	1,680	2,100
CA95 Benly Touring "late" (154cc twin)	600	900	1,350	1,800	2,400	3,000
CA72 Dream Touring "late" (247cc twin)	940	1,410	2,120	2,820	3,760	4,700
CB72 Hawk (247cc twin)	800	1,200	1,800	2,400	3,200	4,000
CL72 Scrambler (247cc twin)	700	1,050	1,580	2,100	2,800	3,500
C77 Dream Touring (305cc twin)	820	1,230	1,850	2,460	3,280	4,100
CA77 Dream Touring "late" (305cc twin)	820	1,230	1,850	2,460	3,280	4,100
CB77 Super Hawk (305cc twin)	600	900	1,350	1,800	2,400	3,000

The Benly Touring's mid-rise handlebars were positioned within easy reach, which provided a more comfortable riding posture.

An extended fender brace was used on the later model Touring 150s, and a rectangular plate was added.

For 1965, four new models joined the Honda parade while two models had reached their twilight. 1965 would prove to be the final year for the CA195T Trail 55 and the CL72 Scrambler 250. Both departing models were replaced with fresh faces in 1966.

New for 1965 was the S65 Sport 65, which was released to dealers on the first day of April. This new model was powered by a single-cylinder, 63cc, overhead-cam motor. Four manual gears were available. A high-mounted exhaust pipe was covered by a slotted heat shield. Sold in the buyer's choice of White, Black or Scarlet Red, the S65 wore a saddle of black and white vinyl. A red tank badge was accented with a silver wing.

A second new 1965 model was the CB160 Sport 160. It carried an extra 7cc's over the CA95 Benly Touring 150, but did so in a much sportier format. In place of the valanced fenders of the Benly, the CB160 wore trim, wheel-hugging sheet metal between the telescopic front forks. A torpedo-shaped exhaust allowed for free breathing. The 161cc

"You meet the nicest people on a Honda" was perhaps the most memorable ad slogan to ever grace the pages of periodicals in the middle '60s, and this version of the CA100 was the bike the happy couples were riding.
Owner: Stuart Covington

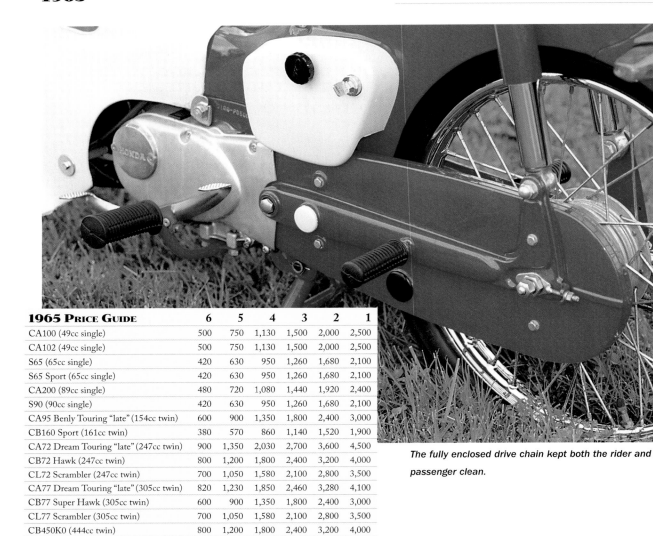

The fully enclosed drive chain kept both the rider and passenger clean.

1965 PRICE GUIDE	6	5	4	3	2	1
CA100 (49cc single)	500	750	1,130	1,500	2,000	2,500
CA102 (49cc single)	500	750	1,130	1,500	2,000	2,500
S65 (65cc single)	420	630	950	1,260	1,680	2,100
S65 Sport (65cc single)	420	630	950	1,260	1,680	2,100
CA200 (89cc single)	480	720	1,080	1,440	1,920	2,400
S90 (90cc single)	420	630	950	1,260	1,680	2,100
CA95 Benly Touring "late" (154cc twin)	600	900	1,350	1,800	2,400	3,000
CB160 Sport (161cc twin)	380	570	860	1,140	1,520	1,900
CA72 Dream Touring "late" (247cc twin)	900	1,350	2,030	2,700	3,600	4,500
CB72 Hawk (247cc twin)	800	1,200	1,800	2,400	3,200	4,000
CL72 Scrambler (247cc twin)	700	1,050	1,580	2,100	2,800	3,500
CA77 Dream Touring "late" (305cc twin)	820	1,230	1,850	2,460	3,280	4,100
CB77 Super Hawk (305cc twin)	600	900	1,350	1,800	2,400	3,000
CL77 Scrambler (305cc twin)	700	1,050	1,580	2,100	2,800	3,500
CB450K0 (444cc twin)	800	1,200	1,800	2,400	3,200	4,000

1965 MODELS

Model	Product Code	Engine Type/ Displacement	Transmission	Year(s) Available
CA100 Honda 50	005	OHV Single/49cc	3-Speed, Auto	1962-70
CA102 Honda 50	006	OHV Single/49cc	3-Speed, Auto	1962-69
CA105T Trail 55	007	OHV Single/54cc	3-Speed, Auto	1963-65
CA110 Sport 50	022	OHV Single/49cc	3-Speed/4-Speed, Man.	1962-69
S65 Sport 65/CS65	035	OHC Single/63cc	4-Speed	1965-69
CA200 Honda 90/C200 Touring 90	030	OHV Single/87cc	4-Speed	1963-66
CT200 Trail 90	033	OHV Single/87cc	4-Speed, Auto	1964-66
S90 Super 90	028	OHV Single/89cc	4-Speed, Manual	1964-69
CA95 Benly Touring 150	206	OHC Parallel Twin/154cc	4-Speed	1963-66
CB160 Sport 160	217	OHC Parallel Twin/161cc	4-Speed	1965-69
CA72 Dream Touring 250	262	OHC Parallel Twin/247cc	4-Speed	1963-66
CB72 Hawk 250	268	OHC Parallel Twin/247cc	4-Speed	1961-66
CL72 Scrambler 250	273	OHC Parallel Twin/247cc	4-Speed	1962-65
CA77 Dream Touring 305	267	OHC Parallel Twin/305cc	4-Speed	1963-69
CB77 Super Hawk 305	275	OHC Parallel Twin/305cc	4-Speed	1961-68
CL77 Scrambler 305	278	OHC Parallel Twin/305cc	4-Speed	1965-68
CB450 Super Sport /CB450KO	283	DOHC Parallel Twin/444cc	4-Speed	1965-68

parallel twin motor drew breath through a pair of Keihin carburetors and shifted through a four-speed transmission.

Regardless of which color you opted for, Black, Scarlet Red, Blue or White, the fenders and side covers were finished in silver. With the Blue & Silver model, the two-person saddle was covered in matching Blue vinyl while the rest of the hues came with a standard Black mount.

With the 247cc CL72 Scrambler 250 making an exit by the end of 1965, an enhanced CL77 Scrambler 305 was rolled out to carry the torch. Wearing a fuel tank, side covers and fenders painted in silver, the bike could be ordered in three hues. The frame, upper forks and headlight shell were sold in Blue, Black or Red. An upswept exhaust featured two separate tubes with a common muffler at the end. A segment of slotted, wrap-around heat shield was applied midway along the length. The 305cc OHC parallel twin sported dual carbs and sent the power through a four-speed transmission.

Pushing the performance envelope ever higher was the all-new CB450 Super Sport. A new series of identification numbers were used. CB450KO referred to the fact that this was be the first year for the model. Subsequent changes to the machine would result in "K1," "K2" etc. as the sequence progressed.

The K1 model was not seen until 1968, but each year that followed took the "K__" designation that was next. The CB450K7 was introduced in 1974, which was the final year for the 450K designation. This alphanumeric system would soon be applied to most of Honda's motorcycles.

The CB450KO featured a 444cc, parallel twin motor with dual overhead cams. This was another example of what would become common practice at Honda. Dual constant velocity (CV) carburetors were applied for smooth delivery of the fuel and air mix. A four-speed transmission with manual clutch was chosen for gear selection.

The only colors sold on the 1965 models were black with silver accents. The fuel tank,

upper fork tubes and headlight nacelle were all black, while the side covers and both fenders were finished in silver. The tubular frame was also done in black. The "K0" and "K1" models wore chrome panels and rubber knee pads on the fuel tank.

The Touring 150's headlight and horn were both encapsulated in the pressed-steel front fork, and the fender valance helped to keep the rider's legs clean and dry.

Like every other aspect of the Honda 50, the rear turn signals were sleek and purposeful.

The well-cushioned saddle remained a comfortable spot when out and about on your Honda.

The latest year brought numerous changes to the Honda lineup as they continued to do their best to satisfy all levels of buyers' needs.

Amongst the models that would be departing before the year was out was the CA200 Honda 90/C200 Touring 90 and the CT200 Trail 90.

Farther up the food chain, the CA95 Benly Touring 150, CA72 Dream Touring 250 and the CB72 Hawk 250 would also slip into the history books this year. To fill the void left by departing models, Honda introduced four new machines.

The CM91 Honda 90 was basically a bigger version of the CA102 Super Cub that first ap-

peared in 1960. A bump in the displacement brought the new total to 89cc, and the CM91 was still started with the use of a button or kick-start pedal. The three-speed gearbox was still automatic.

The new CT90 Trail 90/CT90K0 replaced the recently departed CA105T Trail 55. Going from 54 to 89ccs helped in the forward motion department, and the newest K0 designation would help to track future changes to the model. The upswept, chrome exhaust system remained in place on the K0 and K1 models. Early examples wore a pair of dual overlay sprockets on the rear wheel that were mated to the four-speed automatic transmission. Later

First sold in 1965, the CB160 provided a mid-level platform for those wanting something a bit bigger than the step-through models.
Owner: Greg Mazza

The CB160's 161cc motor was fed by a pair of carburetors and shifted through a four-speed gearbox.

models featured an eight-speed dual-range transmission. The front suspension remained a bottom link system.

The 1966 CA160 Touring 160 could easily play the role of stunt double for the CA95 Benly Touring 150, which was on its way out in 1966. The new machine displaced a few more cc's and wore tires with thin white walls in place of the wider versions seen on the Benly. The rear fender strut was also changed on the new CA160, but no other modifications were seen.

The CL160 Scrambler 160 was based on the successful CB160 Sport of the previous year. Built more for all-around use, the CL160 had a set of dual exhaust pipes that were wrapped in heat shield and converged into one large muffler. *CYCLE* magazine found the new Scrambler to be fairly competent, although not svelte. Being

designed for a multitude of chores, it failed to excel at anything, but still made for a favorable mount. Carrying a weight of 282 lbs., the CL160 was shown with a top speed of 76 mph. The 161cc engine was the same as found in the CB160, but was geared differently for off-road use. Both an electric and kick starter pedal were available to get things moving.

The fenders and side covers were painted Silver, while the options for the remaining sheet metal were shown as Silver, Candy Orange and Candy Blue.

Print ads from Honda seen in the latter part of 1966 included "Head of the line!" as part of their marketing ploy. One such ad included images of the Super 90, Sport 160, Super Hawk and the all-powerful Honda 450. These models and more could be found at the 1,700 Honda dealers located in the U.S..

Typical of many motorcycles of the period, the CB160's fuel tank was clad in chrome panels and rubber knee pads.

The rear wheel was fitted with a drum brake, which delivered suitable stopping power for the lightweight CB160.

The "duck bill" rear fender flap was a common item on Hondas.

1966 PRICE GUIDE	6	5	4	3	2	1
CA100 (49cc single)	400	600	900	1,200	1,600	2,000
CA102 (49cc single)	400	600	900	1,200	1,600	2,000
S65 (65cc single)	420	630	950	1,260	1,680	2,100
CA200 (89cc single)	440	660	990	1,320	1,760	2,200
CM91 (89cc single)	400	600	900	1,200	1,600	2,000
S90 (90cc single)	420	630	950	1,260	1,680	2,100
CA95 Benly Touring "late" (154cc twin)	600	900	1,350	1,800	2,400	3,000
CA160 Touring (161cc twin)	380	570	860	1,140	1,520	1,900
CB160 (161cc twin)	380	570	860	1,140	1,520	1,900
CL160 Scrambler (161cc twin)	400	600	900	1,200	1,600	2,000
CA72 Dream Touring "late" (247cc twin)	800	1,200	1,800	2,400	3,200	4,000
CB72 Hawk (247cc twin)	800	1,200	1,800	2,400	3,200	4,000
CA77 Dream Touring "late" (305cc twin)	820	1,230	1,850	2,460	3,280	4,100
CB77 Super Hawk (305cc twin)	600	900	1,350	1,800	2,400	3,000
CL77 Scrambler (305cc twin)	700	1,050	1,580	2,100	2,800	3,500
CB450K0 (444cc twin)	800	1,200	1,800	2,400	3,200	4,000

1966 MODELS

Model	Product Code	Engine Type/ Displacement	Transmission	Year(s) Available
CA100 Honda 50	005	OHV Single/49cc	3-Speed, Auto	1962-70
CA102 Honda 50	006	OHV Single/49cc	3-Speed, Auto	1962-69
CA110 Sport 50	022	OHV Single/49cc	3-Speed/4-Speed, Man.	1962-69
S65 Sport 65/CS65	035	OHC Single/63cc	4-Speed	1965-69
CA200 Honda 90/C200 Touring 90	030	OHV Single/87cc	4-Speed	1963-66
CT200 Trail 90	033	OHV Single/87cc	4-Speed, Auto	1964-66
S90 Super 90	028	OHV Single/89cc	4-Speed, Manual	1964-69
CM91 Honda 90	034	OHC Single/89cc	3-Speed, Auto	1966-69
CT90 Trail 90 (CT90KO)	053	OHC Single/89cc	4-Spd (early) 8-Spd (late)	1966-68
CA95 Benly Touring 150	206	OHC Parallel Twin/154cc	4-Speed	1963-66
CA160 Touring 160	225	OHC Parallel Twin/161cc	4-Speed	1966-69
CB160 Sport 160	217	OHC Parallel Twin/161cc	4-Speed	1965-69
CL160 Scrambler 160	223	OHC Parallel Twin/161cc	4-Speed	1966-67
CA72 Dream Touring 250	262	OHC Parallel Twin/247cc	4-Speed	1963-66
CB72 Hawk 250	268	OHC Parallel Twin/247cc	4-Speed	1961-66
CA77 Dream Touring 305	267	OHC Parallel Twin/305cc	4-Speed	1963-69
CB77 Super Hawk 305	275	OHC Parallel Twin/305cc	4-Speed	1961-68
CL77 Scrambler 305	278	OHC Parallel Twin/305cc	4-Speed	1965-68
CB450 Super Sport/CB450KO	283	DOHC Parallel Twin/444cc	4-Speed	1965-68

Earlier models from Honda featured rubber fork seal protectors, but the CB160 rode with steel sleeves instead.

You meet the nicest people on a Honda. Like attracts like. A Honda is good-looking, personable. Always gives more than it gets. 200 miles to a gallon of gas. Upkeep minimal. And prices start about $215* The famous four-stroke engine has a will of iron. A model of endurance. World's biggest seller. **HONDA**

FREE: Color brochure, write Dept. MJ, American Honda Motor Co., Inc., Box 50, Gardena, California 90247.   *Plus dealer's transportation and set-up charges.   © 1966 AHM

Perhaps Honda's most memorable ad campaign was that which coined the phrase, "You meet the nicest people on a Honda".

1966

This version of the ad showed folks enjoying their Honda in a bit more rural environment, but having fun nonetheless.

SOME PEOPLE HAVE ALL THE FUN

You can easily see why. A Honda fits right in with suburban life. Parks anywhere. Prices start about $215*. Upkeep is next to nothing. The considerate four-stroke engine gets up to 200 mpg. And keeps quiet ...
models offer a wide rang...
Then there's a thing
styling. Ladies are foreve...
to the store.

BIG VALUES AT YOUR HONDA DEALER'S SUMMER SALES FESTIVAL. *Plus dealer's

SOME PEOPLE HAVE ALL THE FUN

You'll notice they own Hondas. Those famous machines with all the class, the craftsmanship and the wide wonderful range of models. Every one has your interest at heart.
Prices start about $215*. The four-
stroke engine delivers up to 200 mpg. As for upkeep, you haven't a care in the world. 1700 dealer service centers see to that.
All roads lead to Honda. It certainly seems that way. How about a test ride tomorrow? It's the world's biggest seller.

You meet the nicest people on a Honda.

HONDA

FREE: Color brochure, write American Honda Motor Co., Inc., Dept. LQ, Box 50, Gardena, California 90247. *Plus dealer's transportation and set-up charges. © 1966 AHM

Yet another of Honda's often-used phrases claimed that "Some people have all the fun." The CL model was shown being pressed into a variety of duties in this 1966 print ad.

43

1967

For 1967, only one existing model was slated for extinction. The CL160 Scrambler was only introduced the previous year, but a replacement was already being released to fill its shoes.

The first new model released to dealers in 1967 was the CL90 Scrambler 90. March 1 saw this 89cc; single-cylinder model hit the showroom floors. Both the fenders and exhaust were chrome, and the heat-shielded exhaust pipe rode mid-level on the right side of the chassis. No matter whether you chose Candy Red, Candy Blue or Black, the fuel tank was always finished in Silver. A manual clutch allowed changes between the four speeds.

Although the CL160 Scrambler was leaving the team, the CL160D Scrambler 160D was right behind it to take up the slack. The major difference between the leaving and arriving models was the addition of electric start to the "D." Also, where the previous variant wore an all silver motif, the new "D" could be purchased in Silver, Candy Orange or Candy Blue.

Two new 125s were also added to the roster for 1967. July saw the rollout of the CL125A Scrambler 125. The Scrambler class had grown quite popular due to the all-around abilities of the machines carrying the name. High-mount-

The CB77 Super Hawk first appeared in 1961 and ran through 1968. The machine shown here is of 1967 vintage.

The 305cc parallel-twin motor on the CB77 Super Hawk operated with the wet-sump design and took in the air/fuel mix with a pair of carburetors. A four-speed transmission was on board to handle gear changes.

It was common for Hondas to have all of their instrumentation built in to the headlight nacelle, but not all models had a speedometer, tachometer and odometer in one tidy package.

A pair of telescopic forks was a big improvement over the pressed steel variety used on many other Hondas. The silver painted fenders were the stock finish on the Super Hawk.

ed exhaust allowed for some mild off-road riding with less chance of causing fires. The slotted heat shield that wrapped the exhaust tubes kept the rider's legs from doing the same thing. A pair of chrome fenders was joined by your choice of Candy Blue or Bright Yellow frame and upper fork legs. The headlight bucket and gas tank were always done in Metallic Silver. The overhead-cam twin pulled air through a single CV carb and shifted via the four-speed transmission.

One month later, the SS125A Super Sport 125 joined the game. Powered by the same 124cc twin-cylinder motor as the CL 125, the

Super Sport had a low mounted exhaust. The fuel tank was a more angular sporty contour, and along with the fenders was always finished in Silver. The frame, upper forks, headlight bucket, swing arm and shock covers were in your choice of Candy Red, Candy Blue or Black. A side cover "SS125" emblem was done in red and white.

Although new for 1967, the P50 Little Honda, also known as the Motor Wheel, was first seen this year. A 49cc OHC motor was mounted at the rear wheel, hence the nickname. It was basically only a moped, but its rarity is worth noting.

The P50 was started using pedal power, and the bike featured an automatic transmission. It was sold in either Scarlet Red or Sky Blue with Ivory White fenders.

The final entrant for 1967, the CL450 Scrambler 450, was a one-year model. It was an evil twin for the the CB450D Super Sport 450 in name only.

First in June 1967, this new model had a 444cc dual overhead-cam parallel twin motor that sent its spent gases away through a pair of upswept exhaust pipes. One of these pipes was found on each side of the machine. The requisite heat shield was also used on each length of pipe.

Two chrome fenders were blended with upper forks and a headlight nacelle of black. Metallic Silver, Candy Red or Candy Blue would cover the fuel tank and side covers. The side covers were labeled with a short section of angled checkerboard stripe with "450" punctuating the black and white graphic.

1967 PRICE GUIDE	6	5	4	3	2	1
CA100 (49cc single)	400	600	900	1,200	1,600	2,000
CA102 (49cc single)	400	600	900	1,200	1,600	2,000
CM91 (89cc single)	380	570	860	1,140	1,520	1,900
CL90 Scrambler (90cc single)	340	510	770	1,020	1,360	1,700
S90 (90cc single)	400	600	900	1,200	1,600	2,000
CL125A Scrambler (124cc twin)	350	530	790	1,050	1,400	1,750
SS125A (124cc twin)	350	530	790	1,050	1,400	1,750
CA160 Touring (161cc twin)	380	570	860	1,140	1,520	1,900
CB160 (161cc twin)	380	570	860	1,140	1,520	1,900
CL160 Scrambler (161cc twin)	410	620	920	1,230	1,640	2,050
CA77 Dream Touring "late" (305cc twin)	820	1,230	1,850	2,460	3,280	4,100
CB77 Super Hawk (305cc twin)	800	1,200	1,800	2,400	3,200	4,000
CL77 Scrambler (305cc twin)	700	1,050	1,580	2,100	2,800	3,500
CB450K0 (444cc twin)	800	1,200	1,800	2,400	3,200	4,000
CL450 Scrambler (444cc twin)	820	1,230	1,850	2,460	3,280	4,100

1967 MODELS

Model	Product Code	Engine Type/ Displacement	Transmission	Year(s) Available
CA100 Honda 50	005	OHV Single/49cc	3-Speed, Auto	1962-70
CA102 Honda 50	006	OHV Single/49cc	3-Speed, Auto	1962-69
CA110 Sport 50	022	OHV Single/49cc	3-Speed/4-Speed, Man.	1962-69
P50 Little Honda	044	OHC Single/49cc	Automatic	1967-68
S65 Sport 65/CS65	035	OHC Single/63cc	4-Speed	1965-69
S90 Super 90	028	OHV Single/89cc	4-Speed, Manual	1964-69
CL90 Scrambler 90	056	OHC Single/89cc	4-Speed, Manual	1967-69
CM91 Honda 90	034	OHC Single/89cc	3-Speed, Auto	1966-69
CT90 Trail 90	053	OHC Single/89cc	4-Spd (early) 8-Spd (late)	1966-68
CL125A Scrambler	243	OHC Parallel Twin/124cc	4-Speed	1967-69
SS125A Super Sport	244	OHC Parallel Twin/124cc	4-Speed	1967-69
CA160 Touring	225	OHC Parallel Twin/161cc	4-Speed	1966-69
CB160 Sport	217	OHC Parallel Twin/161cc	4-Speed	1965-69
CL160 Scrambler	223	OHC Parallel Twin/161cc	4-Speed	1966-67
CL160D Scrambler	223	OHC Parallel Twin/161cc	4-Speed	1967-68
CA77 Dream Touring 305	267	OHC Parallel Twin/305cc	4-Speed	1963-69
CB77 Super Hawk 305	275	OHC Parallel Twin/305cc	4-Speed	1961-68
CL77 Scrambler 305	278	OHC Parallel Twin/305cc	4-Speed	1965-68
CB450 Super Sport (CB450K0)	283	DOHC Parallel Twin/444cc	4-Speed	1965-68
CB450D Super Sport/CL450 Scrambler	293	DOHC Parallel Twin/444cc	4-Speed	1967

The CB450 was also known as the Black Bomber and was one of Honda's earlier "big" machines.

The Black Bomber's parallel-twin motor displaced 444cc's and featured dual overhead-cam technology.

Dual constant-velocity carbs fed the eager mill with ease and a high level of horsepower was the result.

Set into the top of the CB450's headlight nacelle was a multi-faceted array of gauges and indicator lights.

Typical for most Japanese machines of the day, rubber knee pads were applied to both sides of the chrome-paneled fuel tank.

Model builders who were also Black Bomber fans could assemble a scale kit of their favorite mount.

A single mechanical drum brake was used on the front wheel of the Black Bomber. There was also a drum on the rear, giving the bike adequate stopping power.

A gently sculpted saddle held two CB450 riders in comfort, and the piping made for a nice detail.

The CL77 Scrambler was a perfect bike for riders planning to go both on and off road. Owner: Terry Mitchell

Exhaust exited a set of twin pipes on the Scambler. The pipes were terminated with a two-into-one muffler.

The Honda Custom Group. You take your pick of customized Hondas at your dealer's. Like the Rally here. These models feature a special type of tank, pipe, handlebars, seat. Ride off on your personalized Honda. Wild.

Honda shapes the world of wheels
You wonder how they do it. 20 models so cool and calculating. Any one of 'em would make an ideal companion. Low upkeep. Faithful service. Spectacular performance. That famous Honda four-stroke engine won five out of five '66 Grand Prix Championships, 50cc to 500cc. A world's record. That's Honda's bag. You've got to respect it. See your Honda dealer for a safety demonstration ride.

HONDA
You meet the nicest people on a Honda.

See the "Invisible Circle" color film at your local Honda dealer's. While you're there, pick up a color brochure and safety pamphlet, or write, American Honda Motor Co., Inc., Dept. QS, Box 50, Gardena, California 90247. © 1967, AHM.

A CL77 Scrambler is the central focus of this 1967 ad, while a rare "Rally" model is shown near the top.

Fortified for rugged off-road riding, the Scrambler's handlebars featured a sturdy crossbar.

Designed for use off the smoothly paved roads, the Scrambler fuel tank was devoid of the usual chrome side panels found on other Hondas.

The Scrambler's parallel twin-cylinder motor displaced 305cc's and inhaled through a pair of matching carburetors.

The S90 was introduced in October of 1964 and remained a sporty option for the rider wanting a smaller cycle.
Owners: Kenny and Sylvia Thomas

"Honda shapes the world of wheels" was used on several different print ads, this one featuring the S90 model, along with a few smaller bikes.

Honda shapes the world of wheels
Like a trip to Style City. All those cool classy models. Some 20 in all. Any one of 'em will sharpen your image. Honda leads the field. Craftsmanship like you can't believe. Performance that's no less spectacular. The famous 4-stroke engine is built to go the distance. Honda won five out of five '66 Grand Prix Championships. A clean sweep from 50cc to 500cc. Nobody else has ever done so well. And keep this in mind. Honda draws a crowd. Think you're up to it? See your local Honda dealer for a safety demonstration ride. **HONDA**

You meet the nicest people on a Honda.

S90s built before March of 1968 featured painted silver fenders, while those built after rode with chrome-plated variants.

The S90's 89cc, overhead-cam single delivered power to a four-speed gearbox that was shifted with a manual clutch.

The late run of CA77 Dream Touring 305 models began in 1963 and continued until 1969.

To monitor your speed and distance traveled on the Dream, a single instrument was placed in the top of the headlight housing.

Color-keyed vinyl covered the two-person pillion and a small chrome strip was added for style.

Honda's trademark "Wing" logo found its way onto every model, including the Dream.

To keep things neat and friendly, most of the Dream's components were kept hidden beneath sheet metal housings.

The Dream's rear shocks were also kept concealed beneath tidy sheet metal covers.

A contained rear drive chain kept oil from the rider's pant leg and added to the sterile appearance of the machine.

Displacing 305cc, the Dream's overhead-cam motor lived beneath a newly shaped fuel tank that was revised for the later models.

The Dream's polished rear fender struts added strength to the equation, while also remaining stylish.

This large, two-page spread featured Honda's Custom Group of scooters that could be ordered with a variety of tanks, pipes, bars and seats to create the machine of your dreams.

Take your pick of a Honda. The Trail 90 left. Or the Rally, one of the Honda Custom Group. These models feature a special type of tank, pipe, handlebars, seat. Ride off on your personalized Honda. Wild.

Honda shapes the world of wheels
You've got to hand it to Honda. New designs. New colors. Altogether 20 models to put a glint in your eye. That famous four-stroke engine takes everything in stride. Won five out of five '66 Grand Prix Championships, 50cc to 500cc. A world's record. With Honda, performance counts as well as style. And that tells it like it is. Any questions? See your local Honda dealer for a safety demonstration ride. **HONDA**

For a free color brochure and safety pamphlet write: American Honda Motor Co., Inc., Dept. QF, Box 50, Gardena, California 90247. ©1967, AHM.

Honda's use of movement in their 1960s ads was typical, and almost always featured at least one very happy person in the image.

1968

New models continued to enter the catalog in 1968. Some were replacements for departing versions while others were brand new machines. With every passing year, the Honda lineup offered more variations in their effort to appeal to the widest audience possible.

To meet with the state of Nevada's 5 horsepower minimum licensing requirements, a CL90L Scrambler was introduced late in 1968. The "L" model was nearly identical to the standard CL90, but had red and white "5HP" appliqués of the air filter housing, and was not sold in Black.

Released to dealers on the first day of January 1968, the CL175 Scrambler was an improved variation of earlier models. Built around a tubular steel backbone chassis, the latest Scrambler also featured chrome fenders and exhaust. The newest variant would replace the CL160 Scrambler, which was in its final year of sales. The CL175 also rowed through a 5-speed transmission, and would not be the only 1968 model to do so. The addition of a fifth gear provided a wider range of ratios to meet with a rider's expanding demands. Metallic Silver supplanted the previous Silver, but Candy Blue and Candy Orange remained as available options.

The P50 Little Honda was also dubbed the "Motor Wheel" due to the mounting location of the 49cc OHC power plant. It was actually listed as a moped and may not be a true motorcycle, but is shown here due its uniqueness and rarity.
Owner: Jim Minnis

Another fresh face for 1968 was the CA175 (CD175) Touring. A parallel twin, 174cc motor was suspended from a pressed-steel backbone frame, and four speeds were on tap. Both the tank and side cover emblems read "Honda 175" and Black, Candy Red and Candy Blue were the offered hues. A 6-volt electrical system was on board to handle the lighting duties.

Moving in at a spot closer to the top of the food chain, two new 350cc models were now seen. The CB350 Super Sport rolled in with great fanfare from both Honda and the motorcycle press. *Cycle Illustrated* was greatly impressed by the CB350's 10500 rpm redline and latest five-speed transmission. A lack of engine vibration at any rpm was another feature of the newest member of the Honda family. The motor produced 36 horsepower, which for the day was quite an achievement. The semi-double-loop frame was crafted from pressed steel, and delivered adequate rigidity for the nimble handling machine. A pair of chrome-plated megaphone exhausts added a new sporty flair and the two-tone paint scheme on the 3.2-gallon fuel tank was all-new as well. The headlight bucket and side covers were white, while the fuel tank was sold in your choice of Candy Blue, Candy Red or Green with the lower half being White. The upper segments of the front forks were also finished in whatever color the buyer selected for the fuel tank.

Another "350" first seen in 1968 was the CL350 Scrambler (CL350K0). It was largely the same machine as the CB350, but was fitted with high-mounted chrome exhaust pipes that were covered with slotted heat shields and a black muffler shield.

The saddle covering was not pleated and the CL featured an oval taillight lens. Two-tone paint was again found on the 350, and Daytona Orange, Candy Blue or Candy Red was teamed with a lower section of White. Side covers and headlight shell were also White. Early CL350's featured upper fork legs of Black, while later iterations wore color that matched the primary paint. The same 325cc parallel twin motor shifted through five speeds.

First seen in 1965, Honda's CB450 Super Sport was being sent out to pasture by the end of 1968. To replace the retired model the CB450K1 Super Sport made its entrance in April of 1968. Chrome fenders replaced the painted variety used on the exiting model, and several additional cosmetic changes were also seen on the '68s. In place of the instruments that were melded into the headlight bezel of the previous model, the new K1 had a speedometer and tachometer that stood free, just above the headlight. Both the fuel tank and side covers were now finished in Candy Red, Candy Blue or Black. A stouter license plate support was also mounted to the revised rear fender.

The on-/off-road CL450K1 Scrambler was also introduced in February of 1968 and was equipped in the same fashion as most other

Instead of the typical frame-mounted location, the motor of the P50 was found residing directly at the source. Pedals were used to start the tiny machine and an automatic transmission chose the required gearing.

1968 Price Guide	6	5	4	3	2	1
CA100 (49cc single)	380	570	860	1,140	1,520	1,900
CA102 (49cc single)	380	570	860	1,140	1,520	1,900
S65 (65cc single)	380	570	860	1,140	1,520	1,900
CM91 (89cc single)	380	570	860	1,140	1,520	1,900
CL90 Scrambler (90cc single)	400	600	900	1,200	1,600	2,000
S90 (90cc single)	400	600	900	1,200	1,600	2,000
CL125A Scrambler (124cc twin)	400	600	900	1,200	1,600	2,000
SS125A (124cc twin)	420	630	950	1,260	1,680	2,100
CA160 Touring (161cc twin)	380	570	860	1,140	1,520	1,900
CB160 (161cc twin)	380	570	860	1,140	1,520	1,900
CL160 Scrambler (161cc twin)	380	570	860	1,140	1,520	1,900
CA175 Touring (174cc twin)	360	540	810	1,080	1,440	1,800
CL175K0 Scrambler (174cc twin)	360	540	810	1,080	1,440	1,800
CA77 Dream Touring "late" (305cc twin)	800	1,200	1,800	2,400	3,200	4,000
CB77 Super Hawk (305cc twin)	900	1,350	2,030	2,700	3,600	4,500
CL77 Scrambler (305cc twin)	700	1,050	1,580	2,100	2,800	3,500
CB350K0 (325cc twin)	740	1,110	1,670	2,220	2,960	3,700
CL350K0 Scrambler (325cc twin)	740	1,110	1,670	2,220	2,960	3,700
CB450K0 (444cc twin)	820	1,230	1,850	2,460	3,280	4,100
CB450K1 (444cc twin)	840	1,260	1,890	2,520	3,360	4,200
CL450K1 Scrambler (444cc twin)	840	1,260	1,890	2,520	3,360	4,200

Honda Scramblers. A pair of high exhaust pipes were finished in all-chrome, including the two-piece heat shield. The headlight bucket and upper fork legs were delivered in black and a chrome fender was used on both ends. The same 444cc, DOHC parallel twin motor rested in the frame as in the CB450K1. A "Honda 450" emblem complete with the corporate wing was applied to the fuel tank, which was sold in Candy Red, Candy Blue or Metallic Silver.

1968 also marked the final year for several other models. These machines simply disappeared, not to be replaced with newer models. The P50, CT90 Trail, CL160D Scrambler, CB77 Super Hawk and CL77 Scrambler would all face the final curtain before the year would draw to a close.

1968 MODELS

Model	Product Code	Engine Type/ Displacement	Transmission	Year(s) Available
CA100 Honda 50	005	OHV Single/49cc	3-Speed, Auto	1962-70
CA102 Honda 50	006	OHV Single/49cc	3-Speed, Auto	1962-69
CA110 Sport 50	022	OHV Single/49cc	3-Speed/4-Speed, Manuel	1962-69
P50 Little Honda	044	OHC Single/49cc	Automatic	1967-68
S65 Sport 65/CS65	035	OHC Single/63cc	4-Speed	1965-69
S90 Super 90	028	OHV Single/89cc	4-Speed, Manual	1964-69
CL90 Scrambler	056	OHC Single/89cc	4-Speed, Manual	1967-69
CL90L (5hp) Scrambler	056	OHC Single/89cc	4-Speed, Manual	1968-70
CM91 Honda 90	034	OHC Single/89cc	3-Speed, Auto	1966-69
CT90 Trail	053	OHC Single/89cc	4-Spd(early), 8-Spd(late)	1966-68
CL125A Scrambler	243	OHC Parallel Twin/124cc	4-Speed	1967-69
SS125A Super Sport	244	OHC Parallel Twin/124cc	4-Speed	1967-1969
CA160 Touring	225	OHC Parallel Twin/161cc	4-Speed	1966-1969
CB160 Sport	217	OHC Parallel Twin/161cc	4-Speed	1965-69
CL160D Scrambler	223	OHC Parallel Twin/161cc	4-Speed	1967-68
CA175 Touring (CD175)	237	OHC Parallel Twin/174cc	4-Speed	1968-69
CL175 Scrambler (CL175KO)	236	OHC Parallel Twin/174cc	5-Speed	1968-69
CA77 Dream Touring 305	267	OHC Parallel Twin/305cc	4-Speed	1963-69
CB77 Super Hawk 305	275	OHC Parallel Twin/305cc	4-Speed	1961-68
CL77 Scrambler 305	278	OHC Parallel Twin/305cc	4-Speed	1965-68
CB350 Super Sport (CB350KO)	287	OHC Parallel Twin/325cc	5-Speed	1968-69
CL350 Scrambler (CL350KO)	291	OHC Parallel Twin/325cc	5-Speed	1968-69
CB450 Super Sport (CB450KO)	283	DOHC Parallel Twin/444cc	4-Speed	1965-68
CB450K1 Super Sport	292	DOHC Parallel Twin/444cc	5-Speed	1968-69
CL450K1 Scrambler	294	DOHC Parallel Twin/444cc	5-Speed	1968-69

The 1968 CB450K1 was introduced in April of the same year.
Rick Darke photo

Candy Red, Black or Candy Blue were teamed with chrome "toaster" panels on the tank of the 450K1.
Rick Darke photo

The white piping on the saddle was only seen on the K1 variant of the CB450:
Rick Darke photo

Plenty of chrome added to the visual package on highly capable DOHC twin 450K1.
Rick Darke photo

The new-for-1968 CL350 Scrambler allowed for on- and off-road travel.
Rick Darke photo

The high-mounted exhaust kept the hot pipes away from ground cover.
Rick Darke photo

Decked out in White with a choice of Candy Red, Daytona Orange or Candy Blue, the 1968 CL350 was definitely a handsome machine.
Rick Darke photo

A chrome cross bar and street gauges were used on the 1968 CL450K1.

The bike was first listed in February of 1968. Rick Darke photo

Again designed for street and trail riding, the CL450 was nicely equipped for both in 1968. Rick Darke photo

The winged Honda logo was still a mainstay of the design and trim used on the 1968 bikes.
Rick Darke photo

1969

As any self-respecting motorcycle enthusiast knows, 1969 would see the world of two-wheeled transportation undergo a change that would alter the universe, as we knew it. Honda's introduction of the inline four CB750 set the bar higher than people could even reach before.

Four-cylinder motors had been used in other motorcycles as early as 1911. Ace, Cleveland, Henderson, Indian and Pierce were all American brands that attempted to sell cycles powered by four-cylinder engines. Their mounting was typically inline with the frame versus transverse as seen in the new CB750, and they lacked the technical prowess that was delivered in the 1969 Honda, but were considered state-of-the-art at the time. Of course, Honda

The introduction of the 1969 CB750 Four set the motorcycling world on its ear. The size, power and features were like nothing seen before on a Japanese machine. This bike opened the floodgates for higher performance, comfort and fun.
Owner: Ray Landy

Regardless of what angle you viewed the 750 from, it cut an impressive profile. The chrome four-into-four exhaust looked powerful, yet it was whisper quiet unless you gave the throttle a good twist.

continued to add and replace other models as well, but most were eclipsed by the big CB.

1969 would mark the final year for nearly 20 models in the catalog, while 11 new designations were found. The venerable Dream 305 would make its final appearance in 1969. It had served many Honda owners well.

The smallest of the 1969 models was the CL70 Scrambler (CL70K0). The 72cc, overhead-cam motor delivered power to a four-speed manual transmission. The single exhaust pipe was mounted about midway up the chassis, and was draped in a slotted heat shield. The exhaust, both fenders and the upper fork covers were chrome plated. Fuel tanks were all silver, but the frame could be had in Candy Red or Candy Blue. With the advent of the "K_" alphanumeric system, each cycle would be designated with a subsequent moniker with every alteration. "KO" was used on the first iteration, with the number changing each year a modification would occur.

For 1969, the CT90 Trail (CT90K0) was supplanted by the CT90K1. Major changes

736cc's of displacement were governed by a single overhead cam, and drew life through a set of four individual carburetors. With 68 horses on tap, the heavy 750 was no slouch, and performed admirably when tested by magazines and private owners.

The first CA77 Dream Touring 305 appeared in 1960, and 1969 was the final year for the dependable machine. The model was largely unchanged through its run, but 1963-69 models had a reshaped fuel tank.

included the telescopic front forks in place of the pressed-steel variety used on earlier models. The eight-speed, dual range transmission with an automatic clutch would become standard through the 1979 models. The Scarlet Red or Bright Yellow color options were both paired with a gray-colored shroud for the K1 through K5 versions.

In a break with its own rules, Honda replaced the CA175 Touring with the CA175K3 version. No K1 or K2 models were seen in the catalog. The K3 was built around a tubular steel chassis instead of the pressed-steel type used on the departing version. The cylinders of the newer motor were more vertical than the CA175 as well.

The latest tank emblem read only "Honda," while the side covers wore the "175" badge. The CA175 sported "Honda 175" badges on the tank and the side covers.

A new player in the cast was the CB175K3

Super Sport. First seen in June of 1969, it actually changed within the model year. A two-tone fuel tank was used on the entire 1969 run of CB175K3s, although the layout changed slightly on later versions. The first editions wore the chosen color (Candy Blue or Candy Red) on the top half of the tank, while White was used on the lower section. The "Honda" name was printed in the White section of the paint. Later models saw the color segment extended lower, and the "Honda" name appeared in the color field. Early models also had a non-pleated seat cover, while later offerings wore pleated vinyl on the saddle. The third intra-year change was the covered coil springs on the rear shocks on the later models, whereas the first units had exposed springs.

A 174cc, overhead-cam, parallel twin motor shifted through a five-speed transmission, and a 12-volt electrical system provided the electrics. Both fenders and the low-mounted exhaust megaphones were chrome plated. Spoke wheels and drum brakes were used at both ends of the CB175K3.

For those with an off-road desire, the existing CL175 Scrambler upgraded to the CL175K3 Scrambler. The newest form included fenders; fuel tank, side covers and headlight shell that were all painted the same shade, depending on what was ordered. Candy Blue and Candy Orange were your choices. A silver stripe was used on the tank. To better allow for rugged adventures, the front fender was mounted high above the front tire, replacing the rubber-hugging version used before. The frame was now an all-tubular layout in place of the tubular backbone on the K0 version. The motor's cylinders were also more upright on the new bike.

The CB350K0 Super Sport was replaced by the CB350K1 Super Sport for 1969, and only minimal changes were applied to the '69 model. A second stripe of base color was added to the fuel tank, and the "Honda" name now resided within that stripe. The seat was covered with pleated vinyl and a single reflector was added to the front fender. A rectangular taillight lens was also seen in place of the oval style.

The CL350K1 received the same upgrades as the CB for this year.

Moving up the scales was the newly minted CB450K2 Super Sport, which took the place of the existing K1 variant. The tank was shaped differently and wore a gold accent stripe on the upper contour. Just below this stripe were new metal tank badges, replacing the earlier painted monikers.

The side cover emblems were also finished in gold, and color choices were Candy Red and the new Candy Blue-Green. The rectangular taillight lens also found its way onto the 1969 CB450.

The CL450 was altered from the previous K1 to the latest K2 model. Changes included a gold stripe on the fuel tank, joined by "Honda" painted in white letters. "450 DOHC" side-cover emblems were also done in gold for the latest model. The pleated seating surface and rectangular taillight were also added.

Of course the news everyone had been waiting for was the introduction of the CB750 Four (CB750K0) model released on the 6th of June 1969. The new four-cylinder model embodied the best of everything Honda had to offer, and surpassed anything else on the market. Period advertising claimed: "Sooner or later, you knew Honda would do it." The gatefold ad featured the all-new model in Candy Blue-Green paint, and it looked like nothing the cycling world had seen before.

Beneath the 5-gallon fuel tank resided the inline four that changed all the rules. Displacing 736cc's, and breathing through a set of four carburetors and sending the spent gases through a four-into-four exhaust, these bikes were superior to anything most enthusiasts had ever seen or ridden. Honda claimed the bike produced 68 horsepower at 8500 rpm, and could run up to 125 mph "sans coaching."

The fuel tank on the later CA77 Dream Touring 305s rested above the time-tested 305cc, parallel-twin motor that had served Honda riders faithfully for many years.

1969 PRICE GUIDE	6	5	4	3	2	1
CA100 (49cc single)	360	540	810	1,080	1,440	1,800
CA102 (49cc single)	360	540	810	1,080	1,440	1,800
S65 (65cc single)	380	570	860	1,140	1,520	1,900
CL70 Scrambler (72cc single)	400	600	900	1,200	1,600	2,000
CM91 (89cc single)	380	570	860	1,140	1,520	1,900
SL90 Motosport (89cc single)	380	570	860	1,140	1,520	1,900
CL90 Scrambler (90cc single)	400	600	900	1,200	1,600	2,000
S90 (90cc single)	400	600	900	1,200	1,600	2,000
CL125A Scrambler (124cc twin)	400	600	900	1,200	1,600	2,000
SS125A (124cc twin)	400	600	900	1,200	1,600	2,000
CA160 Touring (161cc twin)	370	560	830	1,110	1,480	1,850
CB160 (161cc twin)	380	570	860	1,140	1,520	1,900
CA175 Touring (174cc twin)	340	510	770	1,020	1,360	1,700
CA175K3 Touring (174cc twin)	340	510	770	1,020	1,360	1,700
CB175K3 Super Sport "early" (174cc twin)	340	510	770	1,020	1,360	1,700
CB175K3 Super Sport "late" (174cc twin)	350	530	790	1,050	1,400	1,750
CL175K0 Scrambler (174cc twin)	360	540	810	1,080	1,440	1,800
CL175K3 Scrambler (174cc twin)	360	540	810	1,080	1,440	1,800
CA77 Dream Touring "late" (305cc twin)	740	1,110	1,670	2,220	2,960	3,700
CB350K0 (325cc twin)	700	1,050	1,580	2,100	2,800	3,500
CB350K1 (325cc twin)	700	1,050	1,580	2,100	2,800	3,500
CL350K0 Scrambler (325cc twin)	740	1,110	1,670	2,220	2,960	3,700
CL350K1 Scrambler (325cc twin)	740	1,110	1,670	2,220	2,960	3,700
SL350K0 Motosport (325cc twin)	440	660	990	1,320	1,760	2,200
CB450K1 (444cc twin)	820	1,230	1,850	2,460	3,280	4,100
CB450K2 (444cc twin)	810	1,220	1,820	2,430	3,240	4,050
CL450K1 Scrambler (444cc twin)	800	1,200	1,800	2,400	3,200	4,000
CL450K2 Scrambler (444cc twin)	800	1,200	1,800	2,400	3,200	4,000
CB750 "Diecast" (736cc four)	1,600	2,400	3,600	4,800	6,400	8,000
CB750 "Sandcast" (736cc four)	3,200	4,800	7,200	9,600	12,800	16,000

Cycle Guide magazine reported a dry weight of 510 lbs. while the Honda ad claimed 445. Although Honda had several DOHC machines in the stable, the new CB750 had only one. Both an electric start and kick-start pedal were aboard to get the big CB running. Once started, a four-into-four throttle cable system was used to activate the bank of carbs. This was a K0 item only. Another rarity of the early models was the "sandcast" alloy cases on the motor. These would be replaced by cases formed with more traditional methods before the 1969 model run was complete.

With all that power on tap, the new Honda needed something better in the braking department too. A single hydraulic disc joined the internally expanding rear drum brake up front. Certainly far better than a double-drum setup, it still wasn't much, especially when compared to today's high-tech components. Zero-to-60 mph times were in the mid 5-second range, and 30-to-0 stopping took nearly 30 feet, according to the Cycle Guide test in the September 1969 issue.

A double-loop, steel tube frame held everything in place and both ends were fully sus-

Fitted with a new seat and fuel tank, the 1969 CB450 Super Sort was all grown up.
Rick Darke photo

1969 MODELS

Model	Product Code	Engine Type/ Displacement	Transmission	Year(s) Available
CA100 Honda 50	005	OHV Single/49cc	3-Speed, Auto	1962-70
CA102 Honda 50	006	OHV Single/49cc	3-Speed, Auto	1962-69
CA110 Sport 50	022	OHV Single/49cc	3-Speed/4-Speed, Man.	1962-69
S65 Sport 65/CS65	035	OHC Single/63cc	4-Speed	1965-69
CL70 Scrambler (CL70K0)	089	OHC Single/72cc	4-Speed, Manual	1969
S90 Super 90/CS90	028	OHV Single/89cc	4-Speed, Manual	1964-69
CL90 Scrambler	056	OHC Single/89cc	4-Speed, Manual	1967-69
CL90L (5hp) Scrambler	056	OHC Single/89cc	4-Speed, Manual	1968-70
CM91 Honda 90	034	OHC Single/89cc	3-Speed, Auto	1966-69
CT90K1 Trail	077	OHC Single/89cc	8-Speed, Auto	1969
CL125A Scrambler	243	OHC Parallel Twin/124cc	4-Speed	1967-69
SS125A Super Sport	244	OHC Parallel Twin/124cc	4-Speed	1967-69
CA160 Touring	225	OHC Parallel Twin/161cc	4-Speed	1966-69
CB160 Sport	217	OHC Parallel Twin/161cc	4-Speed	1965-69
CA175 Touring	237	OHC Parallel Twin/174cc	4-Speed	1968-69
CA175K3 Touring/(CD175K3)	302	OHC Parallel Twin/174cc	4-Speed	1969-70
CB175K3 Super Sport	306	OHC Parallel Twin/174cc	5-Speed	1969
CL175 Scrambler	236	OHC Parallel Twin/174cc	5-Speed	1968-69
CL175K3 Scrambler	307	OHC Parallel Twin/174cc	5-Speed	1969-70
CA77 Dream Touring 305	267	OHC Parallel Twin/305cc	4-Speed	1963-69
CB350 Super Sport (CB350K0)	287	OHC Parallel Twin/325cc	5-Speed	1968-69
CB350K1 Super Sport	287	OHC Parallel Twin/325cc	5-Speed	1969
CL350 Scrambler (CB350K0)	291	OHC Parallel Twin/325cc	5-Speed	1968-69
CL350K1 Scrambler	291	OHC Parallel Twin/325cc	5-Speed	1969
CB450K1 Super Sport	292	DOHC Parallel Twin/444cc	5-Speed	1968-69
CB450K2 Super Sport	292	DOHC Parallel Twin/444cc	5-Speed	1969
CL450K1 Scrambler	294	DOHC Parallel Twin/444cc	5-Speed	1968-69
CL450K2 Scrambler	294	OHC Parallel Twin/444cc	5-Speed	1969
CB750 Four (CB750K0)	300	SOHC Inline Four/736cc	5-Speed	1969-70

Only minor changes, including an extra tank stripe, set the 1969 CL350K1 apart from the 1968 model.
Rick Darke photo

pended. The large, flat pillion made an excellent perch for two riders, and magazines raved about the comfort and handling, despite the high weight reading.

The cost of entry for this brand-new rocket ship was a breathtaking $1,495 in 1969. That price included your choice of Candy Blue-Green, Candy Gold or Candy Ruby Red. A simple gold accent stripe with black pinstripes was also applied to the top curvature of the fuel tank. Both side covers were finished in the selected body color and wore five-sided badges complete with "750" and the Honda "wing".

Sales of the new model were brisk, and the other manufacturers were sent scrambling in an effort to catch up with the four-cylinder beast from Honda. It would be several years before any real competition appeared.

The pleated pillion was also new for 1969.
Rick Darke photo

Side covers and a headlight bucket returned in white for 1969 on the 350K1.
Rick Darke photo

Another list of model alterations awaiting the Honda buyer as new models faded and fresh blood was infused into the catalog in 1970.

The 50cc CA100, first seen in 1962, would make its final showing 1970. The slightly more powerful C70M (C70MK0) would supplant the tiny machine in the new model year. Still the smallest street-legal model from Honda, the CA100 featured electric start and a two-person

saddle complete with passenger foot pegs. The molded front cowling remained white with a choice of Aquarius Blue, Bright Red and Pine Green for the chassis, fenders and fork.

Many of Honda's models would change in incremental fashion and receive the latest "K_ _" designation to mark the revisions. The latest CL70K1 Scrambler now carried its fossil fuel

The CB450K3 Super Sport for 1970 wore a new exhaust and offered two additional color choices to the buyer.
Rick Darke photo

Pleated fork boots were used on the 1970 editions of the CB450 and a front disc brake replaced the drum unit.
Rick Darke photo

1970 MODELS

Model	Product Code	Engine Type/Displacement	Transmission	Year(s) Available
CA100 Honda 50	005	OHV Single/49cc	3-Speed, Auto	1962-1970
C70M Honda 70 (C70MK0)	087	OHC Single/72cc	3-Speed, Auto	1970-1971
CL70K1 Scrambler	111	OHC Single/72cc	4-Speed, Manual	1970
CL90L (5hp) Scrambler	056	OHC Single/89cc	4-Speed, Manual	1968-1970
CT90K2 Trail	102	OHC Single/89cc	8-Speed	1970
CB100 Super Sport (CB100K0)	107	OHC Single/99cc	5-Speed	1970
CL100 Scrambler (CL100K0)	108	OHC Single/99cc	5-Speed	1970
CA175K3 Touring/(CD175K3)	302	OHC Parallel Twin/174cc	4-Speed	1969-1970
CB175K4 Super Sport	315	OHC Parallel Twin/174cc	5-Speed	1970
CL175K3 Scrambler	307	OHC Parallel Twin/174cc	5-Speed	1969-1970
CL175K4 Scrambler	316	OHC Parallel Twin/174cc	5-Speed	1970
CB350K2 Super Sport	317	OHC Parallel Twin/325cc	5-Speed	1970
CL350K2 Scrambler	318	OHC Parallel Twin/325cc	5-Speed	1970
CB450K3 Super Sport	319	DOHC Parallel Twin/444cc	5-Speed	1970
CL450K3 Scrambler	320	DOHC Parallel Twin/444cc	5-Speed	1970
CB750 Four (CB750K0)	300	SOHC Inline Four/736cc	5-Speed	1969-1970
CB750K1 750 Four	300	SOHC Inline Four/736cc	5-Speed	1970-1971

in a freshly shaped tank that was finished in Silver Metallic with the winged Honda logo applied to each side. The speedometer was now housed as an individual gauge versus molded into the headlight bucket as seen on the previous K0. The headlight housing was now also finished to match the chosen frame color of either Candy Sapphire Blue or Candy Topaz Orange. Rear shock springs were now enclosed in cylindrical shrouds.

The 5hp CL90L Scrambler would be seen no longer after the close of the 1970 season.

The CT90K2 received a set of matching gray side covers to better accent the previously added gray shroud. The latest alteration to the handlebars was the addition of the swivel-lock mechanism.

New in the locker room for 1970 was the CB100 Super Sport (CB100K0). Powered by a 99cc OHC motor, it was built with styling that mimicked the bigger street-going variants. A tubular black frame was matched with color-keyed fuel tank, side covers, front forks and headlight shell. Candy Blue, Candy Ruby Red and Candy Gold were the base colors, and all three were mated with a white stripe on the fuel tank and "100" on the side covers. Chrome fenders were fitted over both tires. Rear shock covers were also fitted with color-matched covers. Another 99cc choice for 1970 was aimed at the on/off road crowd. The CL100 Scrambler (CL100K0) was nearly identical to the CB100, but varied in a few details. The upswept exhaust of the CL100 was covered with a two-piece heat shield, and the fuel tank was of a different shape.

Hues were also different in the Candy Sapphire Blue, Candy Ruby Red and Candy Topaz Orange paint choices.

Another Honda making its final appearance in 1970 was the CA175K3 Touring (CD175K3), which had first rolled out only a year before. The CB175K4 Super Sport was there to take the reins. For 1970, the K4 was seen with a two-tone fuel tank decorated with white Honda "wings" on each side and the word "Honda" in black. The side covers now wore

identification of black "175" against a white background. Available colors were altered and Candy Blue Green, Candy Gold and Candy Ruby Red were now the choices.

The CL175K3 Scrambler would be replaced in March of 1970 with the CL175K4 Scrambler. Changes on the K4 edition included chrome fenders that hugged the tires, a black heat shield on the muffler and a white tank stripe that had a new contour. The pillion and fuel tank were also re-shaped for the latest iteration. The upper segment of the front forks, as well as the headlight shell, were also delivered in the color selected by the buyer. Candy Ruby Red, Candy Sapphire Blue and Candy Topaz Orange were on tap for 1970.

The CB350K2 Super Sport was enhanced with a few minor upgrades. The front fender braces were connected to the lower end of the front fork tubes. Previously they were located further up the legs. The front fender-mounted reflector was also moved to each side of the upper fork legs for increased visibility. The latest color scheme included the two-tone tank seen on other 1970 models with matching side covers, upper fork legs and headlight shells. Candy Blue Green, Candy Gold and Candy Ruby Red were the 1970 color options. The CL350K2 Scrambler also experienced some cosmetic changes for the new year. A different profile of the fuel tank was augmented by a white ac-

1970 PRICE GUIDE	6	5	4	3	2	1
CA100 (49cc single)	240	360	540	720	960	1,200
C70MK0 (72cc single)	240	360	540	720	960	1,200
CL70K1 Scrambler (72cc single)	250	380	560	750	1,000	1,250
CB100K0 Super Sport (99cc single)	260	390	590	780	1,040	1,300
CL100K0 Scrambler (99cc single)	220	330	500	660	880	1,100
SL100K0 Motosport (99cc single)	220	330	500	660	880	1,100
CA175K3 Touring 175 (174cc twin)	280	420	630	840	1,120	1,400
CB175K4 Super Sport (174cc twin)	270	410	610	810	1,080	1,350
CL175K3 Scrambler (174cc twin)	270	410	610	810	1,080	1,350
CL175K4 Scrambler (174cc twin)	270	410	610	810	1,080	1,350
SL175K0 Motosport (174cc twin)	360	540	810	1,080	1,440	1,800
CB350K2 (325cc twin)	580	870	1,310	1,740	2,320	2,900
CL350K2 Scrambler (325cc twin)	580	870	1,310	1,740	2,320	2,900
SL350K0 Motosport (325cc twin)	560	840	1,260	1,680	2,240	2,800
SL350K1 Motosport (325cc twin)	560	840	1,260	1,680	2,240	2,800
CB450K3 (444cc twin)	640	960	1,440	1,920	2,560	3,200
CL450K2 Scrambler (444cc twin)	650	980	1,460	1,950	2,600	3,250
CB750 (736cc four)	1,600	2,400	3,600	4,800	6,400	8,000

The 1970 CB750K1 presents a classic and now-familiar profile.

The motor was not changed from the '69 version, but earlier corrections had proved to be all the power plant needed. A 0-to-60 time of 6.2 seconds was recorded by Cycle magazine in its July 1970 issue. High levels of praise for every facet of the machine were also printed in the issue, helping to move the latest 450 from Honda into a new level of desirability.

The 450 Scrambler did not receive the same revisions as the Super Sport, but did have a few minor details addressed. Fuel tank graphics were altered to include a white, tapered stripe, but the side covers remained the same. The muffler heat shield was also modified and was still finished in chrome. Candy Ruby Red, Candy Sapphire Blue and Candy Topaz Orange were the available colors for 1970.

cent stripe, and the selected unit color (Candy Ruby Red, Candy Sapphire Blue or Candy Topaz Orange) was applied to the tank, side covers, upper forks and headlight bucket. The previously black heat shield on the muffler was exchanged for a perforated chrome version.

For 1970, the Honda CB450K3 Super Sport was tweaked into a machine that many magazine editors of the day considered to be a perfect machine. Changes from the 1969 K2 edition were not radical, but were enough to push the latest version into greatness. With a weight just over 420 lbs., and 45 horsepower on tap, the latest CB450 was both nimble and stable.

Medium- and long-range touring were considered as realistic options, despite earlier complaints of harshness and vibration. To assist in the deceleration department, a hydraulic front disc brake was installed on the 1970 model, and really enhanced performance over the drum brake used before. A major improvement on the 1970 CB450 was the application of the front fork "borrowed" from its big brother, the CB750. Not only was the fork a beefier unit, the geometry led to nearly perfect road handling and comfort. The nitrogen-pressurized DeCarbon rear shocks were also fairly substantial.

Last, but certainly not least, there were some changes on the CB750 late in 1970. The CB750K0 remained on the books until the 21st of September, when the CB750K1 was released. The latest version wore smaller side covers that were devoid of the cosmetic slots seen on the previous models. A new version of the side cover badge was also seen on the K1 models. New colors were listed as Candy Ruby Red, Candy Gold, Valley Green Metallic and Candy Garnet Brown.

The only mechanical alteration was the implementation of a two-cable throttle system in place of the 4-into-4 design first used. The new design worked by having one cable pull the throttles open while the other pulled them closed. The big 750 continued to set the pace at Honda dealers, as people grew accustomed to the power and comfort the CB delivered.

White tank stripes help identify the 1970 CL450 K3 and an accessory chrome luggage rack adds to the utility.
Rick Darke photo

The 1970 CL450 featured the peforated muffler heat shield combined with the slotted pipe guards. Rick Darke photo

1971

Overall model changes for 1971 were minor, but alterations were made to nearly every unit in the sales catalog. Constant refinement and improvement were a priority at Honda, and the result was great strides in sales and market dominance.

The CL70K2 was the smallest of the Hondas to receive adjustments in 1971. The always-Silver Metallic fuel tank was trimmed with tapered stripes to match the unit color chosen. Candy Red joined the ranks of Candy Sapphire Blue and Candy Topaz Orange, which were carried over from 1970. The upper portions of the front forks were also finished in the unit color on the 1971 models.

Still a popular choice for the new year, the CT90K3 received a few minor cosmetic changes. Bright Yellow was replaced by Summer Yellow on the color charts, and an accent band of black ran around the frame shroud, near the steering head. The exhaust system was mechanically unchanged, but now featured black piping covered by chrome heat shields.

For the entry-level street rider, the CB100K1 also was dealt a few new hands for 1971. The contour of the saddle was mildly enhanced, and a strip of bright chrome was added to the lower edge. Side cover "CB100" badges were now molded in plastic versus the adhesive graphics of the previous version. In place of the white accent stripe, the lower 1/3 of the fuel tank was finished in white with "Honda" falling within that zone. The 1970 option of Candy Blue Green was replaced with Crystal Blue Metallic.

Changes to the CL100K1 were slightly more dramatic for 1971. The multi-section heat shield, which was previously vented with elongated slots, was now a one-piece unit, perforated with cylindrical openings. A chrome strip was also added to the lower lip of the CL's saddle. The fenders, both front and rear, remained chrome, but the front unit was now suspended with a pair of curved supports on both sides of the fork. Poppy Yellow Metallic supplanted Candy Ruby Red, and a new stripe was seen on the side of the fuel tank. On the Poppy Yellow, a black stripe was applied. With the Candy

Seen here in Strato Blue Metallic, the 1971 CL350 was built for on- and off-road use.

The CL350's 325cc motor provided ample motivation on the streets and trails.

Sapphire Blue or Candy Topaz Orange, the swooping stripe was white. Regardless of color, the new graphic swept gracefully from the rear top edge of the tank, and blended into a flat-sided segment that continued back to the saddle. A molded plastic CL100 badge was also used on both side covers.

To meet with specific market demands, the CL100S0 was a de-tuned version of the CL100K1. The only visible alteration was the "CL100S" badge used on the side covers of the less-powerful model.

Splitting hairs, the CB175K5 Super Sport was almost identical to the K2 model it replaced. The previous paint scheme on the fuel tank included a single pinstripe that separated the upper and lower segments of the housing. The 1971 version sported a pair of stripes that took up the same area of the earlier single stripe. "Honda" now fell into a horizontal space between the front and rear sections of this art. Candy Blue Green was also removed from the options column, but was replaced by Crystal Blue Metallic. The side cover emblems had the same shape and size, but were now cast in plastic and featured a chrome background with the white "175" on a field of black.

All CL175K5 models featured a few more changes than the CB for the latest selling year. The 1971 exhaust heat shield was now an all-chrome piece, and the cooling slots were horizontal in the front section and cylindrical at the muffler. Two of the 1971 colors were new and they joined the remaining Candy Topaz Orange, which was held over. Strato Blue Metallic and Poppy Yellow Metallic were the new hues. Regardless of which look you selected, the tank, side covers, upper fork legs, headlight bucket and both fenders were covered. A new fuel tank graphic was applied and was black no matter which unit color was chosen.

In the 350 class, the CB350K3 was the recipient of a new fuel tank and graphics package. The newly shaped fuel receptacle now featured a reverse backswept accent stripe that was applied in black, regardless of the base color. Base colors were changed to Derby Green Metallic

and Light Ruby Red, with Candy Gold being carried over from 1970. The color was now applied to the tank, side covers and headlight shell and the upper fork legs. A revised "350" badge was also found on each side cover.

The CL350 was virtually unchanged for 1971 save the color choices and tank graphics. Candy Topaz Orange was again an option and was joined by Strato Blue Metallic and Poppy Yellow Metallic. The new tank stripe was black, regardless of the base color applied.

In the 450 division, both the CB and CL models were upgraded cosmetically, but no alterations were made on the mechanical side of the equation. The pillion on the CB450K was revised and finished with a new pleating pattern.

The side covers now boasted "Double Overhead Cam 450" badges. Color changes saw the addition of Valley Green Metallic and Polynesian Blue Metallic to the Candy Gold and Candy Ruby Red, which were carried over from 1970.

The CL variant did have a new one-piece muffler and a newly vented heat shield, also

The 1969 CB175K3 Super Sport was supplanted by the K4 in March of 1970.
Rick Darke photo

Simple guages were still part of the CB175's allure.
Rick Darke photo

Revised tank graphics and the lack of knee pads

distinguished the 1970 CB175K3 from the '69 model.

Rick Darke photo

1971 MODELS

Model	Product Code	Engine Type/ Displacement	Transmission	Year(s) Available
C70M Honda 70 (C70MKO)	087	OHC Single/72cc	3-Speed, Auto	1970-71
CL70K2 Scrambler	111	OHC Single/72cc	4-Speed, Manual	1971
CT90K3 Trail	102	OHC Single/89cc	8-Speed	1971
CB100K1 Super Sport	107	OHC Single/99cc	5-Speed	1971
CL100K1 Scrambler	108	OHC Single/99cc	5-Speed	1971
CL100S Scrambler (CL100SO)	108	OHC Single/99cc	5-Speed	1971
CB175K5 Super Sport	315	OHC Parallel Twin/174cc	5-Speed	1971
CL175K5 Scrambler	316	OHC Parallel Twin/174cc	5-Speed	1971
CB350K3 Super Sport	317	OHC Parallel Twin/325cc	5-Speed	1971
CL350K3 Scrambler	318	OHC Parallel Twin/325cc	5-Speed	1971
CB450K4 Super Sport	319	DOHC Parallel Twin/444cc	5-Speed	1971
CL450K4 Scrambler	320	DOHC Parallel Twin/444cc	5-Speed	1971
CB500K0 500 Four	323	SOHC Inline Four/498cc	5-Speed	1971
CB750K1 750 Four	300	SOHC Inline Four/736cc	5-Speed	1970-71

done in one section, replacing the previous two-piece unit. New tank graphics included the black stripe and two new colors, Strato Blue Metallic and Poppy Yellow Metallic, joined the old standby Candy Topaz Orange. The side covers also wore the "Double Overhead Cam 450" designation.

While the brutish CB750 was winning over new riders every day, some prospective buyers were still a bit daunted by the size and weight of the bigger bike. For those who simply asked for a bit less, the CB500 Four was rolled out in June of 1971. Almost identical in design to its bigger brother, the CB500 was downsized in every dimension, weight included. With the tank half full, the CB500 tipped the scales at only 427 lbs., which was about 80 lbs. fewer than the 750. Also known as the Super Sport 500, this new addition would quickly carve a niche all its own.

Regardless of the enormous weight savings, the CB500 was equipped as nicely as the CB750. Front disc brake, wide, comfortable saddle and a bevy of comfort and convenience features made for a terrific purchase option. The inline four motor produced 50 horsepower at 9000 rpm, making it a bit easier to handle for most riders. Displacing 498cc and governed by a single overhead cam, the smaller motor also

looked a lot like the bigger Honda. A bank of 4 Keihin, 22mm carbs handled the fuel/air delivery, and a new "walking beam" was installed to smooth out throttle response. It provided identical input to all 4 Keihins regardless of the level of input.

The four-into-four exhaust was different than the 750 in both size and its megaphone design. The tail end of each pipe tapered, and then expanded again into a conical shape. Using a drive chain with the same dimensions as the 750's ensured less trouble for the rider. Seems the bigger 750's torque raised havoc on the drive chain, forcing lots of adjustments to keep things rolling smoothly.

With a top speed just shy of 100 mph, the CB500 provided adequate power for almost any rider, especially those who didn't need the monster levels delivered by the 750 version. List price in 1971 was $1,345 for the entire package.

Candy Jet Green, Candy Garnet Brown or Star Light Gold were all seen with a black accent panel on each side of the fuel tank.

Released late in 1970, the CB750K1 returned to the 1971 catalog unchanged. The 1972 K2 variant appeared in March of 1972 and would bring along several modifications.

The CL350 was designed to be a fairly compact machine and handle a wide variety of riding conditions, but any really rough stuff made quick work of the metal front fender.

1971 PRICE GUIDE	6	5	4	3	2	1
C70MK0 (72cc single)	190	290	430	570	760	950
CL70K2 Scrambler (72cc single)	190	290	430	570	760	950
SL70K0 Motosport (72cc single)	210	320	470	630	840	1,050
CB100K1 Super Sport (99cc single)	240	360	540	720	960	1,200
CL100K1 Scrambler (99cc single)	250	380	560	750	1,000	1,250
CL100S0 Scrambler 100S (99cc single)	250	380	560	750	1,000	1,250
SL100K1 Motosport (99cc single)	260	390	590	780	1,040	1,300
SL125K0 Motosport (122cc single)	270	410	610	810	1,080	1,350
CB175K5 Super Sport (174cc twin)	270	410	610	810	1,080	1,350
CL175K5 Scrambler (174cc twin)	280	420	630	840	1,120	1,400
SL175K1 Motosport (174cc twin)	280	420	630	840	1,120	1,400
CB350K3 (325cc twin)	540	810	1,220	1,620	2,160	2,700
CL350K3 Scrambler (325cc twin)	550	830	1,240	1,650	2,200	2,750
SL350K1 Motosport (325cc twin)	540	810	1,220	1,620	2,160	2,700
CB450K4 (444cc twin)	640	960	1,440	1,920	2,560	3,200
CL450K2 Scrambler (444cc twin)	640	960	1,440	1,920	2,560	3,200
CB500 (495cc four)	700	1,050	1,580	2,100	2,800	3,500
CB750 (736cc four)	1,600	2,400	3,600	4,800	6,400	8,000

A single overhead cam stirred the CL350's parallel-twin motor, and five speeds were available.

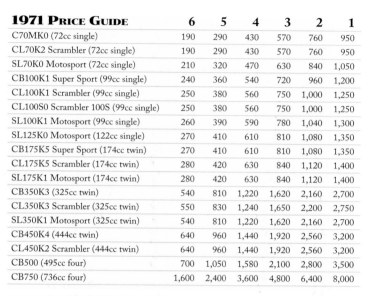

The high-mounted exhaust featured heat shields to prevent brush fires and protected the passenger's legs from burns.

The pointed tank stripe was new for the 1971 CL350s, and was always in Black regardless of what color CL you bought.

1972

1972 proved to be another year of mild revisions to the existing model lineup. Two new names were added to the roster, but even those were more like new lyrics to the same tune.

For the fans of the step-through models, Honda introduced the C70K1. It featured the traditional molded front shroud that provided the rider's legs a bit of respite from the elements and added a touch of style to the diminutive machine. The generous solo seat was now joined by a stout luggage rack that added a bit of functionality to the high-mileage model. With a shroud that was always finished in White, the frame color options were Strato Blue Metallic and Poppy Yellow Metallic. A "Honda 70" emblem was located on the fuel tank and electric start made life easy.

A few minor revisions were made to the

The CB750 was back for another year in 1972, but only minor changes were seen on the latest iteration. The tires and spark wires have been upgraded on this example.
Owner: David Bloom

The 736cc, inline-four motor remained at the top of the heap in the horsepower war, but 1973 would bring some competition from Kawasaki.

Flake Sunrise Orange was chosen for the CB750's side covers, which were carried over from the previous year, badges and all.

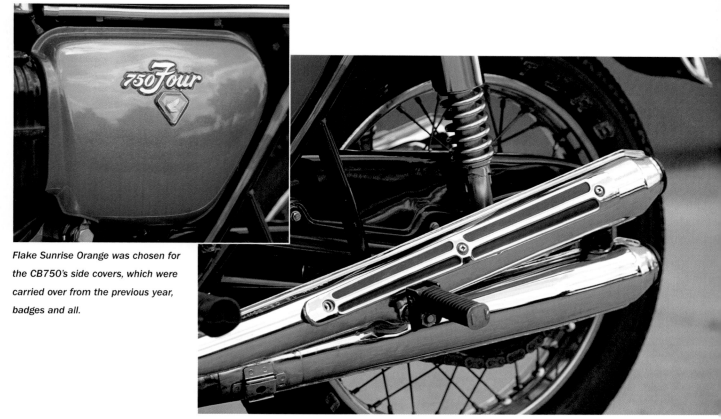

The four-into-four exhaust was another item seen on the 1971 CB750. Heat shields were still in place on the top set of pipes to protect the passenger's legs.

Rubber fork gaitors were still in place on the CB750, but for 1972 the upper fork legs were finished in chrome versus the black paint used before.

The two-place saddle remained a flat, comfortable perch and included a grab strap for the passenger's comfort and safety.

CL70K3 Scrambler, too. The saddle retained the same basic shape, but was now covered in a different vinyl pattern and trim level. The heat shield and exhaust were mounted at a slightly higher location and the shield's venting was changed as well. A segment of black was now inserted within the chrome, and it was perforated by large cylindrical openings.

All fuel tanks on the 1972 models were finished in Special Silver Metallic with a set of red and black pin stripes. Your choice of Candy Sapphire Blue or Candy Ruby Red was applied to the frame. The headlight bucket was black and the upper fork legs were chrome.

Alterations on the CT90K5 Trail were also minor. Previous piping on the seat cover was replaced with a solid black vinyl accented with

a series of rivets along the bottom edges. An auxiliary fuel tank was now mounted to the left of the rear-mounted luggage rack. The black band was removed from the Honda logo on the shroud, and only Mars Orange was offered for 1972.

Cosmetic changes in the graphics were the only variation found on the CB100K2 Super Sport for the latest year. The fuel tank and side covers were finished in white, with two choices of accent graphics. The split panel on the tank was always black on the lower section, but with your choice of Light Scarlet Red or Aquarius Blue on the top. A triangular section on the side cover logo would match whatever color was selected for the tank graphics. 1972 turned out to be the final year for the CB100 model.

The CL100K2 was also in its final year, and would only be fitted with a few minor trim changes. The previous tank graphic was altered to a set of trim, red and white stripes that were found on either a Candy Yellow or Hawaiian Blue Metallic paint. The side covers carried a small red triangle below the "CL100" badge. The shape of the heat shield was radically changed. The contour first clung closely to the diameter of the exhaust, but swelled into a large oblong shape before tapering down to allow the exhaust tube to exit. It was still perforated with small openings to vent heat.

With the exception of new colors being offered, the CL100S2 returned to the fold unchanged for 1972. Candy Yellow or Hawaiian Blue Metallic were now the shades of choice.

For the more aggressive or experienced rider, the CB175K6 was back again with some new trim added to the existing well-built machine. The newly shaped, 2.4-gallon fuel tank was decorated with a curvaceous black stripe that held the "Honda" name within the field. Side covers were also reshaped and now wore a set of horizontal vents in a vertical arrangement at the leading edge. The "175" logo was white against a black background, and red triangle held the Honda wing beneath it. The saddle wore a modified contour with a slight upturn at the rear edge. The frame and headlight shell were black while the tank and side covers could be had in Light Ruby Red or Candy Gold.

The 282-lb. dry weight allowed the CB-175K6 to reach a top speed of 76 mph, and it sold for $894 in 1972.

The Scrambler fans still had the CL175K6 to choose from as well. For 1972, many cosmetic changes were again made, but nothing in the mechanical department. In place of the painted fenders and upper fork segments found on the 1971 models, the 1972s had chrome instead. Both the exhaust and muffler heat shields remained chrome, but their slotting was again altered. The exhaust was wrapped with sheet metal utilizing a series of angled slots, while the reshaped muffler cover still had a set of cylindrical openings. Magna Red or Varnish Blue Metallic were the color choices. On the Magna Red model, striping on the fuel tank was white and yellow. Blue models came with white and orange stripes.

Honda still had two models in the 1972 family powered by 350cc motors, both paral-

1972 PRICE GUIDE	6	5	4	3	2	1
C70MK1 (72cc single)	190	290	430	570	760	950
CL70K3 Scrambler (72cc single)	190	290	430	570	760	950
SL70K0 Motosport (72cc single)	190	290	430	570	760	950
CB100K2 Super Sport (99cc single)	220	330	500	660	880	1,100
CL100K2 Scrambler (99cc single)	220	330	500	660	880	1,100
CL100S2 Scrambler 100S (99cc single)	230	350	520	690	920	1,150
SL100L2 Motosport (99cc single)	230	350	520	690	920	1,150
SL125K1 Motosport (122cc single)	220	330	500	660	880	1,100
CB175K6 Super Sport (174cc twin)	230	350	520	690	920	1,150
CL175K6 Scrambler (174cc twin)	230	350	520	690	920	1,150
SL175K1 Motosport (174cc twin)	230	350	520	690	920	1,150
XL250K0 Motosport (248cc single)	300	450	680	900	1,200	1,500
CB350K4 (325cc twin)	360	540	810	1,080	1,440	1,800
CL350K2 Motosport (325cc twin)	360	540	810	1,080	1,440	1,800
CL350K4 Scrambler (325cc twin)	360	540	810	1,080	1,440	1,800
CB350F (350cc four)	480	720	1,080	1,440	1,920	2,400
CB450K5 (444cc twin)	400	600	900	1,200	1,600	2,000
CL450K2 Scrambler (444cc twin)	400	600	900	1,200	1,600	2,000
CB500 (495cc four)	640	960	1,440	1,920	2,560	3,200
CB750 (736cc four)	1,600	2,400	3,600	4,800	6,400	8,000

1972 MODELS

Model	Product Code	Engine Type/ Displacement	Transmission	Year(s) Available
C70K1 Honda 70 (C70MK1)	092	OHC Single/72cc	3-Speed, Auto	1972-1973
CL70K3 Scrambler	111	OHC Single/72cc	4-Speed, Manual	1972-1973
CT90K4 Trail	102	OHC Single/89cc	8-Speed	1972-1973
CB100K2 Super Sport	107	OHC Single/99cc	5-Speed	1972
CL100K2 Scrambler	108	OHC Single/99cc	5-Speed	1972
CL100S2 Scrambler	108	OHC Single/99cc	5-Speed	1972
CB175K6 Super Sport	342	OHC Parallel Twin/174cc	5-Speed	1972
CL175K6 Scrambler	343	OHC Parallel Twin/174cc	5-Speed	1972
CB350F Four (CB350F0)	333	SOHC Inline Four/347cc	5-Speed	1972-1973
CB350K4 Super Sport	317	OHC Parallel Twin/325cc	5-Speed	1972-1973
CL350K4 Scrambler	345	OHC Parallel Twin/325cc	5-Speed	1972-1973
CB450K5 Super Sport	346	DOHC Parallel Twin/444cc	5-Speed	1972
CL450K5 Scrambler	347	DOHC Parallel Twin/444cc	5-Speed	1972-1973
CB500K2 500 Four	323	SOHC Inline Four/498cc	5-Speed	1972
CB750K2 750 Four	341	SOHC Inline Four/736cc	5-Speed	1972

lel twins. For 1972, an inline four 350 joined the ranks. The CB350F (CB350F0) was again a downsized version of its next-biggest kin, the CB500 Four.

The latest entry into the 350 class was not the lightest (394 lbs. with a half a tank of fuel), nor the quickest, but was a hands-down winner in the smoothness category. Honda had already proven its ability to build strong, inline four power plants, so creating a smaller one didn't seem to be a real challenge. Just like the 750 and 500cc variants, the 350 model ran and idled like nothing else on the market. Sure, there were faster and lighter machines out there, but for those who sought refinement in their two-wheeled craft, the CB350F was the bike of choice.

Another set of Keihin carbs were used, but this time they were 20mm versions. Again, a single overhead-cam motor was used to power the beast. A front disc brake was used to calm it down. With the bike's top speed of just over 98 mph, a good set of brakes was imperative. The fuel tank held 3.2 gallons and oil capacity was listed at 3.2 pints. A four-into-four exhaust was

again used for the most efficient way of moving expended gases from the motor. These were closer in appearance to the CB750 pipes with their long, tapered cones ending with a small inward, reverse taper at the rear.

The tachometer carried a red line of 10,000 rpm, which seemed unbelievably high for the period. The motor seemed to be able to run smoothly and quietly regardless of what was asked of it. The speedometer and tachometer were joined by a small panel of "idiot lights" to help the rider keep tabs on vital signs.

Whether you selected the Candy Bucchus Olive or Flake Matador Red, the fuel tank was trimmed with a set of white and orange pinstripes that outlined the contours of the tank. "350 Four" badges were finished in red and white, and were mounted to each side cover.

Even with the new inline four cylinder brother joining the family, the CB350K4 would return for another year of fun. The parallel twin-powered model would see only minor changes for its penultimate year of sale. The painted headlight shell of 1971 was replaced by a black version for 1972, and the "350" side

A series of vertical slots were used on the 1972 CL175, replacing matching pairs of horizontal openings on the 1971s.

cover badges were enlarged. Light Ruby Red and Candy Gold returned, and they were joined by Candy Bucchus Olive and Gentle Maroon Metallic. This model would sell into the 1973 year, but it would be gone after that.

CL350K4 models would only receive a few minor tweaks for the current year. A reshaped fuel tank was again applied to the existing chassis and a pair of angular slots was cut into the side covers. For a change, the heat shields were left the same in 1972.

Only two color choices, Magna Red and Candy Panther Gold, were seen for 1972. On the red model, white and red stripes adorned the tank. The gold version saw black and red stripes applied. The shape of these new stripes were also different than the black graphic used in 1971.

The 350 Scrambler would also be outfitted with a few new styling touches to set it apart from the 1971 models. The fuel tank was reshaped and now cut a more oval profile. A set of white and orange stripes would be used to accent a choice of Magna Red or Planet Blue Metallic paint. The upper segments of the front forks were done in chrome and the headlight housing was black. Changes to the exhaust system included the use of a three-piece heat

White and orange striping was applied to the Varnish Blue Metallic CL and white and yellow accents were seen on the Magna Red variant.

A 174cc, parallel-twin motor shifted through a five-speed gearbox.

shield and a two-piece muffler. Heat shields were again modified for the latest model. The segments covering the exhaust were vented with rows of angled, vertical slots, while each of the two muffler shields had larger, vertically inclined slots with rounded ends.

The CB450K5 was back for another round, but was the recipient of nothing more than mild cosmetic variations. A total of three colors were now being offered, and all were different from the previous year. Candy Garnet Brown, Light Ruby Red and Candy Bucchus Olive were all offset by a gold accent stripe on the fuel tank. The upper fork legs were now finished in chrome and the headlight casing was black. A narrow chrome strip was also added to the lower edge of the fuel tank this year, and ran through the K7 variants. The CL450K5 also received a few small variations for the new year. A more oval contour was applied to the fuel tank, as were white and orange striping. A black head-

light bucket was offset by chrome upper fork legs. A three-piece heat shield joined a separate two-piece muffler, and all were chromed. Magna Red or Planet Blue Metallic were the hues for 1972.

With the exception of one color option change, the CB500K2 500 Four was unchanged for 1972. Starlight Gold was replaced with Candy Gold, and it was sold alongside Candy Jet Green and Candy Garnet Brown.

For 1972, the CB750K2 was only given trifling changes. Previously, the headlight housing matched the paint, but for 1972 it came in black only. The fork leg uppers are also changed from the color-keyed choice to chrome for 1972. Candy Gold paint would return, but was joined by Brier Brown Metallic and Flake Sunrise Orange.

A different taillight was incorporated as well as new, enlarged side reflectors on the front forks.

A few new faces would be seen in the 1973 class photo while others would see their final year in the Honda academy. Outside the Honda camp, the Kawasaki Z-900 finally appeared, giving the CB750 some real competition.

In the 100cc-and-under class, two models were now gone with two others in their final year of availability. The CT70 was eliminated, and only the 90cc version would remain in 1974, but the CL70 Scrambler disappeared with nothing to take its place. Both the CB100K2

Super Sport and CL100K2 Scrambler were no-shows for 1973.

The CL100S3 Scrambler was seen wearing a new white stripe on the fuel tank and a badge on the side cover reading "100S". A blacked-out exhaust was fitted with a chrome heat shield. The CL100S3 was joined by a slightly larger CL125S Scrambler on New Year's Day 1973. A 122cc motor and different trim told the two apart. September of 1972 saw the new CB125S

With the exception of the new colors, and graphic trim on the fuel tanks, the 1973 CB750 models were the same as seen in 1972.
Owner: Ray Landy

The now-famous four-into-four exhaust and flat, spacious saddle remained intact on the 1973 edition of the big CB.

The side covers were not bashful about proclaiming what model they were affixed to.

(CB125SO) introduced to the family. This new model was powered by a single-cylinder, 122cc OHC mill, and was aimed at the entry-level rider. Both Candy Topaz Orange and Candy Peacock Green were offset with a white and black tank graphic. A pair of chrome fenders were used through 1979.

Subtle changes were seen on the 1973 CB175K7 Super Sport and CL175K7

Scrambler. A chrome grab rail was now found behind their saddles, and the instrument panels were angled back towards the rider's face for better visibility.

In the 350cc arena, the CB350G Super Sport was another '73 New Years Day offering. Unlike the CB350F, a 325cc parallel twin motor drove the G. A pair of CV carburetors and a five-speed transmission was also included in the deal. A swooping set of black and white tank graphics accented your choice of Candy Orange, Tyrolean Green Metallic or Iris Purple Metallic paint. A hydraulic front disc brake was a nice upgrade compared to the drums being used elsewhere. Both the CB350F and CB350K4 Super Sport would bow out before the 1974 models arrived. The CL350K4 was supplanted by the CL350K5.

The latest CB450K6 was trimmed with new tank stripes and was offered in Brier Brown Metallic and Tyrolean Green Metallic. A chrome grab rail behind the seat and angled instruments also made the scene. An additional warning light pod was installed between the

The CB350F was replaced by the CB350F1 in 1974, and tank stripes and side panel badge colors were be the only alterations.
Owner: James L. Townsend

tach and speedometer. The CL450K5 entered 1974 as a K6.

The CB500K2 was in its last year of sale in 1973, and wore a black side panel on the fuel tank and also had its enlarged instruments angled to the rider's eyes.

Honda's big CB750 Four returned in K3 form. Striping on the fuel tanks was now black with white and gold accents. Paint options were Flake Sunrise Orange, Candy Bucchus Olive and Maxim Brown Metallic. No other changes were made to the popular CB, but something would need to be done soon as the Kawasaki began to encroach on its turf.

1973 Price Guide	6	5	4	3	2	1
C70MK1 (72cc single)	190	290	430	570	760	950
CL70K3 Scrambler (72cc single)	190	290	430	570	760	950
SL70K1 Motosport (72cc single)	190	290	430	570	760	950
CL100S3 Scrambler 100S (99cc single)	200	300	450	600	800	1,000
SL100K3 Motosport (99cc single)	200	300	450	600	800	1,000
CB125S0 (122cc single)	220	330	500	660	880	1,100
CL125S0 Scrambler (122cc single)	220	330	500	660	880	1,100
SL125K2 Motosport (122cc single)	220	330	500	660	880	1,100
XL175K0 (173cc single)	260	390	590	780	1,040	1,300
CB175K7 Super Sport (174cc twin)	240	360	540	720	960	1,200
CL175K7 Scrambler (174cc twin)	240	360	540	720	960	1,200
XL250K0 Motosport (248cc single)	320	480	720	960	1,280	1,600
CB350K4 (325cc twin)	360	540	810	1,080	1,440	1,800
CL350K4 Scrambler (325cc twin)	360	540	810	1,080	1,440	1,800
CL350K5 Scrambler (325cc twin)	360	540	810	1,080	1,440	1,800
SL350K2 Motosport (325cc twin)	390	590	880	1,170	1,560	1,950
CB350F (350cc four)	440	660	990	1,320	1,760	2,200
CB450K6 (444cc twin)	380	570	860	1,140	1,520	1,900
CL450K2 Scrambler (444cc twin)	400	600	900	1,200	1,600	2,000
CB500 (495cc four)	600	900	1,350	1,800	2,400	3,000
CB750 (736cc four)	1,400	2,100	3,150	4,200	5,600	7,000

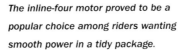

The inline-four motor proved to be a popular choice among riders wanting smooth power in a tidy package.

The CB350F1's upper fork leg covers were color keyed to the chosen hue, which was Flake Matador Red on this example.

Orange and white tank stripes were used on the 1973 CB350F1, while gold was used on the 1974 versions.

The easy-to-read CB350F1 gauges were joined by a small panel of indicator lights to keep the rider fully informed.

1973 MODELS

Model	Product Code	Engine Type/ Displacement	Transmission	Year(s) Available
C70K1 Honda 70 (C70MK1)	092	OHC Single/72cc	3-Speed, Auto	1972-73
CL70K3 Scrambler	111	OHC Single/72cc	4-Speed, Manual	1972-73
CT90K4 Trail	102	OHC Single/89cc	8-Speed	1972-73
CL100S3 Scrambler	108	OHC Single/99cc	5-Speed	1973
CB125S (CB125SO)	324	OHC Single/122cc	5-Speed	1973
CL125S Scrambler (CL125SO)	359	OHC Single/122cc	5-Speed	1973
CB175K7 Super Sport	453	OHC Parallel Twin/174cc	5-Speed	1973
CL175K7 Scrambler	454	OHC Parallel Twin/174cc	5-Speed	1973
CB350F Four (CB350FO)	333	SOHC Inline Four/347cc	5-Speed	1972-73
CB350G Super Sport	344	OHC Parallel Twin/325cc	5-Speed	1973
CB350K4 Super Sport	317	OHC Parallel Twin/325cc	5-Speed	1972-73
CL350K4 Scrambler	345	OHC Parallel Twin/325cc	5-Speed	1972-73
CL350K5 Scrambler	345	OHC Parallel Twin/325cc	5-Speed	1973
CB450K6 Super Sport	346	DOHC Parallel Twin/444cc	5-Speed	1973
CL450K5 Scrambler	347	DOHC Parallel Twin/444cc	5-Speed	1972-73
CB500K2 500 Four	323	SOHC Inline Four/498cc	5-Speed	1973
CB750K3 750 Four	341	SOHC Inline Four/736cc	5-Speed	1973

Powered by a parallel twin-cylinder engine, the 1973 CB350G made good power, considering it was down two pots from its sibling, the CB350F.
Owner: Rick Youngblood

The Candy Orange hue sets the "350" badges off nicely on the CB350G.

Although far from the biggest machine in Honda's lineup, the CB350G was still outfitted with a spacious, well-padded pillion made for two.

1974

As competition from other Japanese manufacturers increased, Honda trimmed the model line to focus each product at a more specific niche. Redundancies were limited as the family tree was pruned.

While this text is devoted to the street models of Honda, a new model for the off-road crowd was introduced that should not go unmentioned. The Elsinore line of off-road machines were named after the famed course in California, and it would soon become a legend amongst those who rode and competed in that segment of the market.

Several new street models were also added to the 1974 catalog, and some returning machines received minor alterations for the latest year. The CT90K5 Trail 90 was one such machine. For the latest models, all turn signal housings were now finished in chrome.

The diminutive CB125S1 returned, and was also trimmed with a few new goodies for 1974. The drum brake on the front wheel was upgraded to a mechanical disc and provided shorter stopping distances. 1973 CB125s had only a speedometer, but the 1974s had a tachometer as well. Cosmetic modifications were also made. The black and white swooping graphic on the fuel tank was replaced with black side panels,

The CB200 was new for 1974, and was aimed at the rider who wanted a small all-around machine.
Owner: Dan Davis

outlined with white pinstripes. The wing emblems found on the side covers were now red, and Candy Topaz Orange was the only sheet metal color offered.

The CB125S1 was a repeat of the previous year, but featured altered tank graphics: "125" badges that were white on a black background. Candy Ruby Red was the only hue available.

In an attempt to fill a new slot in the cycle market, Honda engineers were assigned the task of creating a small, flexible machine that was capable of doing almost everything. It would also have to retail for less than $700. This list of criteria led to the birth of the CB200.

Based on the chassis used on the CB125, the new CB200 was fitted with a 198cc twin-cylinder motor that closely resembled the motor used in the previous 175 models. Weighing in at just a sliver over 300 lbs., the CB200 was petite, yet solid. Typical of all Honda models, it had a fit and finish that was unmatched in the industry.

The angular fuel tank holds 2.4 gallons of fossil fuel, and it was decorated with a vinyl pad on the top surface. Chrome trim added a touch of flair to the overall package. Muscat Green Metallic or Tahitian Red were the offered colors, and either choice was trimmed with black panels, outlined in white, on the sides of the tank.

The side covers were finished in the same color as the fuel tank, and the "CB200" emblems were white. The flat, two-person saddle rests at a height of 30.7 inches, and provides plenty of comfort for both rider and passenger alike. The usual grab strap was found on the seat and a chrome grab rail was fixed behind the rear edge.

The on/off-road variation was the CL200 Scrambler. Powered by the same 198cc, vertical twin mill, there were a few changes on the CL variant. A drum brake was found on both wheels instead of the front disc/read drum combination on the CB. The fuel tank was also different and wore white graphic striping on the sides. The only color sold was Candy Riviera Blue, and this was applied to both tank

The 2.7-gallon fuel tank of the CB200 was trimmed with black panels with white outlines.

"CB200" badges were affixed to the side panels, and they were white with black backgrounds.

A flat, yet well-cushioned saddle was in place for up to two CB200 riders, and the passenger had both a grab strap and rail for support.

The CB550 was a new entry in the 1974 Honda catalog, and this Boss Maroon Metallic example is all original.
Owner: Buzz Walneck

and side covers. "CL200" badges used on the side panels were yellow and white.

With its potential for off-road use, the CL200 was also fitted with a high-mounted exhaust system. Both the exhaust pipes and heat shield were plated in chrome.

All of the 350cc models were eliminated from the 1974 offerings, but a trio of 360cc machines were developed to fill the void. The

CB350 Super Sport was not replaced by another inline four model until the CB400 appeared in the following year.

Two virtually identical 360s were seen in the 1974 lineup, although neither had a four-cylinder motor. The CB360K0 and CB360G had the same 356cc, parallel twin motor, as well as the same frame and bodywork. The CB360G did have a front wheel disc brake to set it apart from the other CB360. Colors for the CB360K0 were Hawaiian Blue Metallic or Candy Orange. The CB360G came in a choice of Hex Green Metallic or Candy Orange.

In typical Honda fashion, an on/off-road variant of the 360 was also sold. The CL 360 Scrambler featured high-mounted exhaust, front drum brake and Muscat Green Metallic paint. The "CL360" emblems on each side panel were finished in yellow and white.

Moving up the food chain, a pair of 450 models remained

1974 PRICE GUIDE	6	5	4	3	2	1
MR50 Elsinore (49cc single)	220	330	500	660	880	1,100
XL70K0 (72cc single)	240	360	540	720	960	1,200
XL100K0 (99cc single)	240	360	540	720	960	1,200
CB125S1 (122cc single)	220	330	500	660	880	1,100
CL125S1 Scrambler (122cc single)	220	330	500	660	880	1,100
XL125K0 (122cc single)	240	360	540	720	960	1,200
MT125K0 Elsinore (123cc single)	260	390	590	780	1,040	1,300
XL175K1 (173cc single)	260	390	590	780	1,040	1,300
CB200K0 (198cc twin)	240	360	540	720	960	1,200
CL200 Scrambler (198cc twin)	240	360	540	720	960	1,200
MT250K0 Elsinore (248cc single)	290	440	650	870	1,160	1,450
XL250K1 Motosport (248cc single)	300	450	680	900	1,200	1,500
XL350K0 (348cc single)	360	540	810	1,080	1,440	1,800
CB350F (350cc four)	380	570	860	1,140	1,520	1,900
CB360G (356cc twin)	360	540	810	1,080	1,440	1,800
CB360K0 (356cc twin)	360	540	810	1,080	1,440	1,800
CL360 Scrambler (356cc twin)	360	540	810	1,080	1,440	1,800
CB450K7 (444cc twin)	380	570	860	1,140	1,520	1,900
CL450K2 Scrambler (444cc twin)	380	570	860	1,140	1,520	1,900
CB550 (550cc four)	400	600	900	1,200	1,600	2,000
CB750 (736cc four)	1,400	2,100	3,150	4,200	5,600	7,000

An inline four-cylinder motor powered the new CB550 to a top speed of almost 100 mph.

in the catalog for 1974. The CB450K7 received different tank stripes that were a combination of black and gold. Candy Orange and Maxim Brown Metallic were the base colors avaiable. The CL450K6 Scrambler was seen wearing a fuel tank from earlier (K1-K4) models and different graphics of white and black. Candy Sapphire Blue Flake was the single color choice. The two-piece muffler was now black with a pair of chrome heat shields. The exhaust remained as chrome with chrome shields. A chrome grab rail was now located behind the saddle and the instrument cluster was leaned back towards the rider.

A new CB550 Four was introduced for the 1974 model year, and was heralded as a terrific all-around machine by periodicals of the day.

Weighing 454 lbs. when fully fueled, the CB550 made for a terrific handling ride. Producing 37.8 horsepower at 8000 rpm made

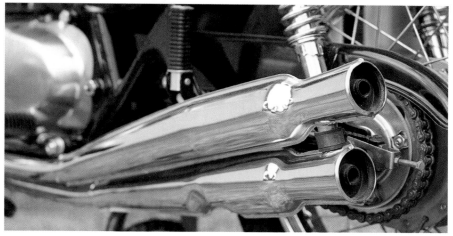

for spirited performance, too. The single overhead-cam motor displaced 544ccs, and ran with a wet sump lubrication system. A five-speed gearbox provided plenty of ratios to match the rider's needs. Capable of nicking 100 mph in top gear, the CB550 delivered plenty of speed with little noticeable effort.

The four-into-four exhaust featured mufflers that first tapered, then expanded again into reverse conical tips. Noise was minimal unless you were whacking the throttle wide open, but even then a polite growl is all you

Each end of the four-into-four exhaust was finished with a reverse cone contour.

A mechanical disc brake was mounted to the CB550's front wheel, while a drum brake was used on the rear.

got from the well-behaved system. West Coast price for the all-new CB550 was $1,600 retail, and Flake Sunrise Orange, Boss Maroon and Freedom Green Metallic were all at your fingertips. Regardless of the color chosen, contrasting black side panels were applied to both sides of the 3.7-gallon tank.

The big CB750 was back in the latest K4 trim. Modifications were trifling, and included wider white stripes on the fuel tank graphics. Numeration on the speedometer was printed in increments of 20. Flake Sunrise Orange was again available, and it was joined by Freedom Green Metallic and Boss Maroon Metallic.

Regardless of which color you chose for the CB550, the side panels of the 1974 models were all accented with black and stripes of gold and white.

Both CB550 side panels were finished in the same hue as the fuel tank, and cast "550Four" badges were affixed.

1974 MODELS

Model	Product Code	Engine Type/ Displacement	Transmission	Year(s) Available
CT90K5 Trail 90	102	OHC Single/89cc	8-Speed	1974
CB125S1	324	OHC Single/122cc	5-Speed	1974
CB200 (CB200K0)	354	OHC Parallel Twin/198cc	5-Speed	1974
CL200 Scrambler	378	OHC Parallel Twin/198cc	5-Speed	1974
CB360 (CB360K0)	369	OHC Parallel Twin/356cc	6-Speed	1974
CB360G	369	OHC Parallel Twin/356cc	6-Speed	1974
CL360 Scrambler (CL360K0)	370	OHC Parallel Twin/356cc	6-Speed	1974
CB450K7 Super Sport	346	DOHC Parallel Twin/444cc	5-Speed	1974
CL450K6 Scrambler	347	DOHC Parallel Twin/444cc	5-Speed	1974
CB550 (CB550K0) 550 Four	374	SOHC Inline Four/544cc	5-Speed	1974
CB750K4 750 Four	341	SOHC Inline Four/736cc	5-Speed	1974

Honda's typical system of upgrading existing models continued for the 1975 model year, but a raft of fresh machines would also make their entrance. Two of their new models would again put the other manufacturers on notice by upping the ante in the respective niches.

The Trail 90, now in its K6 form, received only the slightest of changes. Tahitian Red was found on the frame shroud and side cover to match the body. The "Honda" decal on the frame was done in black lettering.

The CB125 was back and bore the S2 designation. An altered side cover badge was finished in white and yellow. Candy Riviera Blue was also the only color offered for 1975. The

chrome cover seen on the rear shocks of the 1974s was also removed for the latest year.

The CB200T, previously listed as a "K0" was now shown as "T0". New side cover badging was seen as "CB200T" and wore white and yellow paint. Candy Gold Metallic and Custom Silver Metallic were the color selections in 1975. The CL200 Scrambler was gone from the Honda lineup.

Only minor changes were applied to the 360cc models. The CB360K0 became the CB360T0, and sported white and yellow "CB360T" badges on the side covers. A black points cover was also new. Candy Riviera Blue

The CB400 Super Sport became an instant classic for Honda and was joined by two larger Super Sport models in the same year.
Owner: Steve Passwater

Perhaps the most admired feature of the new Super Sport was the heavily contoured four-into-one exhaust system.

The side of the CB400 that was devoid of the exhaust didn't provide much in the eye candy department, but did allow for an unimpeded view of the machine.

Metallic and Light Ruby Red were the available colors. The CL360K1 Scrambler received a new Candy Orange color.

The first of the new models out for 1975 was the CB400F Super Sport. Two other Super Sports would join it, but it was the CB400F that would become an instant classic. Part of this allure was its serpentine four-into-one exhaust. The same configuration four-into-one layout was used on the 550 and 750 Super Sports, but the added twists of the 400's system brought some excitement to the mundane component. The inline four-cylinder motor was built with a single overhead cam and displaced 408ccs. Four carburetors were used to feed the tidy mill.

The CB400F weighed 408 lbs. and boasted 37 horsepower, which meant adequate performance for most riders. The competing machines from Kawasaki, Suzuki and Yamaha were all driven by higher-performance two-stroke power plants, but their performance was harder to handle due to the light switch on-and-off delivery.

The first two years of CB400 Super Sport models would be seen with low, almost flat drag style handlebars. This design provided a more sporting riding crouch without being uncomfortable or radical. The new contours of the fuel tank also added to the desirability of the new CB. A six-speed gearbox allowed the rider to keep the CB400 in the proper ratio to meet with conditions. Rear drum and front disc brakes handled the deceleration of the 400, and was on par when compared to other machines of the day.

Light Ruby Red and Varnish Blue were both offered on the 1975 models. Carrying a retail price tag of $1,395, the smallest Super Sport was snapped up quickly by those who sought performance on a smaller scale.

While probably not as exciting as the new CB400, the CB500T offered a new motor to those wanting something different. The 498cc motor was designed in parallel twin configuration, and was controlled by double overhead cams. The gearbox provided the rider a choice of five ratios. Two-into-two exhaust was used, as were front disc and rear drum brakes.

Glory Brown Metallic paint was accented by gold pinstripes and a saddle covered with tan vinyl was standard. The 1975 CB500T also wore instruments with white numerals on black faces.

Another player in the expanding Honda team was the returning CB550K1. Now wearing instrument faces of dark green and altered tank graphics outlined with gold and black stripes, the K1 was mechanically unaltered. Candy Jade Green or Flake Sunrise Orange were the latest hues available.

Joining the CB550 Four was the CB550F Super Sport model. Sold as the higher-performance sibling to the CB550K1, the Super Sport shared many design traits seen on the CB400 Super Sport. The 544cc motor controlled the valves with a single overhead cam, and fed each cylinder with its own Keihin, 22mm carburetor. The 4.2-gallon fuel tank was shaped much like the smaller 400cc model. Only five speeds are found within the gearbox, down one gear from the six speeds found on the 400. A single disc brake up front was teamed with a drum brake on the rear wheel. Another four-into-one exhaust was used on the 550 Super Sport, setting it apart from Honda's non Super Sport machines.

Side covers finished in paint to match the fuel tank were used on the first 400 Super Sport models.

Nearly every model in the 1975 Honda catalog featured the new dark green instrument faces. The small array of warning lights kept the rider on top of his machine's condition.

Fresh contours of the fuel tank added to the allure of the Super Sport. The Light Ruby Red paint seen here is labeled with the "Honda Super Sport" moniker applied to all the '75 Super Sport models.

A single disc brake at the front wheel helped to slow the 408-lb. 1975 Super Sport.

rear cowling were all unique to the 750 Super Sport. The tank and cowl could be purchased in Flake Sunrise Orange or Candy Sapphire Blue, but the side covers were black and wore "750Four" badges. Spoke wheels rolled at either end. They were slowed by a disc brake on both front and rear wheels. The 1975 models were dressed with silver engines and fork legs. A five-speed transmission provided the power transfer.

The CB750K5 received a few minor changes, and continued to be a favorite amongst buyers seeking a larger machine. Like other models for 1975, the K5 sported dark green instrument faces, and the speedometer now read in increments of 10. Planet Blue Metallic and Flake Apricot Red were only seen on the 750K model.

The side covers and fuel tank were offered in a choice of Candy Sapphire Blue or Flake Sunrise Orange. "Honda Super Sport" was found on the fuel tank while "550 Four" was used on the side covers. The surface of both instruments was finished in dark green with white numerals.

The CB750F Super Sport (CB750F0) was powered by the same 736cc, SOHC motor as the CB750K5, though the Super Sport did exhale through a four-into-one exhaust like the two smaller Super Sports. The fuel tank, seat and

The last, but certainly not least, of the new 1975 models was the GL1000 Gold Wing (GL1000K0). Nothing since the introduction of the CB750 had even come close to the technological advances the new GL delivered.

With Honda abandoning its previous practice of building bigger and bigger inline four motors, the new GL was be driven by a horizontally opposed four-cylinder motor. Displacing 999ccs, the monster mill was fed by a set of four, 32mm Keihin constant velocity carburetors. A four-into-two exhaust provided easy exit for any spent fumes. The matt black pipes were covered with chrome heat shields and tips. Final drive was handled with a drive shaft, thus eliminating much of the rattle that came with the typical chain of the period. Lower maintenance and cleaner operation were two more benefits of the shaft drive, and played into the overall marketing of the new model.

Despite the eerie smoothness of this all-new motor, it was an impressive power plant capable of reaching a top speed in excess of 130 mph.

1975 PRICE GUIDE

	6	5	4	3	2	1
MR50K1 Elsinore (49cc single)	220	330	500	660	880	1,100
XL70K1 (72cc single)	230	350	520	690	920	1,150
XL100K1 (99cc single)	240	360	540	720	960	1,200
CB125S2 (122cc single)	220	330	500	660	880	1,100
MT125K1 Elsinore (123cc single)	260	390	590	780	1,040	1,300
XL175K2 (173cc single)	260	390	590	780	1,040	1,300
CB200T0 (198cc twin)	270	410	610	810	1,080	1,350
MT250K1 Elsinore (248cc single)	290	440	650	870	1,160	1,450
XL250K2 Motosport (248cc single)	300	450	680	900	1,200	1,500
XL350K1 (348cc single)	360	540	810	1,080	1,440	1,800
CB360T (356cc twin)	340	510	770	1,020	1,360	1,700
CL360 Scrambler (356cc twin)	340	510	770	1,020	1,360	1,700
CB400F (408cc four)	400	600	900	1,200	1,600	2,000
CB500T (444cc twin)	360	540	810	1,080	1,440	1,800
CB550 (550cc four)	400	600	900	1,200	1,600	2,000
CB550F (550cc four)	400	600	900	1,200	1,600	2,000
CB750 (736cc four)	600	900	1,350	1,800	2,400	3,000
CB750F (736cc four)	900	1,350	2,030	2,700	3,600	4,500
GL1000 Gold Wing (999cc four, shaft-drive)	1,100	1,650	2,480	3,300	4,400	5,500

Only the Kawasaki Z-1 was able to accelerate harder than the 650-lb. Gold Wing.

Having that much power on tap required brakes that were up to the task of slowing the beast. A trio of hydraulic brakes was found on the GL and provided more than ample stopping power. The rear disc alone was squeezed by a dual-puck caliper and was considered one of the best rear brakes setups ever mounted to a motorcycle.

The styling of the Gold Wing was conservative at best, but held a few surprises. The "fuel tank" was actually a storage compartment that opened for access to the motor and whatever items you chose to stow. Fuel was actually held in a 5-gallon receptacle mounted beneath the saddle. This location provided a lower center of gravity for the ponderous weight of the 'Wing. With mileage hovering around 40 mpg, 200 miles between fill-ups was not unheard of. The spacious seat was also a comfortable perch for 200-mile durations. The handlebars were high

and bent back to make them easy to reach.

Candy Antares Red or Candy Blue Green paint was offset by a chrome fender and spoke wheels on the 1975 GL1000. A "Honda" badge, plated in gold, was affixed to the sides of the storage tank, and "Gold Wing GL1000" graced the side covers. The liquid-cooled motor drew cooled air through the front-mounted radiator that was placed just in front of the frame's down tubes.

All of this technology, power and style carried a steep price. A retail sticker in the neighborhood of $3,000 assured that only the serious rider would apply, but those that did were rewarded with a smooth, fast and great-handling motorcycle. It would be a few more years before the Gold Wing was fitted with fairings, bags and other touring accoutrements, but vendors outside of Honda were quick to address the needs of riders wanting more than a "naked" cruising machine

The rear wheel of the 400 Super Sport was equipped with a drum brake, which aided the disc up front.

A full complement of indicator lights, and a temperature gauge were aboard the 1975 GL. The apparent fuel tank was actually a housing that allowed access to the motor and a quantity of storage space.

Enormous side covers could be removed for access to more of the machines internals, and were festooned with the Gold Wing Gl1000 moniker.

Introduced as a 1975 model, the GL1000 Gold Wing set new standards for both Honda and the rest of touring bike market with its performance, comfort and technological advances.
Owner: Pete Boody

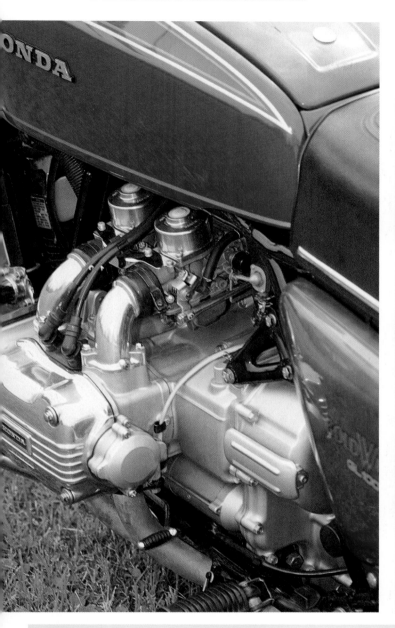

The Gold Wing's opposed, four-cylinder engine displaced 999cc's, as well as most of the competition.

The big four-cylinder motor was liquid cooled, and the radiator kept a supply of reduced-temperature fluids flowing through the cases.

1975 MODELS

Model	Product Code	Engine Type/ Displacement	Transmission	Year(s) Available
CT90K6 Trail 90	102	OHC Single/89cc	8-Speed	1975
CB125S2	324	OHC Single/122cc	5-Speed	1975
CB200T (CB200T0)	354	OHC Parallel Twin/198cc	5-Speed	1975
CB360T (CB360T0)	369	OHC Parallel Twin/356cc	6-Speed	1975
CL360 Scrambler (CL360K1)	370	OHC Parallel Twin/356cc	6-Speed	1975
CB400F Super Sport (CB400F0)	377S	OHC Inline Four/408cc	6-Speed	1975
CB500T (CB500T0)	375	DOHC Parallel Twin/498cc	5-Speed	1975
CB550F Super Sport (CB550F0)	390	SOHC Inline Four/544cc	5-Speed	1975
CB550 (CB550K1) 550 Four	374	SOHC Inline Four/544cc	5-Speed	1975
CB750F Super Sport (CB750F0)	392	SOHC Inline Four/736cc	5-Speed	1975
CB750K5 750 Four	341	SOHC Inline Four/736cc	5-Speed	1975
GL1000 Gold Wing (GL1000K0)	371	SOHC Opposed Four/999cc	5-Speed	1975

1976

After the blockbuster year that saw the 400, 550 and 750 Super Sports and the Gold Wing introduced, 1976 proved to be much quieter when it came to new models. Although not as radical, three new faces did appear in the sales literature. The CL360 Scrambler was gone.

The still-popular CT90 was back for another round, but only minor changes were seen. Shiny

Orange paint was the only hue available; the "Honda" decal pasted to the shroud was now yellow. The rear shocks also featured exposed coil springs, which were plated in chrome.

Another returning model was the CB125S. Aquarius Blue was the annual color selected and the "Honda" appliqué on the tank was red

The CB550 was back for another year in 1976, but only minor changes would make it different from the pervious year's model.
Owner: Buzz Walneck

Candy Garnet Brown was the only color offered in 1976 on the CB550, but the black panel with white and gold stripes made for a tasteful combination.

The CB550K side covers proudly displayed the displacement and cylinder count.

The displacement and power of the CB550 motor provided enough drive to carry two riders in comfort.

Faces of the 1976 instruments wore a lighter green finish than the year before.

Each side of the CB550K sported a four-into-four exhaust system that kept noise to a minimum.

The 1976 CB550 Four was a popular choice for riders wanting both power and an easy-riding machine in one package.
American Honda

with white outlines. The "125S" markings on the side covers were also finished in red and white. A dark brown seat was installed and instrumentation would drop back to a speedometer only. The 122cc single-cylinder motor was now constructed using a two-piece head and the five-speed gearbox was still in place.

CB200T models were treated to new colors, Parakeet Yellow and Shiny Orange. Regardless of which color you chose, side covers were black.

The CB360T now sported a silver points cover, and new fuel tank graphics. Whether you chose Candy Sapphire Blue or Candy Ruby Red, the tank stripes were black and white.

One of the new family members for 1976 was the CJ360T. Wearing bodywork reminiscent of the 750 Super Sport, the CJ was a

better-dressed version of the CB360T it was based on. A two-into-one exhaust also helped to distinguish the CJ from the CB. The sleek fuel tank, altered saddle and rear cowling presented the family resemblance to the bigger 750. Candy Antares Red was the only option, and this was applied to the tank, rear cowl and front fender.

Mechanically, the CB400F Super Sport was unchanged, but a few cosmetic modifications set it apart from the 1975s. Parakeet Yellow replaced Varnish Blue in the catalog, but Light Ruby Red was still a choice. Previous side covers matched the fuel tank, but '76 models wore black. The low handlebars were still employed.

CB500Ts remained for another, and final year. Changes to the last models were green instrument faces, and the addition of Candy Antares Red to the Glory Brown Metallic paint checklist.

Incremental changes continued on the CB550F Super Sports for 1976. Instrument faces were now viewed with light green fascia, and the saddle covering was dark brown. New colors were Flake Sapphire Blue and Shiny Orange. The other 550 model, the CB550K, was also seen with the light green instrument faces, and only one color was offered, Candy Garnet Brown.

New in the 750 class was the CB750A Hondamatic. Blending styling cues from other

1976 MODELS

Model	Product Code	Engine Type/ Displacement	Transmission	Year(s) Available
CT90 Trail 90	102	OHC Single/89cc	8-Speed	1976
CB125S	383	OHC Single/122cc	5-Speed	1976
CB200T	389	OHC Parallel Twin/198cc	5-Speed	1976
CB360T	369	OHC Parallel Twin/356cc	6-Speed	1976
CJ360T	388	OHC Parallel Twin/356cc	5-Speed	1976
CB400F Super Sport	377	SOHC Inline Four/408cc	6-Speed	1976
CB500T 500 Twin	375	DOHC Parallel Twin/498cc	5-Speed	1976
CB550F Super Sport	390	SOHC Inline Four/544cc	5-Speed	1976
CB550K 550 Four	374	SOHC Inline Four/544cc	5-Speed	1976
CB750A 750 Hondamatic	393	SOHC Inline Four/736cc	2-Speed Auto.	1976
CB750F Super Sport	392	SOHC Inline Four/736cc	5-Speed	1976
CB750K 750 Four	341	SOHC Inline Four/736cc	5-Speed	1976
GL1000 Gold Wing	371	SOHC Opposed Four/999cc	5-Speed	1976
GL1000 Ltd Gold Wing	371	SOHC Opposed Four/999cc	5-Speed	1976

750 models and mixing in a two-speed, automatic gearbox brought a fresh choice to the Honda buyer. The same 736cc, inline-four motor was installed, but it breathed through a four-into-one exhaust that was found on the Super Sport variant. Wire wheels and aluminum rims held the rubber in place. Muscat Green Metallic or Candy Antares Red were both options in 1976. The ease of the automatic transmission appealed to some riders, but sales were never as strong as Honda had planned.

CB750F Super Sports were sold in Sulfur Yellow or Candy Antares Red and were found with the light green instrument faces. CB750K models were only sold in Candy Antares Red and featured the latest in light green instrumentation.

The GL1000, introduced in 1975 was only the recipient of a new color option, Sulfur Yellow, and had its gauge faces modified to the newest light green design.

To spice up the Gold Wing offerings a Limited Edition model was also sold alongside the standard model. No mechanical upgrades were used, but a wide array of decorative alterations set the Ltd apart. Gold-colored stripes and badges highlighted custom Candy Brown

1976 Price Guide	6	5	4	3	2	1
XL70 (72cc single)	220	330	500	660	880	1,100
XL100 (99cc single)	220	330	500	660	880	1,100
CB125S (122cc single)	220	330	500	660	880	1,100
MT125 Elsinore (123cc single)	260	390	590	780	1,040	1,300
XL125 (124cc single)	240	360	540	720	960	1,200
XL175 (173cc single)	250	380	560	750	1,000	1,250
CB200T (198cc twin)	260	390	590	780	1,040	1,300
MT250 Elsinore (248cc single)	290	440	650	870	1,160	1,450
XL250 Motosport (248cc single)	300	450	680	900	1,200	1,500
XL350 (348cc single)	360	540	810	1,080	1,440	1,800
CB360T (356cc twin)	340	510	770	1,020	1,360	1,700
CJ360T (356cc twin)	340	510	770	1,020	1,360	1,700
CB400F (408cc four)	400	600	900	1,200	1,600	2,000
CB500T (444cc twin)	360	540	810	1,080	1,440	1,800
CB550 (550cc four)	400	600	900	1,200	1,600	2,000
CB550F (550cc four)	400	600	900	1,200	1,600	2,000
CB750 (736cc four)	600	900	1,350	1,800	2,400	3,000
CB750A (736cc four)	600	900	1,350	1,800	2,400	3,000
CB750F (736cc four)	600	900	1,350	1,800	2,400	3,000
GL1000 Gold Wing (999cc four, shaft-drive)	660	990	1,490	1,980	2,640	3,300

paint. Rims and the spoke wheels were also anodized in gold. The radiator shroud was now plated in chrome and the saddle took on a two-level design. Located inside the faux fuel tank was a limited edition tool kit that came complete with a leather storage bag. The key fob was also finished in the same golden leather as the tool storage bag.

1976 CB750K models were little changed for the new year of sales. Antares Red was the only hue seen in the 1976 catalog.
Owner: Alan Raymond

"750 Four" script was joined by a cloisonné Honda "wing" encased in a field of red on the 1976s.

Four-into-four exhaust remained the standard setup in 1976, and heat shields were still applied to the upper set of mufflers.

Light green faces on the speedometer and tachometer were new for 1976, replacing the dark green look seen on the 1975 editions.

Only minor alterations had been made to the big CB750K models since their inception in 1969. These bikes remained a popular choice for riders wanting power and smoothness in a moderately sized machine.

First introduced as a 1975 model, the Gold Wing returned in 1976 in stock form and this Limited Edition version. This pristine example was purchased from a warehouse in the recent years and shows only 1.3 miles on the odometer.
Owner: Pete Boody

Helping to slow the massive Gold Wing was a rear-mounted disc brake that was squeezed by a dual-puck caliper.

The Gold Wing's rear tire was considered to be massive in its day, but has been eclipsed by 16-inch- wide rubber being used by some of today's custom choppers. The early Gold Wings were classic bikes from any view.

Gold anodized rims and spokes set the 1976 Limited Edition GL1000 apart from the others, and the matching set of brake rotors helped slow the 650-lb. machine down.

The Limited Edition Gold Wings had crests emblazoned onto the side covers.

Beneath the top lid of the storage tank (below) was a leather-bound tool set that was designated for the 1976 Limited Edition GL1000 only.

The radiator and a small storage space are hidden beneath the sheet metal.

The horizontally opposed, four-cylinder motor remained at the heart of the Gold Wing, regardless of which version you bought in 1976.

1977

1977 was a very quiet year overall for new developments at Honda. No new models appeared and three would no longer be listed. Alterations to the remaining models were minor and mostly cosmetic in nature.

The CT90 Trail 90 was proving to be a resilient member of the family and was back for another year. Shiny Orange was the same as seen in 1976, but the "Honda" logo on the frame reverted back to black.

Strangely enough, the CB125S was not seen in the official Honda Motorcycle Identification Guide for 1977, but was again listed for 1978. We can only assume that no changes were made to the '77 model, yet it still existed.

Neither the CB200 nor CB360T were available as of the 1977 sales year. The CJ360T would still be sold for one more year, but would be gone for 1978.

The CB400 Super Sport was in its final year of sale, and a few changes were employed. The fuel tank cap was now recessed and the previous drag style handlebars were raised to mid level. Candy Antares Red models were trimmed with gold and orange tank stripes while the Parakeet Yellow version wore black and red accents.

The CB500T, twin-cylinder model was another casualty, and was no longer offered.

1977 was also the final year for the CB550F Super Sport. Instrument faces for this final year had a dark blue hue, the seat was again delivered in black, and the rubber fork boots were deleted. Candy Sword Blue and Candy Presto Red were both trimmed with a gold tank stripe.

The CB550K was in its penultimate year and also received some minor cosmetic modifications. Excel Black was the only color seen, and the tank was highlighted by a red stripe with gold pinstriping as an outline. The side cover badges still read "550Four K" but were now finished in gold.

In the 750 family, changes were also subtle to the returning faces. The CB750A Hondamatic exhaled through a four-into-two exhaust, replacing the four-into one system first used.

1977 Price Guide	6	5	4	3	2	1
XL75 (75cc single)	220	330	500	660	880	1,100
XL100 (99cc single)	220	330	500	660	880	1,100
CB125S (122cc single)	230	350	520	690	920	1,150
XL125 (124cc single)	240	360	540	720	960	1,200
XL175 (173cc single)	240	360	540	720	960	1,200
XL350 (348cc single)	320	480	720	960	1,280	1,600
CJ360T (356cc twin)	340	510	770	1,020	1,360	1,700
CB400F (408cc four)	400	600	900	1,200	1,600	2,000
CB550 (550cc four)	400	600	900	1,200	1,600	2,000
CB550F (550cc four)	400	600	900	1,200	1,600	2,000
CB750A (736cc four)	600	900	1,350	1,800	2,400	3,000
CB750F (736cc four)	600	900	1,350	1,800	2,400	3,000
CB750K (736cc four)	600	900	1,350	1,800	2,400	3,000
GL1000 Gold Wing (999cc four, shaft-drive)	660	990	1,490	1,980	2,640	3,300

1977 MODELS

Model	Product Code	Engine Type/ Displacement	Transmission	Year(s) Available
CT90 Trail 90	102	OHC Single/89cc	8-Speed	1977
CB125S	383	OHC Single/122cc	5-Speed	1977
CJ360T	388	OHC Parallel Twin/356cc	5-Speed	1977
CB400F Super Sport	377	SOHC Inline Four/408cc	6-Speed	1977
CB550F Super Sport	390	SOHC Inline Four/544cc	5-Speed	1977
CB550K 550 Four	374	SOHC Inline Four/544cc	5-Speed	1977
CB750A 750 Hondamatic	393	SOHC Inline Four/736cc	2-Speed Auto.	1977
CB750F Super Sport	410	SOHC Inline Four/736cc	5-Speed	1977
CB750K 750 Four	405	SOHC Inline Four/736cc	5-Speed	1977
GL1000 Gold Wing	377	SOHC Opposed Four/999cc	5-Speed	1977

Gold pinstripes were applied to the side covers and fuel tank. Candy Sword Blue and Candy Presto Red were seen on the option sheet. The CB750F Super Sport was the first model seen wearing the new Comstar wheels.

These five-spoke rims were assembled using aluminum, and saved some weight as well as looked more contemporary.

A second disc was added to the front wheel as well, bringing a new level of stopping power to the sporting 750. The lower sections of the fork legs and the motor were blacked out on the '77 versions. Candy Presto Red or Black were offered and the tank stripe was red with contrasting gold pinstripes. Only color option changes were applied to the CB750K. Candy Alpha Red or Excel Black found a gold tank stripe outlined with red and white pinstripes. Side cover badges were also finished in gold.

The big GL1000 was the recipient of a few minor tweaks and some new colors. Handlebars were now a bit higher, and reshaped for an easier reach by the rider. Faces of the instruments were changed to black with green lettering. The contoured saddle first used on the Limited Edition 1976 model was attached to the Gold Wing in 1977. Candy Antares Red returned, and was joined by Candy Sirius Blue or Black.

1978

After a year that introduced no new models and showed very few changes, 1978 would be dramatically different. Three previous models, the CJ360T, CB400F Super Sport and CB55F Super Sport were no longer a part of the Honda clan.

Proving its resiliency, the CT90 Trail 90 was still sold. In its annual flip-flop, the "Honda" logo placed on the frame tube was again white. Bright Yellow replaced Shiny Orange as the only color. The handlebars, rear shock coil springs and both wheel hubs were now delivered in black.

Changes to the CB125S were also minimal, and included new tank graphics that consisted of orange, yellow, white and black stripes on a Fire Red base color. New side cover emblems read "CB125S" and were yellow and white for the latest year.

The CM185T Twinstar was introduced for the new sales year. This new entrant offered a bit more machine than the CB125S, but was still a basic model. The 181cc overhead-cam parallel twin motor and four-speed gearbox gave the new rider plenty of power and gears to learn the craft. Two-into-two exhaust gave the spent gases an easy exit. A set of "buckhorn" bars reached back to the rider's hands for a comfortable grip on the controls, and the two-level saddle offered accommodations for a rider and passenger. Candy Antares Red and Candy Sword Blue were ac-

1978 would mark the final year for the SOHC CB750 line. Only minor cosmetic modifications were used on the K model. The CB750K remained a popular choice as it had proven itself to be worthy of many roles.
Owner: Doug Mitchel

cented with tank and side cover stripes of white, gold and black. The "Twinstar" logo on the side covers was a white decal.

To replace the CJ36T and CB400F, a trio of 400cc models was introduced for 1978. While all three models were fairly similar, each appealed to a different rider. The CB400A Hawk Hondamatic shifted through a two-speed, semi-automatic transmission. The rider had to make a selection of the two gears, but no manual clutch was involved. First gear was intended for take-off, while second gear took over from there. With the left hand lever no longer required for clutch control, it is put into duty as a parking brake. The tachometer, normally used to monitor rpm, was supplanted by a series of gear indicator lights in the housing. The 395cc parallel twin motor breathed through three-valve heads and a set of 28mm Keihin constant velocity carburetors.

The CB400A was sold in a choice of Tahitian Red or Candy Sapphire Blue. Striping on the tank and side covers was black and orange and "Hondamatic" appliqués were used on both side covers. The 1978 CB400A Hawk Hondamatic carried a retail sticker near $1,400.

For those buyers who sought an inexpensive middleweight machine that could be shifted manually, the CB400TI Hawk I was right up their alley. The same power plant was used on the Hawk I, but it was fed by a pair of 32mm Keihin CV carbs. In place of the semi-automatic two-speed box found on the Hondamatic,

the Hawk I rowed through a five-speed gearbox. Offered as a lower priced model, the Hawk I rolled with spoke wheels instead of the Comstars, and was kickstart only. A drum brake at both ends was another cost-saving measure. Gauges were limited to a single speedometer and warning lights. Wearing a different fuel tank than the other two Hawks, the I held 3.7 gallons and total weight for the bargain model was 380 lbs. Helios Red or Excel Black was offset by black and orange tank stripes. A price tag of $1,100 allowed the buyer to keep a few more dollars in his pocket.

Appearance wise, the CB400TII Hawk II was close to its siblings. It wore the same Comstar wheels as the Hondamatic, as well as the same 3.4-gallon fuel tank. The big difference in the Hawk II was the equipment. Fitted with both kick and electric start and a hydraulic front disc brake delivered a high level of trim with a price that fell below the automatic model. A speedometer and tachometer were part of the II's package, and the 395cc motor was the same as in the other two offerings. A set of 32mm carbs was also employed on the Hawk II. Tahitian Red and Candy Sapphire Blue were your color options and either choice wore black and orange striping on the tank and side covers. It took approximately $1,300 to ride home on the Hawk II, making it a popular choice among those seeking more traditional machines.

The final new model for 1978 was the CX500. Motivated by a longitudinally mount-

1978 MODELS

Model	Product Code	Engine Type/Displacement	Transmission	Year(s) Available
CT90 Trail 90	102	OHC Single/89cc	8-Speed	1978
CB125S	383	OHC Single/122cc	5-Speed	1978
CM185T Twinstar	419	OHC Parallel Twin/181cc	4-Speed	1978
CB400A Hawk Hondamatic	417	OHC Parallel Twin/395cc	2-Speed Auto.	1978
CB400TI Hawk I	413	OHC Parallel Twin/395cc	5-Speed	1978
CB400TII Hawk II	413	OHC Parallel Twin/395cc	5-Speed	1978
CX500	415	OHV V-Twin/496cc	5-Speed	1978
CB550K 550 Four	404	SOHC Inline Four/544cc	5-Speed	1978
CB750A 750 Hondamatic	393	SOHC Inline Four/736cc	2-Speed Auto.	1978
CB750F Super Sport	410	SOHC Inline Four/736cc	5-Speed	1978
CB750K 750 Four	405	SOHC Inline Four/736cc	5-Speed	1978
GL1000 Gold Wing	431	SOHC Opposed Four/999cc	5-Speed	1978

ed, 80-degree, V-Twin motor, this machine represented a new direction for Honda. Not only was the motor mounted in a different fashion, but also it was used a stressed-member of the frame design that lacked a lower section. Two 35mm Keihin constant velocity carburetors fed 496cc of displacement. The five-speed power was transferred to the rear wheel via a drive shaft. The only other Honda using this system was the Gold Wing, and similar comparisons would be made in later years.

A mechanical drum brake on the rear wheel was teamed up with an 11-inch disc up front that was grabbed by a hydraulic caliper. Comstar wheels were also used on the new CX500. The liquid-cooled motor was kept within operating temperatures by the front mounted radiator, again, much like the Gold Wing. The instruments were mounted in a housing that melded into the headlight bezel. A speedometer, tachometer, temperature gauge and indicator lights made up the array.

A fuel tank that held 4.9 gallons was trimmed with a red stripe outlined with white. Both side covers bore "CX500" badges that were chrome with red trim. The mildly stepped saddle was finished off with a passenger grab rail and a small cowl that blended into the contoured taillight. The CX500 weighed in at just less than 450 lbs. and carried the weight with a low center of gravity due to the motor's configuration and placement. Your choice of Black or Candy Presto Red completed the sales sheet listing.

The balance of the 1978 line was treated to minor cosmetic changes.

The CB550K was the only model in that displacement range, and was little changed from the 1977 model. A sculpted contour saddle gave the rider and passenger more of their own space to perch. Candy Alpha Red or Black were the 1978 hues, and the fuel tank stripe was red with gold pin striping. Side cover alterations saw a "550Four" badge joining a "K" decal and gold striping.

The other semi-automatic model, the CB750A was back for its final year of sale.

1978 Price Guide	6	5	4	3	2	1
XL75 (75cc single)	200	300	450	600	800	1,000
XL100 (99cc single)	220	330	500	660	880	1,100
CB125S (122cc single)	220	330	500	660	880	1,100
XL125 (124cc single)	240	360	540	720	960	1,200
XL175 (173cc single)	240	360	540	720	960	1,200
CM185T Twinstar (181cc twin)	240	360	540	720	960	1,200
XL250 Motosport (249cc single)	300	450	680	900	1,200	1,500
XL350 (348cc single)	320	480	720	960	1,280	1,600
CB400A Hondamatic (395cc twin)	400	600	900	1,200	1,600	2,000
CB400TI Hawk (395cc twin)	320	480	720	960	1,280	1,600
CB400TII Hawk (395cc twin)	340	500	750	1,010	1,340	1,675
CX500 (496cc V-twin)	330	500	740	990	1,320	1,650
CB550 (550cc four)	340	510	770	1,020	1,360	1,700
CB750A (736cc four)	550	830	1,240	1,650	2,200	2,750
CB750F (736cc four)	550	830	1,240	1,650	2,200	2,750
CB750K (736cc four)	550	830	1,240	1,650	2,200	2,750
GL1000 Gold Wing (999cc four, shaft-drive)	640	960	1,440	1,920	2,560	3,200

Comstar wheels were added to the existing model, and Candy Alpha Red or Candy Polaris Blue were your color options.

The 736cc, inline four power plant used on all three of the CB's would see its final year of application in 1978. The CB750F Super Sport retained the black mill for 1978 as well as the black front fork lowers. Candy Presto Red or Black was seen with tank stripes of red with gold striping. The "750 Four" badges used on the side covers were of a more artistic style and stood alone. The CB750K was also left largely alone for the final year in its present form. Candy Alpha Red and Excel Black base colors were accented by gold striping, and finished with gold and red pin striping. The two-stage saddle was also applied providing more separation between rider and passenger.

Side covers for the final SOHC model featured "750 Four" badges and "K" appliqués and gold stripes.

The GL1000 Gold Wing received several upgrades in 1978, but they were mainly cosmetic. A newly designed exhaust system was finished in all chrome and provided better breathing for the 999cc motor. Wheels were changed from spokes to Comstars and an instrument pod was added to the top of the storage tank. Faces of the gauges were now black with red markings.

1979

Unlike some model years, 1979 was rife with new models and changes to existing bikes. A few model designations were unaltered, but the motorcycles they were now attached to were a whole new breed of Hondas.

It was the final year for the CT90 Trail model, although a CT110 replaced it in 1980. The 1979 wore a coat of Tahitian Red paint and the "Honda" shroud decal was now larger, but still done in white.

The CB125S returned for another year. Changes were again minor, the biggest of which was the replacement of the front disc brake with a leading show drum. Light Ruby Red paint was trimmed with a red and black tank stripe and the "CB125S" side cover decal was now red and black.

The Twinstar CM185T was in its last year and received only cosmetic modifications. The same colors were sold in 1979 as in 1978, but striping was now red with gold accents. "Twinstar" decals used on the side covers were also gold.

Only two CB400 Hawks were seen in 1979, with the CB400A removed from the catalog. Both the Hawk I and II were unaltered from the previous year, except for color options. Both

The CBX Super Sport was first sold in the 1979 model year, and captured the attention of high-performance riders everywhere.
Owner: Tom Ronan

versions were sold in a choice of Candy Antares Red or Black, and touted side cover stripes of gold and orange.

New to the 400cc family were the CM400A Hondamatic and the CM400T. With the exception of a different gearbox, these two models were the same machine. The CM400A featured Honda's two-speed, semi-automatic transmission, while the CM400T rowed manually through five gears. The 395cc, parallel twin fitted with three-valve heads was found in both models. Both models breathed through new "shorty" exhaust pipes and rolled on blacked-out Comstar wheels with silver alloy rims. Diameter of the front wheel was reduced to 18 inches to enhance the "custom" look as well as dropping the saddle height lower to the ground. Teardrop tanks held 2.5 gallons of fuel and were sleeker than those used on the CB400 Hawks. Deeply sculpted saddles were teamed with pullback bars for a more comfortable riding stance and gave the CMs a different profile similar to some of Hondas bigger bikes. Both of the new CM models tipped the scales at 394 lbs. when dry.

The CM400T retailed for $1,748, while the CM400A cost an extra $150. Both the A and T variants were sold in Candy Presto Red or Candy Holly Green with orange and red pinstripes. Side cover artwork was white and red. One-hundred-mph speedometers were also used on both variations.

The CX500 gang would expand to three models in 1979, proving the popularity of the 80-degree V-Twin motor that bowed in 1978. The base model CX500 was the beneficiary of some fresh styling cues, but was unaltered mechanically. The alloy Comstar wheels were still being used, but the black rim covers were not applied. Brake and clutch levers were finished with black anodizing and a rectangular master cylinder was installed on the bars. Black or Candy Presto Red featured maroon tank stripes highlighted with gold pinstripes. Side cover "CX500" badges were gold with red trim.

Two new CX500 models were added for 1979, but both were still powered by the

The CBX's massive 1047cc motor was a stressed member of the chassis and delivered 103 horsepower, according to Honda's ratings for 1979 models.

same 496cc, 80-degree V-Twin mill found in the standard CX500. The CX500C Custom featured a sleeker teardrop fuel tank, deeply sculpted saddle and pullback handlebars. A different style of Comstar wheels featured black spokes outlined with natural highlights. The inner face of the rims were also black, but had naturally finished fascia. Truncated exhaust pipes delivered a slightly more aggressive tone to match the custom lifestyle. Candy Plum Red or Candy Universal Blue was trimmed with gold stripes on the tank and side covers, along with gold "CX500 Custom" appliqués. The bobbed rear fender was chrome, while the svelte, tire-hugging front fender matched the chosen body color.

The Deluxe was the third and final CX500 model for 1979. Fitted with the same fuel tank and side covers as the base CX500, the Deluxe stood apart in several ways. The CX500D wore the same black and silver Comstar wheels as the Custom, but had full-length exhaust canisters and a pair of chrome fenders. Candy Presto

Steering the CBX was accomplished by grabbing hold of the die-cast handlebars that stretched up to the rider's grip. The fuel tank held more than 5 gallons, but limited mileage was the trade-off for the CBX's amazing power.
Owner: Ray Landy

The large, ribbed taillight lens was also used on the 1979 Gold Wings, but the CBX featured the sculpted "duck tail" rear cowling that the GL1000 lacked.

Dual disc brakes on the front Comstar wheel were teamed with an even larger rotor on the rear wheel, providing plenty of stopping power.

Red was tastefully highlighted with gold stripes and emblems. More upright bars and a cushier, chrome trimmed saddle provided a compliant and comfortable riding posture. The face of the CX500D speedometer ran all the way to 120 mph.

1979 brought no listing for the CB550K, but a new model arrived to fill the shoes of the missing 550cc machine. Touted as a "boulevard beauty and back-road bandit," the CB650 was designed to appeal to a wide variety of riders.

The CB650's 627cc, SOHC inline four motor shifted through a five-speed gearbox and delivered the power to the rear wheel via chain drive. A four-into-two exhaust saved some weight over the four-into-four systems used on many four-cylinder machines. With a saddle height of only 31.5 inches and a dry weight of 437 lbs., the CB650 delivered ample power in a fairly lightweight package. Subtle, two-tone paint schemes of Candy Muse Red and Maroon or Black and Red were also benefactors of gold pinstripes. Comstar wheels were black highlighted with silver and a pair of chrome fenders were applied. A front disc brake was joined by a drum on the rear wheel, providing plenty of stopping power for the CB650's weight.

Honda's class of 750cc machines would receive the largest dose of change for 1979, and the results were a milestone for the company. First off, the CB750A Hondamatic was removed from the lineup. The 3-year run of the semi-automatic version had proven that the majority of riders at that level prefer to shift their own, thus eliminating the need for such a model in that class.

It had been 10 years since the first CB750 rolled onto the scene, and the time had come for a makeover on the time-tested machines. Not content to apply a new coat of paint to existing models, Honda went all out when creating the updated machines for the 750 class.

All three 750 models—CB750K, CB750K Limited Edition and CB750F—were now powered by a 749cc, DOHC, 16-valve motor that delivered impressive performance. A set of four 30mm Keihin carburetors fed the expanded motor's dimensions and an accelerator pump provided a quicker response when the throttle was twisted.

The new design was 1.5 inches narrower and one-half inch shorter than the previous SOHC motor, but weighed 6 lbs. more.

The new CB750K and Limited Edition models were fairly similar, but still had some major differences. The base model K rolled on chrome spoke wheels and you had a choice between three solid colors. Candy Muse Red, Candy Bayard Brown and Black were all trimmed with gold striping. Both fenders, as well as the four-into-four exhaust were de-

1979 PRICE GUIDE	6	5	4	3	2	1
XL75 (75cc single)	180	270	410	540	720	900
XL100 (99cc single)	190	290	430	570	760	950
CB125S (122cc single)	220	330	500	660	880	1,100
XL125S (124cc single)	220	330	500	660	880	1,100
XL185S (180cc single)	240	360	540	720	960	1,200
XR185 (180cc single)	240	360	540	720	960	1,200
CM185T Twinstar (181cc twin)	240	360	540	720	960	1,200
XL250 Motosport (249cc single)	280	420	630	840	1,120	1,400
CB400TI Hawk (395cc twin)	320	480	720	960	1,280	1,600
CB400TII Hawk (395cc twin)	340	500	750	1,010	1,340	1,675
CM400A Hondamatic (395cc twin)	400	600	900	1,200	1,600	2,000
CM400T (395cc twin)	420	630	950	1,260	1,680	2,100
CX500 (496cc V-twin, shaft-drive)	340	510	770	1,020	1,360	1,700
CX500C Custom (496cc V-twin, shaft-drive)	340	510	770	1,020	1,360	1,700
CX500D Deluxe (496cc V-twin)	340	510	770	1,020	1,360	1,700
XL500S (498cc single)	320	480	720	960	1,280	1,600
XR500 (498cc single)	320	480	720	960	1,280	1,600
CB650 (627cc four)	340	510	770	1,020	1,360	1,700
GL1000 Gold Wing (999cc four, shaft-drive)	640	960	1,440	1,920	2,560	3,200
CBX (1,047cc six)	1,300	1,950	2,930	3,900	5,200	6,500

livered in chrome. The K also had a taillight that was housed in a wrap-around tail section that extended from the rear of the saddle. The Limited Edition CB750K was painted in two-tone Candy Muse Red and Red with gold stripes keeping the two apart. Both side covers were fitted with special "10th Anniversary CB750K" emblems that were coated with green and gold. Black Comstar wheels were highlighted with silver. The same front disc and rear drum found on the K was present.

A freestanding taillight was also used on the Limited Edition model.

Perhaps the most exciting entry in the 750 class was the all-new CB750F. Still powered by the same motor as the other two entries, it was fabricated with several independent features that enhanced performance further. Almost every facet of the F's design was aimed at the sporting rider, and went far beyond the cosmetic alterations seen on previous Super Sports from Honda. Carburetor jetting was adjusted to better suit the CB750F's demands as well as the altered breathing characteristics of the four-into-two exhaust. The new layout of the exhaust kept the lower tubes within the dimensions of the frame, thus providing improved cornering clearances.

The CB750F motor was housed in a frame that featured downtubes that were 0.4mm thicker than those used on the K and Ltd. Ed. models, resulting in a stiffer chassis. All-aluminum Comstar wheels also played into the sporting nature of the F while also saving a few ounces. The F was slowed by a trio of disc brakes, one on the rear wheel and two up front, and hydraulic calipers grabbed all three rotors. A fully prepped CB750F weighed 542 lbs. and carried 4.1 gallons of fuel when topped off.

In the appearance department the F model also wore different bodywork and graphics than the other two 750s. A sweeping fuel tank blended directly into the notched side covers that swept back to meet with the duck tail housing that held the brake light in place. When ordered in Black, the machine was trimmed with a set of swooping red and orange stripes. With Pleiades Silver Metallic, black and red stripes were applied.

A 150-mph speedometer was used on the F model, along with the other instrumentation found on the two siblings. Capable of turning in mid-12-second quarter-mile times, and having a top speed of just over 124 mph, the 1979 CB750F set new standards for production machines. With the exception of Kawasaki's 750 triple, the 1979 F was the fastest 750 available

to the consumer.

It's probably a safe bet to say that most motorcycle manufacturers would be content to release eight new models in a single year, but Honda had one more trick up its 1979 sleeve. The CBX Super Sport rolled onto the marketplace and instantly got the attention of every enthusiast on the block. With its massive inline six-cylinder motor suspended from the frame, it made a new argument for unlimited highway speeds.

Honda had much success with six cylinder machines in the Gran Prix world as far back as the 1960s, but the CBX was its first civilian model offered. Dual overhead cams and four valves per cylinder metered the 1047cc beast. Needless to say, a valve adjustment was not for the faint of heart or those pinching pennies. Six individual Keihin carburetors handled the fuel and air mixture. Honda claimed an output of 103 horsepower for the new model, raising the bar several notches higher in one fell swoop.

Lacking any front downtubes, the CBX used the massive motor as a stressed member to keep the chassis stiff. A six-into-two exhaust provided a swift exit for spent fumes and looked amazing at the same time. By angling the first three-into-one junction upwards, the cornering clearance was little affected by the snake pit of

1979 MODELS

Model	Product Code	Engine Type/ Displacement	Transmission	Year(s) Available
CT90 Trail 90	102	OHC Single/89cc	8-Speed	1979
CB125S	383	OHC Single/122cc	5-Speed	1979
CM185T Twinstar	419	OHC Parallel Twin/181cc	4-Speed	1979
CB400TI Hawk I	413	OHC Parallel Twin/395cc	5-Speed	1979
CB400TII Hawk II	413	OHC Parallel Twin/395cc	5-Speed	1979
CM400A Hondamatic	448	OHC Parallel Twin/395cc	2-Speed Semi-Auto	1979
CM400T	447	OHC Parallel Twin/395cc	5-Speed	1979
CX500	415	OHV V-Twin/496cc	5-Speed	1979
CX500C Custom	449	OHV V-Twin/496cc	5-Speed	1979
CX500D Deluxe	470	VH V-Twin/496cc	5-Speed	1979
CB650	426	SOHC Inline Four/627cc	5-Speed	1979
CB750F Super Sport	445	DOHC Inline Four/749cc	5-Speed	1979
CB750K 750 Four	425	DOHC Inline Four/749cc	5-Speed	1979
CB750K Limited Edition	425	DOHC Inline Four/749cc	5-Speed	1979
GL1000 Gold Wing	431	SOHC Opposed Four/999cc	5-Speed	1979
CBX Super Sport	422	DOHC Inline Six/1047cc	5-Speed	1979

What better way to arrive at the airfield than on Honda's CX500 as shown in this brochure art from 1979?

tubes. A five-speed transmission provided the rider with his gear selections. With the alternator and ignition hardware placed behind the crankshaft, overall width of the motor was only slightly more than the CB750 mill.

An enormous 5.3-gallon fuel tank was hoisted on top of the frame's backbone, and had a hard time keeping up with the CBX's voracious appetite for explosive liquid. Slowing the 606-lb. contraption was handled by three rotors squeezed by hydraulic calipers. A pair of 276mm discs up front and an even bigger 296mm out back did a fine job of bringing the CBX down from speed. Aluminum Comstar wheels held the rubber in place, and the 1979 version were delivered in its natural silver state. A large ducktail cowling was wrapped around the taillight assembly and matched the body color selected. Candy Glory Red and Perseur Silver were the paint choices listed for the '79 models. Both side panels were black, regardless of the color purchased. A single gold stripe

adorned the tank and tailpiece. A wide black "racing" stripe ran the complete length of the fuel tank and tail section, and was outlined with gold.

The 1979 was the priciest model in the lineup at $3,998, and even the mighty Gold Wing sold for a mere $3,698. Kawasaki's KZ1300 in-line six sold for an astounding $4,400 the same year.

The GL1000 was sold alongside the CBX and continued to offer the touring rider a primary choice for long distance rides. Changes were few, and 1979 would be the last year for the 999cc motor. Turn signals on the 1979s were now rectangular, as was the taillight, which was borrowed from the CBX parts bin. Brake and clutch levers were finished in black, and silver Comstar wheels remained standard.

Candy Limited Maroon, Candy Grandeur Blue and Candy Burgundy were the 1979 colors for the GL1000.

1980

Compared to the nine new models introduced for 1979, 1980 would seem fairly tame, yet there were still a few additions to the lineup.

The CT90 Trail had grown to be a CT110 for 1980, but few other changes were implemented. Only four speeds were now available in contrast to the previous eight-speed arrangement. Ignition was now fired with points. This new CT110 would be sold through the 1986 model year, but since changes would be few, this will be the last listing in this book.

Light Ruby Red was still applied to the CB125S for 1980, but tank and side cover graphics were simplified. "Honda" decals on the fuel tank were now gold with a black outline while "CB125S" side cover appliqués were gold with red and black perimeters. 1980 models saw a set of color-matched fenders in place of the chrome units used earlier. Housings of the turn signals were now supplied in black plastic replacing the chrome style.

CM185Ts were no longer a part of the Honda team, but a slightly larger CM200T Twinstar stepped up to the plate. Powered by a 194cc parallel twin motor, the CM200T was for the most part an enlarged CM185T. A pair of shorter mufflers were the only mechanical alteration between the two. Candy Presto Red or Candy Holly Green were decorated with

The overall appeal of the CX500 did not go unnoticed by law enforcement agencies, and they were often pressed into official duty or used as parade units.
Owner: Elgin Police Department

gold "Twinstar" and white and gold "CM200T" decals.

The 400cc roster was trimmed by the loss of the Hawk I and Hawk II, but a new player stepped into the mix. The CB400T looked like a smaller version of the CB750F, including the bodywork that swept from fuel tank to tail section in one flowing line. Solid black Comstar wheels were fitted to both ends and a chrome fender was applied at the front end. A single piston brake caliper grabbed the disc attached to the front wheel. A rear drum remained on duty out back. The 395cc parallel twin featured three-valve heads and a six-speed gearbox. When buying the Custom Silver Metallic, red and black stripes were affixed while the Black version presented orange and yellow bands.

The semi-automatic CM400A was back, but only cosmetics were altered. Base colors were unchanged, but the Candy Presto Red now wore bright red pinstripes while the Candy Holly Green units had contrasting light and dark green lines. An 85-mph speedometer was also installed on the 1980 and 1981 units. The same modifications were applied to the CM400T.

Entering the 400cc fray as an entry-level model, the CM400E was stripped of the more expensive hardware, but offered a competent package to the first-bike buyer. Wire wheels replaced the Comstars and a front wheel drum brake was used instead of the disc found on other Honda 400s. Instrumentation was limited to speedometer only.

Any color you wanted as long as it was Black was offered but orange and red pinstripes livened things up a bit. Tank emblems were white while "CM400E" side cover art was orange and white.

Moving up the food chain, the base model CX500 was no longer sold, but the CX500C and CX500D returned.

The Custom came in your choice of Candy Plum Red or Black, and both hues were accented with gold and red striping. The Deluxe was only sold in Candy Presto Red with red and gold trim. "CX500 Deluxe" side cover decals were gold.

Both CX500s were now limited to an 85-mph speedometer.

The base CB650 was de-contented to make allowances for the new CB650 Custom. The CB650 now sported wire wheels, but still had a front disc brake. A set of chrome airbox trim panels was added as well as altered saddle and side covers. A simple pinstripe was applied to your choice of Black or Candy Bourgogne Red paint. A four-into two exhaust was also still in-

Equipped with a full set of warning lights, siren and radio, this CBX500 was available for a variety of duties.

1980 was the second year of sale for the CB750F and owners were adding personal touches to make the new machine their own. This one has a bolt-on case guard and aftermarket saddle.
Owner: M&R Cycle Specialist, Inc.

The sweeping new bodywork of the revised 750 brought new levels of sales to Honda dealers.

More refined side covers were trimmed with fresh graphics for a coherent design theme throughout the 750F.

cluded in the less decorated model.

Slotting in above the CB650 was the new CB650C Custom. A pair of black Comstar wheels and a four-into-four exhaust set the Custom apart from the lower level 650. Black or Candy Muse Red were the options, and the chrome airbox covers were also applied to the Custom.

One departure and one arrival would occur in the 750 family of 1980 Hondas. The CB750K Limited Edition was only intended as a single-year model, so 1980 was never in its cards. Rolling in for the latest model year was the CB750C Custom. In keeping with the "custom" mentality, a teardrop tank, stepped saddle and pullback bars were all part of the appearance package. A single disc brake was found on the front Comstar and a drum was used on the aft wheel. Candy Muse Red or Cosmo Black Metallic completed the Custom's list of tricks.

The CB750F Super Sport now had blacked-out Comstar wheels and an 85-mph speedometer. The same body colors were seen, but the Black now had only red stripes while the Pleiades Silver Metallic saw red and black enhancements. The CB750K lost the taillight cowling and the stoplight was now supported on a bracket jutting from the rear fender. The 85-mph speedometer was commonly applied to all motorcycles of the period due to government restrictions.

Candy Bayard Brown was no longer a color choice, but Candy Muse Red and Excel Black remained.

Another custom model in the 1980 catalog was all new. The CB900C Custom was powered by a larger-displacement DOHC, four-valve motor, and a new variation was the dual-range, five-speed gearbox that gave the rider 10 speeds from which to select.

Unlike the smaller CB750 models, the new CB900C was shaft-driven adding smoothness as well as reducing maintenance needs. A four-into-four exhaust system was all chrome. Gold and red pinstripes were applied to your choice of Candy Muse Red or Candy Poseidon Blue.

In response to a new European ruling that

limited horsepower ratings for motorcycles to 100, the CBX was actually detuned for 1980. Honda was forced to build one CBX to meet the restrictions of U.S. and European markets or sell two different versions. With volume of CBX sales not high enough to justify a double build, all 1980 CBXs were limited to 98 horse-power. 1979 models produced 103. Air-adjust-able front forks were a part of the 1980 CBX structure, and Comstar wheels were now black. Even the mighty CBX was forced to wear an 85-mph speedometer for the new year. Perseur Silver was no longer offered, but Black and Candy Glory Red were in the lineup for the '80 CBX.

There were two bits of good news for fans of the Gold Wing in 1980. An opposed four-cylinder motor would still power the GL, but displacement was bumped to 1085cc's. The all-silver Comstar wheels were replaced with the highlighted black models and a pair of single-piston hydraulic brakes grabbed solid discs on

A pair of more powerful disc brakes were added to the CB750F equation, as were the Comstar wheels.

Hard angles and smooth contours created an unforgettable shape on the latest CB750F.

This ducktail section added another bit of flair to the sporty F model 750.

Replacing the time-tested single overhead cam motor with a DOHC version in 1979, Honda provided riders with smoother power than ever before.

the front wheel. The same maximum speed of 85 mph was indicated on the speedometer face. All emblems and pinstripes are gold, whether you bought the Candy Muse Red or Black version of the GL1100.

The big Interstate joined the GL family. By taking the already amazing Gold Wing and adding a full-coverage fairing and a set of hard saddlebags and rear storage box, long-range riding was a definite possibility. Of course, the new equipment added 100 lbs. to the already-ponderous 636-lb. base model, but once you were rolling the weight seemed to fall away. For those who wanted more than the sound of the scenery rushing by, an AM/FM radio, complete with helmet intercoms, could be added to the mix. The unit was made by Clarion and designed to fit the Gold Wing only. The entire assembly was easily removed with a key for safety and security. Two speakers were mounted in the fairing and flanked the bank of additional instruments.

The rear-mounted storage box swallowed two full-face helmets, but didn't leave space for much else. Each saddlebag was fitted with a waterproof vinyl liner that kept the chosen contents dry and out of the elements. A weight limit of 20 lbs. for each housing was listed. A pair of pockets in the fairing allowed for another 5 lbs. each.

The base price for the GL1100 Interstate was $4,898. The radio package added another $574.60. This was a lofty price for the period, but it bought the long-distance rider a capable machine with great creature comforts.

1980 PRICE GUIDE	6	5	4	3	2	1
C70 Passport (72cc single)	180	270	410	540	720	900
XL80S (80cc single)	190	290	430	570	760	950
XL100S (99cc single)	190	290	430	570	760	950
CB125S (122cc single)	220	330	500	660	880	1,100
XL125S (124cc single)	220	330	500	660	880	1,100
XL185S (180cc single)	240	360	540	720	960	1,200
CM200T Twinstar (194cc twin)	240	360	540	720	960	1,200
XL250 Motosport (249cc single)	280	420	630	840	1,120	1,400
CB400T Hawk (395cc twin)	320	480	720	960	1,280	1,600
CM400A Hondamatic (395cc twin)	380	570	860	1,140	1,520	1,900
CM400E (395cc twin)	400	600	900	1,200	1,600	2,000
CM400T (395cc twin)	400	600	900	1,200	1,600	2,000
CX500C Custom (496cc V-twin, shaft-drive)	340	510	770	1,020	1,360	1,700
CX500D Deluxe (496cc V-twin, shaft-drive)	340	510	770	1,020	1,360	1,700
XL500S (498cc single)	300	450	680	900	1,200	1,500
XR500 (498cc single)	300	450	680	900	1,200	1,500
CB650 (627cc four)	340	510	770	1,020	1,360	1,700
CB650C Custom (627cc four)	320	480	720	960	1,280	1,600
CB900C Custom (902cc four, shaft-drive)	350	530	790	1,050	1,400	1,750
CBX (1,047cc six)	1,200	1,800	2,700	3,600	4,800	6,000
GL1100 Gold Wing (1,085cc four, shaft-drive)	700	1,050	1,580	2,100	2,800	3,500
GL1100I Gold Wing Interstate (1,085cc four, shaft-drive)	840	1,260	1,890	2,520	3,360	4,200

1980 MODELS

Model	Product Code	Engine Type/ Displacement	Transmission	Year(s) Available
CT110 Trail 90	459	OHC Single/105cc	4-Speed	1980
CB125S	383	OHC Single/122cc	5-Speed	1980
CM200T Twinstar	465	OHC Parallel Twin/194cc	4-Speed	1980
CB400T Hawk	413	OHC Parallel Twin/395cc	6-Speed	1980
CM400A Hondamatic	448	OHC Parallel Twin/395cc	2-Speed Semi-Auto.	1980
CM400E	447	OHC Parallel Twin/395cc	5-Speed	1980
CM400T	447	OHC Parallel Twin/395cc	5-Speed	1980
CX500C Custom	449	OHV V-Twin/496cc	5-Speed	1980
CX500D Deluxe	470	OVH V-Twin/496cc	5-Speed	1980
CB650	460	SOHC Inline Four/627cc	5-Speed	1980
CB650C Custom	460	SOHC Inline Four/627cc	5-Speed	1980
CB750C Custom	425	DOHC Inline Four/749cc	5-Speed	1980
CB750F Super Sport	445	DOHC Inline Four/749cc	5-Speed	1980
CB750K 750 Four	425	DOHC Inline Four/749cc	5-Speed	1980
CB900C Custom	461	DOHC Inline Four/902cc	10-Speed	1980
GL1100 Gold Wing	463	SOHC Opposed Four/1085cc	5-Speed	1980
GL1100 Gold Wing Interstate	463	SOHC Opposed Four/1085cc	5-Speed	1980
CBX Super Sport	422	DOHC Inline Six/1047cc	5-Speed	1980

The 1981 Honda lineup was status quo for the most part, but a few new bikes were introduced. The new faces were variations on a theme, but still new entries in the books.

The diminutive CB125S soldiered on, and now wore Black paint with gold and red stripes. Side cover art was printed in solid red. A newly installed capacitor discharge ignition was also found on the 1981 CB125s. The next larger model, the CM200T Twinstar, was also back for sale in 1981. The previous 6-volt system was bumped to 12 for 1981 and a capacitor discharge ignition was also new. A chrome passenger grab rail was added behind the rear seat, and two new colors for the CM200T were sold. Candy Bourgogne Red or Candy Sword Blue both featured appliqués with different color

trim. Red paint received blue outlining of the "CM200T" and the blue model wore red outlining.

Many of Honda's 1981 models were now sold wearing two-tone paint, and the CM400A was among the lucky.
Owner: Matt Jonas

CB400T Hawks were given a few cosmetic upgrades, and still looked a lot like their larger siblings, the CB750F and new CB900F. A fresh design was applied to the front fender and was now painted to match the chosen body color. The rear taillight cowl had a bolder spoiler molded into it to complete the big brother affect. Black Comstar wheels were highlighted on the edges and a dual-disc front brake seized the rotor. Pleiades Silver Metallic versions saw black and blue stripes and the Black models wore accents of orange and blue.

The semi-automatic CM400A for 1981

The 395cc parallel-twin motor proved itself as a durable power plant and was installed on several models besides the Hondamatic.

was finished in two-tone paint schemes. Gold "CM400A" emblems and pinstripes adorned either Candy Sword Blue with Blue Gray Metallic or Candy Bourgogne Red with Red Brown Metallic.

The CM400C gave the CM400 family one new member. Shifting through a five-speed gearbox versus the semi-automatic two-speed was about the only mechanical difference between the two. Other minor contrasts were in

the dual-piston front brake and Black Comstar wheels with highlights. Again, there was a pair of two-tone paint sets to choose from. Candy Muse Red mated to Metallic Brown, or Cosmo Black Metallic paired with Metallic Blue. Gold pinstripes accented both the fuel tank and side covers.

The entry-level CM400E claimed a few small victories in the modification department. The speedometer now resided atop a chrome base, and the turn signal housings were also changed to chrome versus black as was used on the 1980s.

The addition of two-tone paint was the only significant change for the 1981 CM400Ts.

Candy Bourgogne Red was set with Metallic Bronze, or you could get the Candy Sword Blue and Metallic Light Blue option. Gold pinstripes were used in either case.

The CX500 clan was joined by two new members and minor changes were applied to the Custom and Deluxe versions.

The CX500C Custom steered through a pair of leading-axle front forks in 1981 and '82. Two-tone color sets now ruled the roost at Honda and the Custom received the Candy Bourgogne Red with Red Brown Metallic or Cosmo Black Metallic with Blue Metallic. Again, gold stripes helped keep the two chosen colors apart. The CX500D Deluxe delivered more ride control with the addition of air-adjustable front forks in 1981. Cosmo Black Metallic was the single color listed and it was trimmed with orange and gold pinstripes.

The new GL500 Silver Wing was introduced as a new 1981 model. Based on the chassis and power train of the CX500 models, the Silver Wing wore all-new sheet met-

A simple gear indicator was used in place of the usual tachometer on the CM400A. The semi-automatic gearbox was shifted without a clutch, requiring only a nudge to the foot shift lever.

al that included a modular saddle and storage design that allowed the rider to configure his machine to fit his changing needs. A two-person saddle with no storage space was the most basic setup. By replacing the rear section of the saddle with a small trunk, a moderate amount of travel gear could be stowed. The third option involved the installation of a large trunk that also included a backrest for the rider. The Silver Wing mainly provided space for two riders and no storage or one rider with his choice of capacities.

The pair of rear coil over shocks used on the CX models was replaced by a Pro-Link rear suspension that resided between the frame tubes and delivered a more compliant and adjustable ride. Only solid colors were sold on the Silver Wing. Candy Muse Red or Cosmo Black Metallic both sported gold pinstripes.

Taking mid-level touring to the next level, the GL500 Silver Wing Interstate also entered the freeway for 1981. Rolling on the same chassis and suspension as the base Silver Wing, the Interstate provided the rider with protection from the elements by employing a full-coverage fairing. The Interstate also expanded the stowage capacity by allowing for a set of hard saddlebags to join the modular seat and rear storage compartments. To compensate for the extra weight, the GL500 Interstate slowed with a pair of slotted disc brakes on the front wheel. Selected bodywork was cloaked in a choice of Candy Muse Red or Cosmo Black Metallic, both with gold accents.

Adjustable air suspension was finding its way onto more Hondas for 1981, and the CB650 was among the models now fitted with them. Newly designed "CB650" logos were on the side covers, and Black was replaced by Cosmo Black Metallic, but no other changes were applied. Another application of the adjustable air forks was found on the CB650C Custom. The fork style was also changed to leading axle for 1981.

A pair of hydraulic disc brakes was also thrown into the mix. In keeping with the two-tone custom theme, the CB650C was coated with Candy Universal Blue and Metallic Blue, or Candy Muse Red and Metallic Brown.

Similar revisions were seen on the CB750C for 1981. Leading-axle forks were implement-

ed, but they were not air adjustable. Dual front disc brakes helped to bring the now-two-toned machine to a halt. Candy Universal Blue with Blue Metallic or Cosmo Black Metallic with Blue Metallic were applied to the fuel tank and side covers.

Comstar wheels were used on nearly every Honda model by 1981, and the CM400A sported the all-black versions.

The Candy Sword Blue and Blue Gray Metallic paint option was selected on this CM400A.

Super Sport CB750F units now featured a front fender complete with its own small duck-tail spoiler that was painted unit color. A pair of slotted front disc brakes were squeezed by twin-piston calipers. The same two base colors were seen in 1981, but the silver machines were accented with black and blue stripes. K models were fitted with air-adjustable front forks and newly shaped mufflers. Excel Black was replaced by Cosmo Black Metallic.

The CB900 listings expanded by one. The CB900C Custom was given the now typical two-tone finish, with Candy Muse Red/Brown Metallic or Cosmo Black Metallic/Blue Metallic as your choices. Leading-axle, air-adjustable forks were also employed for 1981.

The CB900F Super Sport was all-new for 1981. Built in the same tradition as the CB750F model, the 900F touted higher performance and sexier bodywork to the sport-minded rider. A four-into-two exhaust was mated to the 902cc, 16-valve motor to save weight and enhance breathing. A trio of disc brakes was on board to slow the Super Sport, and the front discs were slotted. Black models were accented by orange-red stripes, and the Pleiades Silver Metallic versions wore dark blue-light blue accents.

Having lost some of its bite in 1980, the CBX was pointed in a more "sport-touring" direction for 1981. The big six-cylinder monster was fitted with a sleek frame-mounted fairing and hard-sided saddlebags. For shorter trips, the saddlebags were easily detached.

The tail section was also smoother and devoid of the ducktail look used on the 1979 and 1980 units. Every inch of the new bodywork was covered in Magnum Silver Metallic and highlighted with black stripes that were outlined in red. The added weight of the new trim gave Honda reason to upgrade the front disc brakes to internally vented rotors for added cooling. Rear coil-over shocks were replaced with the adjustable Pro-Link suspension.

No mechanical changes were made to the GL1100 or Interstate for 1981. Pinstriping on both machines was now orange and gold, and was applied to the buyer's choice of Candy Muse Red or Cosmo Black Metallic paint.

1981 MODELS

Model	Product Code	Engine Type/ Displacement	Transmission	Year(s) Available
CB125S	383	OHC Single/122cc	5-Speed	1981
CM200T Twinstar	465	OHC Parallel Twin/194cc	4-Speed	1981
CB400T Hawk	413	OHC Parallel Twin/395cc	6-Speed	1981
CM400A Hondamatic	448	OHC Parallel Twin/395cc	2-Speed Semi-Auto	1981
CM400C Custom	447	OHC Parallel Twin/395cc	5-Speed	1981
CM400E	447	OHC Parallel Twin/395cc	5-Speed	1981
CM400T	447	OHC Parallel Twin/395cc	5-Speed	1981
CX500C Custom	449	OHV V-Twin/496cc	5-Speed	1981
CX500D Deluxe	470	OHV V-Twin/496cc	5-Speed	1981
GL500 Silver Wing	MA1	OHV V-Twin/496cc	5-Speed	1981
GL500 Silver Wing Interstate	MA1	OHV V-Twin/496cc	5-Speed	1981
CB650	460	SOHC Inline Four/627cc	5-Speed	1981
CB650C Custom	460	SOHC Inline Four/627cc	5-Speed	1981
CB750C Custom	MA5	DOHC Inline Four/749cc	5-Speed	1981
CB750F Super Sport	445	DOHC Inline Four/749cc	5-Speed	1981
CB750K 750 Four	MA4	DOHC Inline Four/749cc	5-Speed	1981
CB900C Custom	461	DOHC Inline Four/902cc	10-Speed	1981
CB900F Super Sport	438	DOHC Inline Four/902cc	5-Speed	1981
GL1100 Gold Wing	463	SOHC Opposed Four/1085cc	5-Speed	1981
GL1100I Gold Wing Interstate	463	SOHC Opposed Four/1085cc	5-Speed	1981
CBX Super Sport	MA	DOHC Inline Six/1047cc	5-Speed	1981

Meet a bike that'll make you want to ride forever.

A bike that'll make you feel in control on the longest stretch of highway. Or shortest city street.

A bike that'll make you look like a million. And feel like one.

It's the CM400A from Honda. Like the CM400T, it's a mid-size cruiser that's designed to deliver high times and low maintenance.

There's a custom stepped seat. A wide rear tire that puts lots of rubber on the road. Pull-back handlebars for a laid-back look. A rich, two-tone teardrop tank. Black Comstar™ wheels. Plus shorty-style mufflers.

And, like the T, the A is more than just another pretty face. Out on the road, it gets all fired up with a 395 cc four-stroke, twin-cylinder engine with maintenance-free electronic ignition.

As well, there are special counterbalancers, improved front forks, rear shocks that pamper the road (you, too), a powerful front disc brake and more.

In fact, the only real difference between these two middleweight miracles is the transmission.

The A's got a sweet and easy two-speed semi-automatic. It means there's a little less work, so you have more time to enjoy the scenery.

See Honda's 1981 CM400A. In Candy Red. Or Candy Blue.

In looks, it stands far above the crowd.

In motion, it gets you far ahead of the crowd —almost automatically.

Instrumentation has special night-time lighting for easy reading.

Sleek, lean and oh-so beautiful two-tone gas tank holds 10 litres.

ELECTRIC STARTER

LOW, LOW SEAT HEIGHT LETS YOU SIT WITH BOTH FEET FIRMLY ON THE GROUND.

NO-MAINTENANCE COMSTAR™ WHEELS WITH TUBELESS TIRES

STANDARD TOOL KIT HIDDEN UNDER THE SEAT.

HONDAMATIC TRANSMISSION, THE ONLY TWO-SPEED SEMI-AUTOMATIC IN ITS CLASS.

MAINTENANCE-FREE CD IGNITION

SEE SEE HONDA CM400A

Mirrors standard equipment

The line of CM400 models was becoming a favorite choice amongst mid-level riders.

Another of Honda's popular "custom" models was the big CB900C. Sporting two-tone paint for 1981, it was a true classic.

Step up and meet the king of our Customs. The CB900C.

At the heart of it all beats a powerful 902 cc, DOHC, 16-valve engine that'll take you off the ramps and on to the highways in seconds.

And all that power at your fingertips is unleashed through a unique and innovative transmission system.

First, power's routed through a five-speed transmission, and then through a dual-range gear box for 10 speeds in all. There's low range for rocket-like acceleration and responsive riding. Or high range for low-rev cruising.

The power then gets to the ground through a clean, quiet, low-maintenance shaft drive.

As well, the CB900C's transistorized, low-maintenance ignition system gives off high voltage sparks from idle to redline. Four-valves-per-cylinder Pentroof combustion chambers guarantee good breathing for combustion efficiency and a rush of power when you really need it.

But how a motorcycle looks is just as important as how it performs. So we've designed the 1981 CB900C to look lean and just a little bit mean.

With pull-back handlebars. An even cushier low-riding stepped seat. Wide-section tubeless tires with raised white lettering. Black Comstar wheels with polished edges. A slick two-tone teardrop tank. A four-into-four exhaust system with upswept chrome mufflers. And for the finishing touch, Candy Red or Black Metallic.

The CB900C.

It jumps at the chance to be ridden. And seen.

Five-speed transmission routes power through this dual-range intermediate gear box.

Smooth ride and easy load adjustment come standard with inter-connected air shocks.

AIRCRAFT-STYLED INSTRUMENT PANEL INCLUDES WARNING INDICATOR FOR LOW AIR-PRESSURE IN SHOCKS.

LEADING-AXLE AIR-ASSISTED FRONT FORKS.

DUAL-DISC BRAKES HAVE IMPROVED PAD MATERIAL FOR QUIETER OPERATION

WIDE-SECTION TUBELESS TIRES WITH RAISED WHITE LETTERS.

AUTOMOTIVE-TYPE OIL COOLER HELPS KEEP ENGINE OIL AT CONSISTENT TEMPERATURE

SEE SEE HONDA CB900C

Mirrors standard equipment

Relegated to the "sport touring" class in 1981, the CBX was delivered complete with fairing and saddlebags.
Owner: Matt Jonas

All four of
Honda's 1981
CM400 varieties
could be found
in one product
brochure.

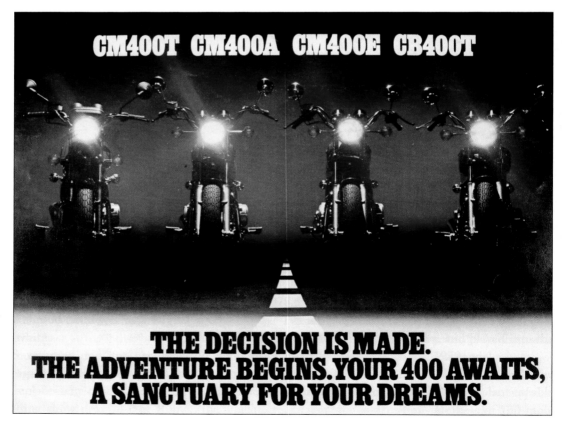

The CBX's revised tail section was flanked by a set of removable saddlebags, adding a new level of convenience for the long distance rider.

Magnum Silver Metallic with black and red striping was the only color sold on the CBX for the 1981 model year.

To better handle the demands of the long distance rider and his luggage, the Honda Pro-Link rear suspension was installed on the 1981 CBX.

A matching set of internally ventilated front disc brakes helped bring the big CBX down from speed.

1982

A myriad of new and upgraded models would grace the showroom floors of Honda dealers for 1982. This group of bikes would forecast much of Honda's future for years to come.

Looking the part of a bigger machine, but being driven by a 49cc two-stroke motor, the new MB5 was put into service in a multitude of ways. From a sporty pit bike to a street-legal form of miserly transport, the MB5 did it all. The reed-valve motor held a single cylinder within its walls and shifted through a five-speed gearbox. A gloss black exhaust pipe was responsible for venting spent gases. Both tires were wrapped around three-spoke alloy rims, and a disc brake was used on the front wheel. The Helios Red had a blue stripe on the tank, while the Black version wore red trim.

Candy Imperial Blue coated the metal on the 1982 CB125S and tank striping of light and dark blue meshed with gold "Honda" and "CB125S" decals. No other changes were made.

In its last year of sale, the CM200T Twinstar saw mainly cosmetic changes. Both rear shocks were now adjustable five-ways, and Candy Muse Red was the only hue offered. Contrasting pinstripes and the "CM200T" art were both done in maroon.

Joining the ranks for 1982 was the CM250C Custom. Powered by a slightly larger 234cc, parallel twin motor, the CM250C Custom looked a lot like the CM200T of the same year. Unlike the four-speed CM200T, the CM250C rowed through five gears. Being a custom, two-

A one-year only model, the MB5 was a sporty alternative for a rider seeking simple and inexpensive transportation.
Owner: Dale Evans

tone paint was the rule. Candy Muse Red was teamed with Candy Antares Red, or if you preferred, Cosmo Black Metallic was mated to Gray Metallic. Side cover graphics were finished in gold.

Several 1981 400cc machines were replaced by 450cc versions for 1982, and another variation was first seen as well.

The first of the new 450cc models was the CB450SC Nighthawk. It was the smallest of the new Nighthawk family and wore distinctive sheet metal and graphics. The 447cc parallel twin SOHC mill was complete with a six-speed transmission. Highlighted black Comstar wheels held white letter tires and rolled beneath a chrome fender up front. A new color, Candy Wineberry Red, joined the old standby Cosmo Black Metallic. Both colors were offset with tank and side cover stripes of chrome. Tank side "Honda" graphics were gold, and delivered a highly appealing overall look to the new model.

Powering the MB5 was a 49cc, two-stroke motor that shifted through a five-speed gearbox.

The Hawk was still included in the new lineup, but was now powered by the larger 447cc motor. The larger power plant was also finished in black for 1982, and stripes on the Black model were changed to orange and red. The 400cc Hondamatic had also grown to the 450cc dimension for 1982, and a few other alterations were found. Comstar wheels were now black with highlights. The motor's cases and cylinders were also black, while the case covers remained silver. Two-tone finishes remained a popular offering, and not just the "custom" machines were given that treatment. Candy Muse Red was joined by Candy Antares Red, while Candy Empire Blue found a partner in Candy Dark Blue. The unpopular 85-mph speedometer remained.

The CM450C was the recipient of the same changes and colors as the CM450A. With the

The 1982 MB5 was equipped with a pair of circular instruments housed in a rectangular cluster.

Both front and rear wheels were of the three-spoke Comstar variety and finished in black with polished rims.

exception of the newly installed 450cc motor, the CM450E was unchanged. Candy Muse Red and Candy Imperial Blue replaced the Black seen in 1981. All of the 450cc models now carried the oil cooler that was previously only applied to the Hondamatic. The increase in displacement generated more heat, and by dropping operating temperatures Honda was able to maintain its reputation for durability.

New for 1982, the CX500TC featured a CX500 V-twin motor, complete with turbocharging and fuel injection.
Owner: Dennis Rockwell

Further setting the CX500TC apart from other Hondas were the gold anodized rims used on both the front and rear end.

Covering all of the 1982 CX500TC's hardware was a sleek bodywork package, enhancing the space-age approach of the turbo model.

Besides all the high-tech hardware, the CX500TC bore graphics that included day-glo red accents that were applied to an overall Pearl Altair White.

In contrast to the freestanding headlights of most motorcycles, the guiding light of the TC was smoothly integrated into the flowing fairing.

The CX family lost one model in the CX500D. Changes to the CX500C were minor with only a second puck being added to the front brake caliper. Fresh two-tone mixes were Candy Muse Red with Red Brown Metallic or Cosmo Black Metallic with Gray Metallic.

Wanting to add more power to the CX500 motor without bumping displacement, Honda made the next obvious choice: turbocharging. Built using the Pro-Link equipped GL500 chassis, the new CX500TC brought a raft of new features to the Honda front. The IHI turbo unit supplied an enormous 17.4 lbs. of boost, and many components within the V-Twin motor were enhanced to maintain durability. Oil capacity was increased through the use of finned sump to keep things slippery.

Once the turbo equation had been deciphered, Honda realized that carburetion would not be able to deliver the fuel and air mixture efficiently to the cylinders. The decision to incorporate a fuel injection system now gave the engineers a new challenge. Feeding an engine this small with fuel injection had never been approached, so Honda devised its own system. A digital computerized fuel injection design was compact and complex, but meted out fuel to meet with the power demands of the blown mill.

The motor displaced one more cc than the CX500C, but still delivered the power to the rear wheel via drive shaft. Three 277mm disc brakes were used to slow the Turbo from speed.

To showcase all of this new gadgetry, the CX500TC was wrapped in all-new bodywork. The Pearl Altair White and Moonstone Silver Metallic paint was trimmed with panels of day-glo red, along with dark and light gray. To further the individuality of the model, special Comstar wheels were anodized in gold. Lower fork legs were also coated in gold paint to continue the theme. A semi-gloss black, two-into-two exhaust was gilded with large "TURBO" badges near the exits. A 5.3-gallon housing was used for fuel storage.

The CX500TC weighed close to 600 lbs. when loaded up with all required fluids and a full tank of gas. Carrying a retail price of $4,898, it was certainly not the choice of a bargain hunter, but for the cost it delivered a high degree of performance in a 500cc package.

When compared to the complexity of the CX500TC, the FT500 Ascot seems almost primitive. Named for the famous dirt track in Southern California, it provides simplicity and performance. Powered by a single-cylinder, 498cc OHC motor devoid of any breathing device it's an amazing contrast. The FT500 is brought to life with the touch of a button, and the blacked-out motor exhales through an equally black two-into-one exhaust. Cast wheels are finished in black and silver and the

The 1982 Silver Wing Interstate delivered many features and lots of comfort to the rider wanting something smaller than the GL1100.
Owner: Mike McGuire

The Interstate's Black Comstar wheels were highlighted with silver and the front wheel sported a pair of slotted disc brakes.

A trio of hard-sided storage compartments awaited the rider's travel wares.

The spacious two-person saddle was accessorized by the passenger backrest, giving both inhabitants a comfortable perch on the Interstate.

The same 80-degree V-twin motor used in the CX500 Custom and GL500 Silver Wing was at home in the better-dressed 1982 Interstate.

bodywork comes in your choice of Monza Red with gray and silver stripes or Black with red and orange art. The headlight and instruments are rectangular in shape, and the 85mph speedometer ruling was still in use.

Both versions of the GL500 Silver Wing received the same minor alterations for 1982. Cosmo Black Metallic was no longer offered, but Sterling Silver Metallic stepped in to fill the gap. A vacuum-operated fuel valve, complete with reserve, was installed on the smaller touring machines.

The 1982 CB650 was now missing its Custom sibling, but was joined by a new Nighthawk. Changes to the CB650 included a second piston being added to the front brake and only one color, Candy Muse Red, was offered.

Joining the Honda fray was the CB650SC Nighthawk. Powered by a blacked-out 627cc,

SOHC inline four motor, this new entry had styling that set it apart from the non-Nighthawks in the catalog. A serpentine chrome stripe that was either Candy Flair Blue or Cosmo Black Metallic was applied to the bodywork. A chrome four-into-four exhaust added style and improved breathing.

Valve adjustment was now achieved via screen-style system and a chain drive was still in use for motivation.

The 750cc group got three all-new faces, with changes made to the returning members as well. The CB750C stopped with a second set of new pistons on its two front calipers, and the engine was delivered in nearly all-black. Two-tone paint remained, and Candy Muse Red/Candy Antares Red or Candy Empire Blue/Candy Blue were seen as the choices. The CB750F Super Sport saw even fewer alterations. A blacked-out mo-

1982 MODELS

Model	Product Code	Engine Type/Displacement	Transmission	Year(s) Available
MB5 (MB50)	166	2-Stroke Single/49cc	5-Speed	1982
CB125S	383	OHC Single/122cc	5-Speed	1982
CM200T Twinstar	465	OHC Parallel Twin/194cc	4-Speed	1982
CM250C Custom	KB4	OHC Parallel Twin/234cc	5-Speed	1982
CB450SC Nighthawk	MC9	SOHC Parallel Twin/447cc	6-Speed	1982
CB450T Hawk	ME0	SOHC Parallel Twin/447cc	6-Speed	1982
CM450A Hondamatic	MC1	SOHC Parallel Twin/447cc	2-Speed Semi-Auto	1982
CM450C Custom	MC0	SOHC Parallel Twin/447cc	6-Speed	1982
CM450E	MC2	SOHC Parallel Twin/447cc	6-Speed	1982
CX500C Custom	449	OHV V-Twin/496cc	5-Speed	1982
CX500TC Turbo	MC7	OHV V-Twin/497cc	5-Speed	1982
FT500 Ascot	MC8	OHC Single/498cc	5-Speed	1982
GL500 Silver Wing	MA1	OHV V-Twin/496cc	5-Speed	1982
GL500 Silver Wing Interstate	MA1	OHV V-Twin/496cc	5-Speed	1982
CB650	460	SOHC Inline Four/627cc	5-Speed	1982
CB650SC Nighthawk	460	SOHC Inline Four/627cc	5-Speed	1982
CB750C Custom	MA5	DOHC Inline Four/749cc	5-Speed	1982
CB750F Super Sport	MC3	DOHC Inline Four/749cc	5-Speed	1982
CB750K 750 Four	MA4	DOHC Inline Four/749cc	5-Speed	1982
CB750SC Nighthawk	ME1	DOHC Inline Four/749cc	5-Speed	1982
VF750C V45 Magna	MB1	DOHC V-Four/748cc	6-Speed	1982
VF750S V45 Sabre	MB0	DOHC V-Four/748cc	6-Speed	1982
CB900C Custom	461	DOHC Inline Four/902cc	10-Speed	1982
CB900F Super Sport	MB7	DOHC Inline Four/902cc	5-Speed	1982
GL1100 Gold Wing	MB9	SOHC Opposed Four/1085cc	5-Speed	1982
GL1100A Aspencade	MB9	SOHC Opposed Four/1085cc	5-Speed	1982
GL1100I Gold Wing Interstate	MB9	SOHC Opposed Four/1085cc	5-Speed	1982
CBX Super Sport	MA2	DOHC Inline Six/1047cc	5-Speed	1982

In its final year of sale, the once-mighty CBX was relegated to "sport touring" status and lost much of the allure it enjoyed during its first days on the market. Still a great bike, it had simply been eclipsed by other offerings available.
Owner: Steve Searles

A pair of hard-sided saddle bags and a full-coverage fairing provided protection for the CBX rider and his belongings.

Air-adjustable front forks allowed for many comfort levels, and a full complement of gauges greeted the rider.

tor and the addition of an orange stripe on the Black version were the only changes from 1981. The CB750K saw slotted front discs grabbed by a pair of twin-piston calipers, and the only hue was Candy Imperial Blue.

The first new 750 entrant was another version of the Nighthawk. It shared many cosmetic cues with the smaller 650 and 450 models and was powered by a 749cc, DOHC inline four. Candy Flair Blue and Cosmo Black Metallic were both accented with the chrome stripes seen on other Nighthawks.

Two brand-new 750s were sold for the first time in 1982 and, except for sharing a power plant, they were nothing alike. The VF750C Magna and VF750S Sabre were both driven by a four-cylinder motor that was arranged in a V-four format. A 90-degree divide between the banks was used and four-valves were found atop each cylinder. Liquid cooling was employed to keep all four jugs running at the same temperature. A six-speed gearbox was included to keep the motor within its optimum rpm range. The sixth gear was listed as an overdrive, but was actually only another selection that dropped rpm at highway speeds. Shaft drive was installed on both machines for smooth and quiet operation.

The VF750C was designed in the "cruiser" or "custom" theme. A deeply sculpted, two-person saddle was mated with a set of pull-back handlebars. A low-rise backrest complete with an aluminum "sissy bar" also graced the V45 Magna. A shortened rear fender and minimalist front fender were both finished in chrome. Suspension on the Magna was handled by a pair of coil-over shocks in the rear and the usual hydraulic fork up front.

Cast wheels were used to keep both tires in place, and a pair of grooved disc brakes were used up front. A drum brake was found on the rear hoop. Candy Maroon or Candy Imperial Blue covered the fuel tank and side covers.

The VF750S Sabre, while being powered by the same motor as the Magna, was another animal altogether. Draped in sleek bodywork that began at the fuel tank and melded into the rear tail section, the Sabre even looked different than its sibling. A more sedately sculpted saddle also featured a rear-mounted grab-rail and contoured tail section. Different cast wheels were found on the Sabre, but a chrome fender was still utilized on the front. The Sabre rode with Honda's Pro-Link suspension on the rear. The use of this suspension required an inch longer wheelbase on the Sabre.

Another drastic difference between the Magna and Sabre was the Sabre's exotic, full-feature instrument console. In addition to the usual speedometer and tachometer, there was a clock that doubled as a stopwatch, tripmeter, fuel and temperature gauges and an array of LCD warning lights. This bank of information was welcomed by some riders, but confused others with too much data.

1982 CB900C models were fitted with slotted front brake discs and dual piston calipers. Two-tone choices were altered and now included Candy Muse Red with Candy Antares Red or Candy Empire Blue with Candy Blue. Only stripe color was changed on CB900F. The previous orange-red stripe on the Black version were changed to a pair of orange and red, and the Pleiades Silver Metallic now claimed black and blue graphics.

The Gold Wings were slowly evolving and each year saw the installation of more creature comfort and performance features. The naked GL1100 rolled on larger rubber both fore and aft, and dual piston calipers compressed slotted discs up front. Self-canceling turn signals found their way into the GL1100's network as well. Cosmo Black Metallic was joined by Candy Wineberry Red and Black in 1982.

Next on the GL1100 order sheet was the Aspencade. Taking the Interstate's level of comfort and performance higher, the new Aspencade bristled with more toys and storage capability. An enlarged passenger backrest included storage pouches on both sides for easy access to small items. The Type II audio system put the controls at the rider's fingertips by placing them on the handlebars. An on-board compressor made adjusting the suspension a breeze.

Two-tone paint also set the Aspencade apart from Interstate sibling—a choice of Sterling Silver Metallic and Tempest Gray Metallic, or Sorrel Brown Metallic with Harvest Gold Metallic.

On the Silver two-tone, the saddle was covered in silver and black vinyl. The Brown version had a pillion covered with two shades of brown vinyl. The Interstate also had the newest slotted front disc brakes and dual-piston calipers and was sold in the same colors as the base GL1100.

Once the CBX had been de-tuned, then shifted into "sport touring" mode, buyer interest began to wane. The once-mighty six-cylinder machine would see its final year of sale in 1982. Changes for the final year of production included Pearl Altair White paint with light blue, dark blue and black stripes. A rear passenger grab rail was also installed, but all else remained the same as the CBX rode into its final sunset.

Seated behind the ample fairing and windscreen, the CBX rider was shielded from wind and the elements.

Still a sight to behold, the CBX's inline-six motor had set the world on fire when first seen in 1979.

1983

With 11 models departing after 1982 and 11 models being added in 1983, Honda continued to play with its mix of product to try to satisfy as many riders as possible.

The CM250C was the only remaining model in that cc range as the CM200T was no longer offered. The biggest change on the 1983 versions was the use of a belt drive in place of the drive chain. Cleaner, quieter operation was the result of the switch. The motor of the CM250C was painted black with highlighted cooling fins, and silver heads and external cases. Black was the only color listed with chrome and red strip-ing. "250 Custom" side cover art was red and gold.

In the 450 group, the CB450T and CM450C were missing. The CB450SC Nighthawk was back with a few alterations. Cast-alloy wheels replaced the Comstars and a speedometer printed with a top speed of 105 was installed. The chrome stripes were replaced with black on the Candy Wineberry Red, and gray on the Black versions. The CM450A also featured the newest cast-alloy wheels and the 105-mph speedom-

Joining the single-cylinder FT500 Ascot in 1983 was the V-twin VT500FT Ascot. This example has been fitted with some Hondaline accessories.
Owner: Marion Robinson

Silver side panel graphics were applied to the Pearl Siren Blue copies of the VT500FT.

Blackchrome covered the two-into-one exhaust and a drum brake on the rear wheel was joined by a disc up front.

The VT500FT Ascot was driven by a V-twin motor.

The low-rise handlebars of the Ascot lent to a mildly aggressive riding posture, but were still comfortable enough to ride all day.

First seen in 1982 as a 500cc model, the CX650TC was back in 1983 as a 650. The previous gold-anodized wheels and day-glo artwork were replaced by more sedate silver wheels and red and blue graphics. The insurance industry made hay on those wanting to own AND ride their turbocharged motorcycles.
Owner: Matt Jonas

eter. Color choices changed to Black with Achilles Black Metallic or Candy Regal Brown with Chestnut Gold Metallic. A blacked-out motor with silver accents was installed in the CM450E, and the 105-mph speedometer also made its way onto the latest model. Black and Candy Regal Brown were the 1983 hues.

The addition of a new Ascot family led to only minor changes for the returning FT500 model. A 120-mph speedometer was used, and stripe colors changed to white and blue on the Monza Red with silver and red on the Black. The new entry into the Ascot family album was the VT500FT Ascot. Powered by a 491cc, V-Twin motor, the VT500FT delivered a different power band to the rider. The liquid-cooled motor sent power through a six-speed gearbox

and exhaled through a two-into-one exhaust that was finished in black chrome. Cast-alloy wheels and a front disc brake completed the hardware parade. Pearl Siren Blue models featured silver side panels and the Candy Bourgogne Red rode with black panels.

One of the two new Shadow model was the VT500C, and it was powered by a 491cc, V-Twin OHC liquid-cooled motor. Shaft drive and a six-speed transmission were all a part of this cruiser-style machine. A blacked-out motor tied into the image and chrome pipes led the exhaust away from the cylinders. Candy Wineberry Red or Black were both fitted with chrome side panels, while the rear fender was delivered in unit color.

Cast-alloy ComCast wheels replaced the previous Comstars across the model line and the VT500C Shadow was one of the machines wearing the cast hoops.

The Nighthawk line grew by one model in

The CX650TC cut an interesting profile from any angle.

1983 MODELS

Model	Product Code	Engine Type/ Displacement	Transmission	Year(s) Available
CM250C Custom	KB4	OHC Parallel Twin/234cc	5-Speed	1983
CB450SC Nighthawk	MC9	SOHC Parallel Twin/447cc	6-Speed	1983
CM450A Hondamatic	MC1	SOHC Parallel Twin/447cc	2-Speed Semi-Auto	1983
CM450E	MC2	SOHC Parallel Twin/447cc	6-Speed	1983
FT500 Ascot	MC8	OHC Single/498cc	5-Speed	1983
VT500C Shadow	MF5	OHC V-Twin/491cc	6-Speed	1983
VT500FT Ascot	MF8	OHC V-Twin/491cc	6-Speed	1983
CB550SC Nighthawk	ME4	DOHC Inline Four/572cc	6-Speed	1983
CB650SC Nighthawk	ME5	SOHC Inline Four/655cc	6-Speed	1983
CX650C Custom	ME8	OHV V-Twin/674cc	5-Speed	1983
CX650TC Turbo	ME7	OHV V-Twin/674cc	5-Speed	1983
GL650 Silver Wing	ME2	OHV V-Twin/674cc	5-Speed	1983
GL650I Silver Wing Interstate	ME2	OHV V-Twin/674cc	5-Speed	1983
CB750SC Nighthawk	ME1	DOHC Inline Four/749cc	5-Speed	1983
VF750C V45 Magna	MB1	DOHC V-Four/748cc	6-Speed	1983
VF750F Interceptor	MB2	DOHC V-Four/748cc	5-Speed	1983
VF750S V45Sabre	MB0	DOHC V-Four/748cc	6-Speed	1983
VT750C Shadow	ME9	SOHC V-Twin/749cc	6-Speed	1983
CB1000C Custom	MG1	DOHC Inline Four/973cc	5-Speed/10-Speed	1983
CB1100F Super Sport	MG5	DOHC Inline Four/1062cc	5-Speed	1983
GL1100 Gold Wing	MB9	SOHC Opposed Four/1085cc	5-Speed	1983
GL1100A Aspencade	MB9	SOHC Opposed Four/1085cc	5-Speed	1983
GL1100I Gold Wing Interstate	MB9	SOHC Opposed Four/1085cc	5-Speed	1983
VF1100C V65 Magna	MB4	DOHC V-Four/1098cc	6-Speed	1983

1983 with the introduction of the CB550SC. Both the 550 and 750 versions of this bike benefited from a new engine architecture that included hydraulic valve lash adjusters. By moving the alternator behind the bank of cylinders, a narrower motor was achieved. The inline four-cylinder, 16-valve motor displaced 572cc's. A chrome four-into-two exhaust system added to the "custom" appearance of the new Nighthawk, as the trend continued. The 550 drove through six speeds and a shaft drive. Candy Presto Red or Black were the color choices.

The CB650 was no more, but the CB650SC Nighthawk stayed on to carry the torch for 650 buyers. The inline four motor was bumped to 655cc's, and hydraulic valve adjusters were now a part of the design. Honda's new "TRAC" anti-dive forks were employed on the 650 Nighthawk and added a measure of control under hard braking. Shaft drive, cast-alloy wheels and triple disc brakes rounded out the hardware list for the 1983 model. Pearl Siren Blue or Candy Wineberry Red were highlighted by the four-into-two exhaust complete with "bologna slice" mufflers.

The entire range of CX and GL 500 models had moved closer to the head of the class with their displacement bumped to 674ccs for 1983. The CX650C rolled off of showroom floors wearing a new fuel tank, saddle and wheel design. A blacked-out engine wore silver heads and exhaled through a chrome two-into-two exhaust. Black or Wineberry Red covered the fuel tank, as well as the side covers, but the side covers also had large chrome panels to complete the ongoing custom look of many Honda models.

The turbo-fed CX650TC changed little outside of the enlarged mill. Colors used did change and Pearl Shell White and Candy Aleutian Blue were accessorized by red and blue stripes. The turbo-only wheels were now silver and the lower fork legs were black.

Both GLs were also upgraded to the new 674cc motors in 1983. A set of cast alloy wheels was also put in place on the latest versions, and even color choices were shared by the GL650

Silver Wing and Interstate models. Two-tone choices of Candy Wineberry Red with Bramble Red Metallic or Nimbus Gray Metallic with Achilles Black Metallic were on the menu. "Silver Wing" and "Interstate" badges were all finished in gold.

The 750 models lost two and gained two models for 1983. Gone were the CB750C and the revered CB750F Super Sport. The CB750SC Nighthawk would remain the only inline four-powered model. The big Nighthawk now showed 150 mph on its speedometer and rode on cast-alloy, ComCast wheels that were black with highlighted "spokes." New colors for the CB750SC were Black with a gray stripe outlined in white, or Candy Wineberry Red with a black stripe and white outlines.

1983 VF750C V45 Magnas and the VF750S V45 Sabres also saw the addition of a 150 mph speedometer. Front brake discs were still grooved, but they changed from straight to curved. Candy Maroon or Black were used on the Magna, while Candy Wineberry Red or Black graced the Sabre in 1983.

One of the new models from Honda was the sporty VF750F Interceptor. By canting the 748cc, V-four motor at a different angle in the frame and wrapping the bike in sleek bodywork, it gave off a distinct racing glow. The two-tone color schemes did little to dispel this effect. Pearl Shell White was teamed with your choice of Candy Aleutian Blue or Candy Bourgogne Red. Final chain drive and a 16-inch front tire also played into the sporting nature of the Interceptor. It would go on to achieve much success at racetracks across the U.S.

Although similar in appearance to its smaller offspring the VT500C Shadow, the VT750C Shadow packed a lot more punch. Two spark plugs were used in each of the V-Twin's heads to ensure complete burn. The 45-degree layout of the motor included three-valve heads, and although it was liquid cooled, it sported cylinder fins like an air-cooled model. Honda claimed an output of 67 horsepower for the V-Twin, which was mated to a six-speed transmission.

Both 900cc models were banished from the

V45 INTERCEPTOR

...E RIDER.
And now we come to the final—though
...st important—element in the Interceptor's
...sign: You. Which, in the final analysis, is
...y we built this motorcycle. Make no
...stake, the V45 Interceptor is not for
...rybody. But if you want a motor-
...le like no other in the world today,
...ou want to come as close as you
...sibly can to feel what it's like to
...e the checkered flag at Daytona
...aguna Seca or Loudon, then
...V45 Interceptor waits for you to
...e command.
It is the ultimate riding experience.

...ATURES:
...gh-performance, 748 cc engine
...duces 86 horsepower.
...uid-cooling system with
...n radiators.
...re-designed rectangular
...tion frame.
...e-speed close-
...o transmission.

- Sealed O-ring drive chain.
- Cast aluminum alloy swing arm.
- Air-adjustable front forks with three-way adjustable rebound damping.
- Air-adjustable Pro-Link rear suspension with

four-way adjustable rebound damping.
- TRAC anti-dive control helps reduce the weight transfer effect to the front wheel under braking.
- Triple disc brakes with twin piston calipers.
- 16-inch front wheel provides precise steering.

- Special ComCast alloy wheels.
- Road racing-type tire sizes and profiles.
- Self-adjusting hydraulic clutch.
- Integrated fork brace.
- Adjustable handlebars.

kingdom for 1983, but a brace of even better bikes rolled in to save the day. Riding in to save the custom rider's needs was the new CB1000C Custom. A 973cc, inline four motor featured dual overhead cams and four valves per cylinder. The shaft-drive machine had 10 speeds. The five-speed gearbox featured a sub-transmission that provided another five gear ratios. The latest ComCast alloy wheels were installed at both axles and a duo of front disc brakes was joined by a drum brake on the rear hub. Being a Custom, the bars reached back to the rider and two-tone paint was in charge. Black and Achilles Black Metallic or Candy Regal Brown and Chestnut Gold Metallic were the selections. The taillight housing was seen as an integral part of the rear fender on this 1983 only model.

For the sport rider who wanted all the cubic inches Honda could muster, the CB1100F Super Sport was introduced for 1983. Its combination of an inline four-cylinder motor that displaced 1062cc's made the loss of the 750, 900 and CBX Super Sports easier to grasp. A Black Charcoal four-into-two exhaust saved some weight over a four-into-four system and

allowed for greater cornering clearance. Triple disc brakes were on hand to slow the speed-hungry machine. A five-speed gearbox and chain drive completed the performance aspects of the big Super Sport. A frame-mounted bikini fairing wrapped around the rectangular headlight and added to the sporting appearance. Pearl Shell White was coordinated with your choice of Candy Pearl Maui Red or Candy Pearl Capiolani Blue. ComCast wheels were black with silver highlights. The CB1100F was also a one-year only model.

In the Gold Wing camp, changes were evolutionary. The undressed GL1100 now rolled on 11-spoke cast wheels and slowed with the assistance of Honda's "TRAC" anti-dive forks. A 150-mph speedometer was also added to the '83 versions. Black or Candy Regal Brown were the color choices. The Aspencade also got the 11-spoke wheels and TRAC anti-dive forks. A digital, liquid crystal diode dashboard replaced the analog gauges. Your two-tone choices were Nimbus Gray Metallic with Achilles Black Metallic or Candy Wineberry Red with Bramble Red Metallic. The GL1100I Interstate benefited from the same changes

Once the V45 Interceptor hit the streets, it became an instant winner for both street and racing riders.

Simple name badges coated in gold were all the Sabre needed to make its identity known.

A hot rod V-four motor powered the V45 Sabre cruiser, and many accoutrements made it a great value, too.
Owner: M&R Cycle Specialist, Inc.

Displacing 748cc into four cylinders, the Sabre's V motor also ran with four valves per cylinder and shifted through six speeds.

Flowing bodywork and a blacked-out motor gave the V45 an aggressive, yet graceful look.

Encapsulated within an angular housing were all the instruments and indicators needed to track the actions of your V45 Sabre.

Mounted to cast wheels, a pair of disc brakes slowed the rider safely and quickly on the Sabre.

The 1983 CB1100F combined the traits of a big, inline-four motor with a sporty chassis and great looks. Sadly, it was only available for one year, then disappeared from catalogs.

made to the Aspencade save the digital dash. A 150-mph speedometer made its way onto the Interstate and Black or Candy Regal Brown were listed as color options.

Finally in 1983, the VF1100C V65 Magna was rolled out and quickly won the hearts of those wanting the fastest scooter on his block. A 1098cc, V-four, DOHC motor sounded fast by description and it proved its salt when you twisted the throttle. With a rating of 105 horsepower at 9500rpm, the V65 had no equals. A copious mass of torque hurt no one except for the competition. Being

liquid cooled, the V65 sported a large radiator on its front down tubes, but didn't appear too obvious or distracting. Carrying all this power on a wheelbase of nearly 63 inches insured that things would remain stable, or at least help to keep the front wheel on the ground during acceleration. The deeply sculpted saddle and pull-back bars said "custom" but the V65 was more muscle bike than cruising machine. Part of the V65's profile came from the 16-inch rear tire and 18-inch front. A triplicate of disc brakes were all halted with dual-piston calipers. The V65 retailed for $3,898 when first introduced for 1983.

1984

1984 would prove to be a year of many changes for Honda as typical model lineup alterations were joined by those forced by a round of government regulations.

The CB125S would only see one more year of sale beyond 1984, so changes were again minimal. Turuna Red was grafted with a set of white and dark blue stripes and the Honda wing decal was a combination of gray and white. A circular headlight and a 12-volt electrical system rounded out the modifications on the '84 models.

The CM250C was the smallest of the Hondas to go missing for 1984, and the CM450A, CM450E and CB450SC Nighthawk models were also axed, but fresh metal awaited the 500cc rider. The CB450SC

The VF500F Interceptor was new for 1984 and shared many traits with its big brothers, the VF750F and VF1000F.

Owner: Steve Passwater

The VF500F's V-four motor displaced 498cc's and featured dual overhead cams and four valves per cylinder. Liquid cooling kept the whole operation under control.

Despite being the smallest of the three Interceptors, the VF500F wore the name proudly.

The four-into-two exhaust was finished in black chrome and made for a nice contrast against the red, white and blue paint.

Nighthawk would return in 1985.

A smaller version of the already popular VF750C V45 Magna appeared as the VF500C V30 Magna. A 498cc V-four motor delivered 64 horsepower and, when compared to the larger V65 Magna, claimed more ponies per liter. The biggest mechanical difference on the V30 was the final chain drive in place of the shaft used on the other Magna offerings. Weighing only 401 lbs. dry, the baby Magna fit the needs of many smaller or less-experience riders. Although it made smaller riders feel safe and secure, the spacing of the pegs, bars and saddle made a nice perch for larger riders as well. Dressed with the typical pull-back bars, stepped saddle and teardrop tank, the little Magna lost no points in the styling department, either.

Another new entry, the VF500F Interceptor, shared the 498cc V-four motor found in the V30 Magna, but was packaged as a sport bike. The VF500F was also a smaller clone of its bigger brothers the VF750F and the new VF1000F. The mini-Interceptor tipped the scales at 408 lbs. and Honda claimed a horsepower rating of 68. With a weight savings of 100 lbs. over its VF750 brethren, the appeal was obvious. A redline of 12500 rpm showed what Honda had in mind for the new 498cc sport machine.

The VF500F shared some key components with the 750 version in the air-adjustable front shocks with TRAC anti-dive and the Pro-Link rear suspension. Sixteen-inch ComCast wheels were found at both fore and aft. A frame-mounted half-fairing and low-mounted chin spoiler kept the family resemblance strong. Candy Alamoana Red with Black and Shasta White, alongside Candy Aleutian Blue with Fighting Red and Shasta White were the color choices in 1984.

Virtually untouched for the new year, the VT500C Shadow returned. Candy Scorpio Red or Black adorned both the fuel tank and side covers, replacing the previous chrome side covers.

The single-cylinder FT500 Ascot was removed from the 1984 listings, but the VT500FT remained for its final year of sale. Black replaced Pearl Siren Blue, and a three-tone tank decal was applied in place of the two-tone seen on 1983 models.

The CB550SC Nighthawk was also discontinued for 1984.

Only mild cosmetic changes were applied to the CB650SC Nighthawk. Black or Candy Bourgogne Red paints were new to the Nighthawk and the "TRAC" emblem was relocated beneath the axle on the front fork legs.

First appearing in 1979, the entire line of CX and GL machines was dropped from the family tree for 1983.

Honda faced another challenge during this time period after a certain Milwaukee builder of big V-Twin machines began to complain that it was unable to compete with 750cc-and-up machines being sold by the Japanese manufacturers. In an effort to level the playing field, a steep tariff was placed in imported motorcycles displacing more than 750ccs. To comply with this new ruling, Honda, along with every other Japanese builder, began selling 700cc ma-

Honda's TRAC, anti-dive suspension did a great job of keeping the V500F under control during hard braking. Both front discs were grasped by dual-piston calipers.

1984 MODELS

Model	Product Code	Engine Type/ Displacement	Transmission	Year(s) Available
CB125S	441	OHC Single/124cc	5-Speed	1984
VF500C V30 Magna	MJ8	DOHC V-Four/498cc	6-Speed	1984
VF500F Interceptor	MF2	DOHC V-Four/498cc	6-Speed	1984
VT500C Shadow	MF5	OHC V-Twin/491cc	6-Speed	1984
VT500FT Ascot	MF8	OHC V-Twin/491cc	6-Speed	1984
CB650SC Nighthawk	ME5	SOHC Inline Four/655cc	6-Speed	1984
CB700SC Nighthawk S	MJ1	DOHC Inline Four/696cc	5-Speed	1984
VF700C V45 Magna	MB1	DOHC V-Four/699cc	6-Speed	1984
VF700F Interceptor	MB2	DOHC V-Four/699cc	5-Speed	1984
VF700S V45 Sabre	MB0	DOHC V-Four/699cc	6-Speed	1984
VT700C Shadow	ME9	SOHC V-Twin/694cc	6-Speed	1984
VF750F Interceptor	MB2	DOHC V-Four/748cc	6-Speed	1984
VF1000F Interceptor	MB6	DOHC V-Four/998cc	5-Speed	1984
VF1100C V65 Magna	MB4	DOHC V-Four/1098cc	6-Speed	1984
VF1100S V65 Sabre	MB3	DOHC V-Four/1098cc	6-Speed	1984
GL1200 Gold Wing	MG9	SOHC Opposed Four/1182cc	5-Speed	1984
GL1200A Aspencade	MG9	SOHC Opposed Four/1182cc	5-Speed	1984
GL1200I Gold Wing Interstate	MG9	SOHC Opposed Four/1182cc	5-Speed	1984

Introduced in 1984 to comply with the newly introduced tariffs on motorcycles over 750cc, the CB700SC Nighthawk S models were all new.
Owner: Rick Youngblood

The 696cc, inline-four Nighthawk S motor delivered plenty of punch and stayed well within the latest government guidelines.

chines in 1984. By applying a bit of ingenuity to the situation, the only thing the restricted machines lost were a few cc of displacement. Performance changed little.

One all-new model to meet with the International Trade Commission's round of lunacy was the CB700SC Nighthawk S. The 696cc displacement fell just under the wire, and was divided into four cylinders arranged inline. Most of this new motor was coated in black, but highlighted fins, valve covers and case covers were silver. A set of four velocity stacks were also finished in silver but were non-functional. Four valves per cylinder and a six-speed gearbox drove through a shaft drive, an uncommon feature on a sport machine. Black chrome was applied to the four-into-two exhaust to continue the dark theme of the new Nighthawk. A pair of disc brakes on the front wheel were joined by a drum on the rear allowing the S to be pulled down from speed smoothly. The bikini fairing, fuel tank, side covers and tail section were all treated to a two-tone paint scheme of either black and red or black and blue.

Carrying a dry weight of only 470 lbs., the new Nighthawk S delivered terrific performance from the new cc limited class of bikes.

A reduced-capacity 699cc motor was installed in the 1984 VF700C Magna. Except for a new wheel design, the mid-range Magna remained unchanged.

Introduced in 1983 and instantly garnering a multitude of awards, the VF750F and its de-tuned twin, the VF700F, were both back. Having to pay a stiff tariff on any cycle over 700ccs, Honda did not bring many of the 750 Interceptors into the U.S, for 1984 and, except for a few minor graphic changes, the bike was left untouched. The VF700F was a virtual twin of the bigger 750 version, but sold for $800 less and lost a bit of its previous performance. The bike remained a popular choice among buyers, even having lost some of the bite of the original.

The VF700S Sabre had also been trimmed of 699cc to meet with the new guidelines, but picked up a black exhaust system and a color-

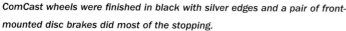

ComCast wheels were finished in black with silver edges and a pair of front-mounted disc brakes did most of the stopping.

keyed front fender in exchange. New colors were listed as Black with Maroon or Black with Pleiades Silver Metallic and Red. The Maroon version claimed silver trim stripes and the Silver model wore red. All "Honda" and "Sabre" badges were gold.

The VT700C Shadow was also a victim of the new 700cc rule. The smaller 694cc power plant was the only change listed for the 1984 model.

Both the CB1000C and CB1100F models were gone. To help to ease the pain, the VF1000F Interceptor was introduced. By using the successful formula used to build the VF750F and increasing some key dimensions, the bigger Interceptor was everything its younger brother was and more. Displacing 998cc, and fitted with larger valves, the VF1000F produced 113 horsepower, 27 more than the VF750F. An aluminum radiator replaced the brass model found on the 750 also. A 17-inch rear wheel is employed and front fork tubes are 41mm complete with improved TRAC anti-dive control. Twenty-seven lbs. of extra weight

brought the VF1000F's total to 514, but the weight was handled with ease by the enhanced motor. Shasta White was accented with Candy Aleutian Blue and Candy Bourgogne Red. The big VF1000F was only sold for one year.

The VF1100C V65 Magna was little changed except for colors. ComCast wheels now featured five pairs of twin spokes that were highlighted with silver. Black or Candy Andromeda Red were both seen on the showroom floors.

By adding another 100cc, Honda was able to bring out two new models in the V65 Sabre and Gold Wing.

New for 1984 was the VF1100S V65 Sabre. By installing the 1098cc motor used in the Magna into a larger and longer frame, the V65 Sabre was born. Additional tweaks to the motor gave the Sabre even more power than the V65 Magna, and that was a tall order. A pair of circular gauges flanked a rectangular panel containing a variety of monitoring and warning indicators. The big Sabre looked much like its smaller 700cc sibling, and came in a choice

Every Nighthawk S was fitted with the color-matched bikini fairing direct from the factory. It provided the rider with a bit of wind protection and gave the instrument panel a place to hide.

Introduced as a 1983 model, the VF1100C V65 Magna faded from view after the 1986 model was done.
Owner: Rick Youngblood

Combining old-world dial and high-tech digital gauges provided the rider with a wide array of information on the V65 Magna.

The padded two-tier seat was a nice blend of style and comfort.

1098cc of power resided within the cases of the V-four motor and six speeds were fed to a shaft drive.

The V65 cut an aggressive profile.

Helping to keep the passenger aboard during acceleration, the padded backrest served many purposes.

of Black with Pleiades Silver Metallic and Red stripe, or Black and Maroon with a silver stripe.

All three models in the Gold Wing family received complete makeovers and emerged better than ever. The increase in engine size to 1182cc was only the tip of the iceberg as every facet of the design was rejuvenated to meet with increasing competition from Yamaha and Kawasaki. Chassis geometry and altered wheel sizes brought the latest 'Wing closer to the ground and enhanced cornering clearance. The 16-inch front and 15-inch rear wheels were wrapped with Dunlop rubber to enhance comfort and handling of the big GL. The base GL1200 and Interstate featured a set of fork-mounted gauges to monitor bike functions, but the Aspencade held a bank of digital gauges within its capacious fairing. The Aspencade also housed an on-board air compressor that was used to supply the GL's air-ride suspension, as well as fill a beach ball if required. The Aspencade also had the luxury of a fine audio system that can be augmented with a CB radio. All controls for the sound system were mounted with the fairing or on towers near the grips for easy access at speed. When fully equipped, yet devoid of fuel, the Aspencade tipped the scales at more than 755 lbs.

The Interstate was still well equipped but paled a bit in comparison to the Aspencade. Analog gauges could be accented with a sound system and, like the base GL, was only sold in solid colors. The 1984 GL1200 was sold in Black or Candy Wineberry Red. The Interstate was not offered in Black, but the Red was listed along with Pearl Siren Blue and Senior Gray Metallic. The Aspencade sported a choice of three, two-tone combinations: Pearl Saturn Red/Century Brown Metallic, Premium Beige Metallic/Grace Brown Metallic and Pearl Siren Blue/Achilles Black Metallic.

Joining the pair of disc brakes on the front wheel, a third rotor was found at the aft as well.

Being liquid-cooled, the V65 Magna's big V-four needed a big radiator to keep things at a manageable temperature.

1985

1985 would turn out to be a fairly quiet year for Honda in the new model department, although a few models were reaching the end of the line.

First appearing as a 1973 model, the CB125S1 was in its last year in 1985. A rectangular headlight replaced the round 1984 unit, and changes to the striping were the only revisions. The same Turuna Red was now trimmed with blue and white stripes, while the "Honda" and "CB125S" décor were completed in white.

With a combination of "Milwaukee" styling and Honda know-how, the CMX250C Rebel cruised onto the scene for 1985 and was an instant success. Riding on a chassis that provided a low, 26 inch saddle height, the new Rebel was especially appealing to smaller riders eager to join in on the fun. The Rebel proved to be a favorite choice for the rider wanting low maintenance and a stable platform to learn on.

A 234cc, parallel twin motor was joined by a five-speed gearbox giving even the neophyte rider plenty to do. A set of classic chrome spoke wheels measured 15 inches at the rear and 18 inches at the front, adding to the traditional styling. A black frame was highlighted by chrome side covers that looked remarkably similar to the battery boxes being used on the machines from Harley-Davidson. The teardrop tank only added to this illusion. Candy Supreme Red or Pearl Stellar Black were first offered on the Rebel and nothing but a simple brown/orange/yellow Honda wing adorned the fuel tank.

Rolling in to fill the void left by the departed VF1000F Interceptor, the 1985 VF1000R created an instant buzz both in the media and amongst buyers.

After vanishing for the 1984 year, the CB450SC Nighthawk was back for 1985. Pricing was the key feature of this competent 447cc machine, and the only changes were in the paint department. Candy Empire Blue with light blue stripes or Candy Andromeda Red with red striping were the color choices.

Fresh graphics and a revised instrument cluster graced the VF500C V30 Magna, and Candy Andromeda Red was replaced by Candy Wineberry Red. The VF500F Interceptor also received new gauges and altered graphics for 1985. Previous glitches in the crankshafts had been addressed and corrected. Black accents used in 1984 were replaced by Candy Blue, and Fighting Red was knocked out by Candy Red on the '85s. The VT500C Shadows now wore polished engine covers and enlarged cooling fins on the cylinders. A more-aggressive two-place saddle was extended to include an upswept backrest for improved passenger comfort.

Chrome was applied to the round headlight housing and Black or Candy Glory Red were the 1985 hues.

The lone remaining Ascot for 1984, the VT500FT, was gone for 1985.

The Nighthawk was the only 650 family member and did not receive much attention for

The race-ready VF1000R featured a long list of advanced features that delivered a new level of power and handling for the street rider.

the new year. Improvements to the TRAC anti-dive system and revised brake rotors were the most useful changes, while side cover graphics and speedometer faces were listed as cosmetic. Candy Scorpio Blue or Candy Empire Red were the paint selections.

Nighthawk S models were mostly unchanged with the exception being a white outline around the red or blue color panels used on the tariff beaters. Speedometer faces were now printed with their speeds listed in increments of 10, beginning at 5.

Adding some comfort and appearance features to the VF700C Magna only improved the breed. Cast wheels were now comprised of 5 individual spokes and were black with silver highlights. A black side stand and rear fender delivered in unit color rounded out the paint and details. A rear passenger sissy bar complete with padded backrest was now a standard feature on the 700 Magna. Candy Scorpio Red joined Black in the option column.

1985 would be the final year for VF700F Interceptor production, and the hugely popular VF750F Interceptor had already been escorted from the building. A more easily adjusted TRAC system on the front forks and revisions

to the brake rotors and calipers joined fresh handlebars and mirrors. Subtle changes were also made to the color schemes with Candy Alamoana Red supplanting Candy Bourgogne Red on the palette.

1985 VF700S Sabre models rode on Pro-Link rear suspension complete with roller bearings in the linkage. All 1985 700 Sabres were finished in Black with Monte Rosa Silver metallic insets. A choice of red or blue accent stripes was the only decision to be made. VT700C Shadow models also now featured polished engine covers that complemented either Black or Candy Glory Red paint.

The VF750F Interceptor was eliminated from the 1985 lineup, and another casualty was the VF1000F Interceptor. Those bemoaning the loss didn't cry for long with an all-new model rolling onto showroom floors: the VF1000R. This was a true race-inspired machine that was powered by a 998cc, 90 degree V-four motor that pumped out 117 horsepower, thanks in part to 36mm CV carburetors and 11.1 compression.

A box-section frame of steel and a swing arm of box-section aluminum provided stiffness and light weight resulting in dry weight of only 525 lbs.

1985 MODELS

Model	Product Code	Engine Type/ Displacement	Transmission	Year(s) Available
CB125S	441	OHC Single/124cc	5-Speed	1985
CMX 250C Rebel	KR3	OHC Parallel Twin/234cc	5-Speed	1985
CB450SC Nighthawk	MC9	SOHC Parallel Twin/447cc	6-Speed	1985
VF500C V30 Magna	MJ8	DOHC V-Four/498cc	6-Speed	1985
VF500F Interceptor	MF2	DOHC V-Four/498cc	6-Speed	1985
VT500C Shadow	MF5	OHC V-Twin/491cc	6-Speed	1985
CB650SC Nighthawk	ME5	SOHC Inline Four/655cc	6-Speed	1985
CB700SC Nighthawk S	MJ1	DOHC Inline Four/696cc	5-Speed	1985
VF700C V45 Magna	MK3	DOHC V-Four/699cc	6-Speed	1985
VF700F Interceptor	MB2	DOHC V-Four/699cc	5-Speed	1985
VF700S V45 Sabre	MB0	DOHC V-Four/699cc	6-Speed	1985
VT700C Shadow	ME9	SOHC V-Twin/694cc	6-Speed	1985
VF1000R	MJ4	DOHC V-Four/998cc	5-Speed	1985
VF1100C V65 Magna	MB4	DOHC V-Four/1098cc	6-Speed	1985
VF1100S V65 Sabre	MB3	DOHC V-Four/1098cc	6-Speed	1985
VT1100C Shadow	MG8	SOHC V-Twin/1099cc	5-Speed	1985
GL1200A Aspencade	MG9	SOHC Opposed Four/1182cc	5-Speed	1985
GL1200I Gold Wing Interstate	MG9	SOHC Opposed Four/1182cc	5-Speed	1985
GL1200L Gold Wing Ltd. Ed.	MG9	SOHC Opposed Four/1182cc	5-Speed	1985

A 6.2-gallon fuel tank was cloaked in wind-tunnel designed fairing that looked racy and provided a modicum of protection from the elements. Black, star-shaped Comstar wheels were teamed with a pair of floating rotor front disc brakes and stout 41mm fork legs. The lower fork legs were finished in red to match the seat and front fender. The primary bodywork was a patriotic combination of Fighting Red, Shasta White and Candy Aleutian Blue.

VF1100C Magnas now included more easily adjustable brake and clutch levers, and improved self-canceling turn signals that employed push-to-cancel switches. Black and Pearl Vintage Red were the 1985 hues. The 1100 Sabre also received the screw-adjustment levers and self-canceling turn signals. The same colors used on the VF700S Sabre applied to the bigger 1100 model.

The addition of the VT1100C Shadow grew that family line to three different models bearing the same name. Five-hundred and 700cc varieties were still sold alongside the big-twin model. Displacing 1099cc, the new Shadow was fired with two spark plugs per cylinder and carried the rider on a 29.1-inch saddle height. A chubby 15-inch rear tire was slowed by a drum, while the taller 18-inch front rubber was anchored by a brace of discs. Without fluids the VT1100C weighed a moderate 531 lbs.

Changes to the Gold Wing listings brought the elimination of the naked GL1200 in 1985. Touring riders wanted more than a plush chassis and powerful motor, and the better-dressed models were outselling the stripped-down model by a wide margin. Improvements to the remaining Aspencade and Interstates included dropped gear ratios for smoother take-offs, better ventilation through the existing airflow system and altered self-canceling turn signals.

Joining the 1985 Gold Wings was the best-dressed model of them all, the GL1200L Limited Edition. For those who even the lavish accoutrements of the Aspencade weren't enough, the Limited Edition would more than likely fill their every need. By adding a bevy of electronic enhancements to the already well-equipped Aspencade, the "L" was a show-stopper. An on-board travel computer, electronic cruise control, and computerized fuel injection were the most notable selling points. Cornering lights and rear-mounted stereo speakers added another layer of frosting to the cake. A liquid crystal diode (LCD) panel even showed you what time zone you were traveling in, or what mileage had passed on your journey. An interior light on the rear trunk and special tool kit rounded out the long list of desirable features.

Delivered in Sunflash Gold Metallic and Valiant Brown Metallic, two-tone paint, and sold in very limited numbers, the 1985 GL1200L was truly a limited edition.

1986

VF1000R High-performance 998cc DOHC liquid-cooled V-4 engine with 10.7:1 compression ratio produces incredible horsepower • Advanced gear-driven cam shafts • Close-ratio five-speed transmission • 41mm front forks with adjustable rebound damping • TRAC* anti-dive control • Pro-Link* rear suspension • Rectangular section frame • Wheelbase: 59.1 inches • Seat height: 31.9 inches • Fuel capacity: 6.2 gallons, including 1.2 gallon reserve • Dry weight: 538 pounds

INTERCEPTOR™/750 INTERCEPTOR™ High-performance 699/748cc DOHC liquid-cooled V-4 engine produces astounding horsepower†† • Advanced gear-driven camshafts • Close-ratio six-speed transmission • Air-adjustable 37mm front forks • TRAC* anti-dive control • Pro-Link* rear suspension • Rectangular section aluminum frame • Wheelbase: 58.3 inches • Seat height: 30.7 inches • Fuel capacity: 5.3 gallons, including 1.1 gallon reserve • Dry weight: 445.2 pounds

INTERCEPTOR High-performance 699cc DOHC liquid-cooled V-4 engine • Advanced gear-driven camshafts • Close-ratio six-speed transmission • Air-adjustable 37mm front forks • TRAC* anti-dive control • Pro-Link* rear suspension • Rectangular section aluminum frame • Wheelbase: 58.3 inches • Seat height: 30.7 inches • Fuel capacity: 5.3 gallons, including 1.1 gallon reserve • Dry weight: 445.2 pounds • Limited availability

500 INTERCEPTOR™ Powerful 498cc DOHC liquid-cooled V-4 engine produces an incredible 68 horsepower†† • Close-ratio six-speed transmission • Race-designed rectangular section frame • Air-adjustable front forks • TRAC anti-dive control • Air-adjustable Pro-Link rear suspension with adjustable rebound damping • 16-inch front wheel • Wheelbase: 55.9 inches • Seat height: 31.5 inches • Fuel capacity: 4 gallons, including 0.5 gallon reserve • Dry weight: 412.3 pounds

When compared to some of Honda's more tumultuous years, 1986 was fairly quiet. Several familiar faces would no longer be seen, but a few new friends would be introduced.

The 250 Rebel was back on the front line but few changes were seen. In the first year of sale, the 250 Rebel outsold every other available motorcycle, so Honda was not motivated to mess with success. The Pearl Stellar Black was joined by Candy Eiger Blue for '86, and the blue model still rode with a black chassis. The blue unit did, however, get a silver and black "Rebel" decal and a black, gray and silver appliquè on the tank. Its sibling, the CMX250 Limited, wore a gold badge of distinction. Available only in Pearl Stellar Black, the Limited was festooned with swirling gold artwork on the tank and rear fender. Cylinder head covers, fuel cap and carburetor covers were also finished in gold. Rings of the headlight and speedometer did not miss the application of the amber hue. Cases of the engine, lower fork legs and brake and clutch levers were all chrome plated.

1986 would be the final year for the CB450SC Nighthawk. Candy Flair Blue with silver pinstripes or Candy Glory Red with black stripes were offered and the front fender matched the selected paint. Side cover decals were also silver for the last year of production.

With hopes of grabbing the attention of first-time 250 Rebel buyers, or perhaps those

For 1986, Honda buyers had their choice of four different V-four-powered sport bikes, each catering to a slightly different set of rules.

that simply wanted more of the same, Honda brought out the CMX450C Rebel for 1986. By enlarging the cooling fins of the existing Hawk 450 motor and installing in into a larger "Harley-esque" machine, the Rebel appealed to a new audience of riders. A six-speed gearbox was fed by the 447cc, SOHC parallel twin mill. Décor was sparse on the Pearl Stellar Black or Monte Rosa Silver Metallic paint, but a Honda wing on the tank and "Rebel Four-Fifty" decal on the battery cover did add to the blend.

In the sport bike category, the VF500F Interceptor was in its final year of sale. Cosmetic alterations included all-black wheels, and a seat, front fender and lower fork legs wearing red. Only one combination of Fighting Red, Shasta White and Candy Blue was sold.

The VF500C V30 Magna, CB650SC Nighthawk and VF700S Interceptor were three more no-shows for 1986.

The VT500C Shadow would also be gone at the end of the 1986 model year and Candy Scorpio Red was the only color listed for the final examples.

Honda's first tariff beater, the CB700SC Nighthawk S, bowed out at the end of the latest year and only cosmetics would change. The entire motor, both wheels and the faux velocity stacks were all delivered in an all-black motif. The two-tone combinations were listed as Black with Candy Alamoana Red panels and orange divider stripes, or Candy Aleutian Blue with Shasta White panels and red striping.

A chrome side stand was the only change found on the 1986 VF700C Magna. Candy Glory Red replaced the Candy Scorpio Red paint used in 1985.

A pair of new models were seen for 1986 and would set the stage for things to come from Honda. The VFR700F and VFR750F Interceptors were entirely new creations and set the performance bar several feet higher. The 700 variant was built to accommodate the remaining tariffs, and the 750 was designed to crush the racing world into submission. Both v-four motors featured gear-driven cams and were reduced in both size and weight. A claim of more than 100 horsepower for the 750 was evidence of the successful new design, and the 700 was not far behind. Honda also claimed dry weight for either machine to be less than 440 lbs., partly due to their all-aluminum chassis and rear swing arm assemblies. The four-valve, liquid-cooled motors displaced 698 or 748cc, depending on the model selected. Six-speed transmissions and chain drive were part of both

1986 MODELS

Model	Product Code	Engine Type/ Displacement	Transmission	Year(s) Available
CMX 250C Rebel	KR3	OHC Parallel Twin/234cc	5-Speed	1986
CMX250CD Rebel Ltd.	KR3	OHC Parallel Twin/234cc	5-Speed	1986
CB450SC Nighthawk	MC9	SOHC Parallel Twin/447cc	6-Speed	1986
CMX450C Rebel	MM2	SOHC Parallel Twin/447cc	6-Speed	1986
VF500F Interceptor	MF2	DOHC V-Four/498cc	6-Speed	1986
VT500C Shadow	MF5	OHC V-Twin/491cc	6-Speed	1986
CB700SC Nighthawk S	MJ1	DOHC Inline Four/696cc	5-Speed	1986
VF700C V45 Magna	MK3	DOHC V-Four/699cc	6-Speed	1986
VFR700F Interceptor	MK8	DOHC V-Four/698cc	6-Speed	1986
VFR700F2 Interceptor	MK8	DOHC V-Four.698cc	6-Speed	1986
VT700C Shadow	MK7	SOHC V-Twin/694cc	6-Speed	1986
VFR750F Interceptor	ML7	DOHC V-Four/748cc	6-Speed	1986
VF1000R	MJ4	DOHC V-Four/998cc	5-Speed	1986
VF1100C V65 Magna	MB4	DOHC V-Four/1098cc	6-Speed	1986
VT1100C Shadow	MG8	SOHC V-Twin/1099cc	5-Speed	1986
GL1200A Aspencade	ML8	SOHC Opposed Four/1182cc	5-Speed	1986
GL1200I Gold Wing Interstate	ML8	SOHC Opposed Four/1182cc	5-Speed	1986
GL1200SE-I Aspencade SE-I	ML8	SOHC Opposed Four/1182cc	5-Speed	1986

equations as well. Regardless of the model you rode home, Fighting Red, Shasta White and Candy Aleutian Blue covered the body panels. Front fenders on both were red only.

For a different look in the same machine, the VFR700F2 was also sold in 1986. Finished entirely in Pearl Crescent White, and topped off with a blue pillion, the F2 stood out from the other machines of the day. F2 instrumentation was also housed in squarish pods instead of the round gauges seen on the other two models. Devoid of any engine designation or stripes, the F2 stood out by being plain.

With growing interest in the cruiser market, Honda wasted no time in modifying the VT700C Shadow to new levels for 1986. Perhaps borrowing several styling cues from the Low Rider models sold at Harley dealers, the new Shadow was longer, lower and more radical.

A revised wheelbase of 63 inches and a saddle height of only 27.4 inches added to the mystique. The rather small fuel tank was mated to another holding cell mounted under the saddle. This arrangement allowed for looks and a decent cruising range. A deeply sculpted, two-person saddle led to an upswept rear fender edge, adding to the "Milwaukee" feel. A pair of cast, five-spoke rims and exaggerated pull-back handlebars complete the stage. Chrome side covers set off the Candy Brilliant Red or Black paint, which is applied to the fuel tank and fenders. Honda "wing" and "Shadow" decals are finished in an orange and gold freckled pattern.

With only this year remaining on its agenda, the VF1000R was little changed. A composite headlamp now encased dual bulbs and both brake and clutch levers were silver. A set of forged aluminum handlebars could be adjusted to better suit the rider's size and posture and a fork bridge finished in anodized gold was found on the front forks.

The V65 Sabre was eliminated in 1986 and the VF1100C V65 Magna was in its twilight year. The Magna's polished side cases now highlighted the mostly black motor and a chrome side stand added some flash. All brake discs now included inner-opening cutouts and a fiber-optic anti-theft system was included in the package. Candy Glory Red took over where Pearl Vintage Red once stood.

The VT1100C Shadow was mostly unchanged, but an all-black model was offered alongside the black and silver. Whether buying the all-black or two-tone, the side covers were finished in the same silver and black paint. The all-black version simply had a fuel tank of solid black. A gold "Shadow" side cover decal replaced the silver used in 1985.

Evolutionary changes arrived for the Gold Wings. Dolby noise reduction was added to the sound system on the Aspencade. A splash guard was added to the rear fender to better tame errant fluids. Three new two-tone color options were listed for the GL1200A: Twilight Beige Metallic with Mahogany Red, Pearl Marlin Blue with Spiral Blue Metallic and Trophy Silver Metallic with Tempest Gray Metallic were your 1986 choices. The Interstate received the same rear splash guard, but only two color options, Candy Wineberry Red or Black, were listed.

The top of the Gold Wing lineup, the GL1200SE-I Aspencade was introduced for 1986. This best-dressed model featured all the best qualities of a "standard" 'Wing and added some ups and extras to set it apart. The Pearl Splendor Ivory and Camel Beige Metallic paint was unique, and the fuel-injected motor made for easier starting and smoother acceleration at all speeds. A comprehensive bank of electronics was at the rider's fingertips with the tank-mounted display and control panel.

Dolby noise reduction was also added to the sound system on the SE-I, and a pair of angular speakers were added to the tops of the rear box for added passenger enjoyment. Both ends of the suspension could be easily adjusted from the saddle with the onboard air compressor system. An extensive tool kit went to the buyer of the SE-I Aspencade, as did many miles of open-road adventure.

1987

It was a year of attrition as nine 1986 models were pulled from the catalog. A pair of brand-new sport bikes would be a harbinger of things to come from Honda.

The 250 Rebel was still a popular choice for those just getting their feet wet in motorcycling, or whose feet needed to be closer to the ground. 1987 would be the last year for the small Rebel until its return almost a decade later. The '87s Rebels were sold in Black with brown tri-color tank decals, or in Candy Wineberry Red complete with a matching red frame. Artwork on the red models was a combination of gray, silver and white. Silver brake and clutch levers were also seen on the 1987 units.

The CB450SC Nighthawk was gone, but the bigger CMX450C Rebel remained for another round. Splashier tank graphics and polished control levers were about the only modifications made. An enlarged fuel tank decal now read "Rebel Honda" and Black or Candy Glory Red were offered as base colors.

Both the VT500C Shadow and VF500F Interceptor were de-listed in 1987, but Honda's first new sport bike would help to ease the pain. As good as the VF500F had been, it was quickly eclipsed by sport machines from Kawasaki, Suzuki and Yamaha. Honda needed something better to combat the influx of fast-improving rides.

With a 598cc, inline four motor capable of producing 83 horsepower, and a super slippery set of bodywork, the CBR600F Hurricane broke all records in the 600 class of Japanese machines. The new motor was employed as a stressed member of the "diamond-type" frame and helped to keep dry weight just below 400 lbs. The inline engine was liquid cooled, featured 16 valves and shifted through a six-speed gearbox. A four-into-one exhaust handled spent fumes. A trio of disc brakes were mounted to the 17-inch front and rear wheels, both finished in red. The Hurricane itself was sold in Pearl Crystal White with Fighting Red or Black with Monza Red. The 600 Hurricane would not be the last bike with this technology or name in the Honda lineage.

Eliminations in the 700cc group included the Nighthawk S and VFR700F Interceptor. Retaining a spot was the VF700C Magna, albeit with numerous changes. New styling exaggerated the Magna's cruiser status. Vented side covers, black-wrinkle paint on the air cleaner and a solid disc rear wheel were among the changes.

A small chin spoiler was also added to the lower front downtubes of the frame, just in front of the 699cc motor. An exotic, upswept four-into-four exhaust was fitted with four individual mufflers. Candy Wave Blue or Candy

1987 MODELS

Model	Product Code	Engine Type/ Displacement	Transmission	Year(s) Available
CMX 250C Rebel	KR3	OHC Parallel Twin/234cc	5-Speed	1987
CMX450C Rebel	MM2	SOHC Parallel Twin/447cc	6-Speed	1987
CBR600F Hurricane	MN4	DOHC Inline Four/598cc	6-Speed	1987
VF700C V45 Magna	MN0	DOHC V-Four/699cc	6-Speed	1987
VFR700F2 Interceptor	MK8	DOHC V-Four.698cc	6-Speed	1987
VT700C Shadow	MK7	SOHC V-Twin/694cc	6-Speed	1987
CBR1000F Hurricane	MM5	DOHC Inline Four/998cc	6-Speed	1987
VT1100C Shadow	MM8	SOHC V-Twin/1099cc	5-Speed	1987
GL1200A Aspencade	ML8	SOHC Opposed Four/1182cc	5-Speed	1987
GL1200I Gold Wing Interstate	ML8	SOHC Opposed Four/1182cc	5-Speed	1987

Bourgogne Red were the 1987 color choices.

Another 1987 casualty was the VFR750F Interceptor, leaving only the VFR700F2 in its wake. A digital ignition system was the only hardware upgrade, but a new hue was offered for the latest editions. The all Pearl Crescent White package was joined by a mostly Candy Wave Blue version. The blue unit featured a small section of silver on the bodywork as well as silver wheels, saddle and graphics.

Having been redesigned for the 1986 model year, the VT700C Shadow returned in 1987 wearing only different graphics. Candy Brilliant Red was replaced by Candy Glory Red, and the "Honda" decal used on the tank was black with a gold outline stripe. The Honda "wing" was now a combination of brown, gold and yellow.

To mask the pain caused by the loss of the VF1000R and VF1100C V65 Magna, Honda whipped up a little something called the CBR1000 Hurricane. Similar in design to the smaller 600cc model, the 998cc version produced 130 horsepower and claimed a top speed nearing 160 mph. Wrapped in an all-encompassing set of bodywork, the Hurricane was as sleek as it was fast. The 16-valve, inline four motor was also liquid cooled and put its power through a choice of six speeds. Final drive was by chain. A trio of drilled disc brakes slowed the 490-lb. (dry) machine to halt. Three different

two-tone options were sold in 1987. Black with Monza Red rolled on red wheels and featured black tank art. The Alaska Blue with Atlanta Gray or Winterlake Blue with Atlanta Gray were sold with silver wheels and graphics.

The cruiser class was still dominated by Honda's VT1100C Shadow, and several changes were applied to the 1987 models. A pair of elongated exhaust pipes swept backwards towards the new shaft drive and accented the long look of the machine. A new saddle design added to the lengthy appearance. One gear was removed from the gearbox for a new total of four. Yellow spark plug wires were also added along with a silver tank stripe. Black or Candy Wineberry Red sheet metal rode on a black frame.

Only two versions of the GL1200 Gold Wing were sold in 1987, and changes were minimal. A redesign of the plush king and queen saddles now included three-stage foam for increased comfort.

The Aspencade had three new two-tone color combos on the menu. Candy Wineberry Red with Dusky Red Metallic, Black with Tempest Gray or Pleiades Silver Metallic with Spiral Blue Metallic. The Interstate was still available in solid colors—Pearly Beige Metallic or Amethyst Gray Metallic.

Further decline in the Honda lineup for 1988 focused each segment more intently on the models being sold, whether returns of the previous year or new designations. Not a single model was offered under 600cc as even the bigger machines became more compact and easier to manage.

Both 250 and 450 versions of the Rebel were gone for 1988, leaving beginning riders to look elsewhere for entry-level motorcycles.

The CBR600F Hurricane blew in wearing only new colors. Fighting Red paired with Pearl Crystal White or Medium Gray Metallic with Granite Blue Metallic were seen in the catalogs.

A fresh member of the cruiser family was introduced as the VT600C Shadow VLX. Powered by a liquid cooled, V-Twin motor that displaced 583cc's, the VLX had a four-speed gearbox and chain drive. Furthering the Milwaukee mystique, the VLX had only one rear shock which rode beneath the lower frame rails much like the "Softail" models from Harley. This arrangement gave the illusion of a hard tail chassis with the comfort of suspension. A triangular air cleaner sat nestled in the V of the motor, all of which was silver. Whether you bought the Candy Wave Blue or Candy Wineberry Red, the frame of the VLX was painted to match.

Racing onto the 1988 pages of the sales brochures was the new NT650 Hawk GT. Built around a 647cc V-Twin motor, the Hawk GT featured an aluminum spar frame that was both lighter and stiffer than previous designs. The rigidity of this new design was proven by the application of a single-sided swingarm on the rear end. This combination provided almost anyone with a terrific all-around machine that was both sporty and comfortable. Big enough for highway use yet nimble enough for local errands the Hawk GT filled a new niche for

Honda. A pair of disc brakes were mounted to the alloy, six-spoke rims and a two-into-one exhaust routed the gases cleanly on their way. Tempest Gray Metallic or Candy Tanzanight Blue units were trimmed with "Hawk Honda" decals on the tanks and "GT 647" art on the side covers.

With the recovery of Milwaukee-built machines well under way, the International Trade Commission rescinded its earlier tariff on imported motorcycles larger than 750cc.

With the restriction lifted, several Hondas were pulled from the lineup. The VF700C Magna, VFR700F2 Interceptor and VF700C Shadow were all eliminated from the production lines.

Although shackled by the ITC ruling in 1987, the V45 Magna underwent a massive makeover. 1988 found the previous restrictions gone, and the V45 Magna returned in all its glory as the VF750C. Besides the bump in displacement the latest V45 Magna was mostly the same as the newly designed 1987. The chin spoiler returned but was now color-matched to the fuel tank chosen. "Magna" tank art was now applied in silver, and bodywork could be had in Black or Candy Bourgogne Red.

With the displacement limits gone, the VT700C Shadow returned in 1988 as the VT800C. Outside the enlarged V-Twin motor, changes were few. Wire wheels replaced the cast units seen on previous versions and two-tone fuel tank paint was mated to chrome on the side covers. Silver "Shadow" tank art was found on the Black and Candy Glory Red models while gold "Shadow" graphics were applied to the Candy Wineberry Red and Dry Silver Metallic option.

Modifications to the CBR1000F Hurricane were also limited to new color options. Starlight Silver Metallic was joined with Karakorum Gray while Granite Blue Metallic found a partner in Monza Red.

Color options on the returning VT1100C Shadow didn't change from the 1987 models, but a few details were altered. The silver stripe found on the fuel tank was now removed and black spark plug wires were installed. Frames on the 1988 models matched the selected color of the sheet metal.

While the balance of the 1988 Honda lineup may have seemed kind of lackluster, changes in the Gold Wing arena would be dramatic. Since its inception in 1975, the flat-four motor had increased in size to 1200cc, and accessories had grown to meet with riders' growing demands. Despite efforts by other manufacturers to close the gap left by the dominating Gold Wing, very little progress was made. With the introduction of the latest GL1500, all hope was lost.

Not only did Honda jump displacement to 1520cc, but they did so by adding another pair of cylinders. The opposed-six motor was even smoother and more powerful than any previous iterations, leaving the competition scratching their heads in wonder.

Everything that was loved about the previous 'Wings was still in place, but every aspect was polished to a new luster. Along with all the usual hardware came some new features that improved the breed further. By adding two cylinders and a bevy of new gear, weight was growing rather vast.

A GL1500, when loaded with all required fluids pushed the scales to a high of 882 pounds. Considering the amount of trickery aboard this may not seem unlikely, but try rolling it around a parking lot. To ease the burden of moving your new GL into spaces or your garage, a reverse gear was installed. Not a true reverse gear perhaps, but a system that supplied a running GL with enough power in neutral to feed a mechanism that propelled the machine backwards. Even uphill movement could now be achieved with little effort. If the machine was to fall over while being reversed a shut off switch killed the motor to prevent further damage.

A full compliment of electronic wares were aboard the latest Gold Wing and everything was easier than ever to use. The major controls could even be accessed while wearing winter gloves, a plus for those inspired enough to ride when the mercury dropped.

The responsibility of slowing the new GL1500 was in the capable hands of three 296mm brake discs, one on the rear wheel and two up front. Twin-piston calipers were on hand to anchor the discs. The front rotors were dressed with plastic covers that also helped to direct air onto the calipers for cooling assistance. A cast aluminum 18-inch wheel was held in the front forks while a 16-inchrim rolled out back. The fuel tank held 6.3 gallons and the saddle height was a respectable 30.5 inches.

Swaddled in a fresh new set of sleek bodywork, new colors were also applied to the bigger and better GL. Two-tone still reigned supreme, and their were three pairs listed in 1988. Dynastic Blue Metallic with Pewter Gray Metallic, Phantom Gray Metallic mated with Checker Black Metallic or Martini Beige Metallic and Haze Brown Metallic were all at your fingertips. A base price of $9998 was all it took to get yourself into the saddle.

1988 MODELS

Model	Product Code	Engine Type/ Displacement	Transmission	Year(s) Available
CBR600F Hurricane	MN4	DOHC Inline Four/598cc	6-Speed	1988
VT600C Shadow VLX	MR1	SOHC V-Twin/583cc	4-Speed	1988
NT650 Hawk GT	MN8	SOHC V-Twin/647cc	5-Speed	1988
VF750C V45 Magna	MN2	DOHC V-Four/748cc	6-Speed	1988
VT800C Shadow	MR6	SOHC V-Twin/800cc	4-Speed	1988
CBR1000F Hurricane	MM5	DOHC Inline Four/998cc	6-Speed	1988
VT1100C Shadow	MM8	SOHC V-Twin/1099cc	4-Speed	1988
GL1500 Gold Wing	MN5	SOHC Opposed Six/1520cc	5-Speed	1988

Model listings for 1989 remained fairly compact for Honda, but several new entrants were introduced, keeping things interesting.

The needs of the small sport bike market were addressed with the fresh CB400F CB-1. Having an inline four motor slung beneath its frame, the CB-1 had a resemblance to the Hawk GT, but lacked the spar frame and single-sided swing arm. Within the walls of the 399cc, dual-overhead cam motor were gear-driven camshafts and liquid cooling. A four-into-one exhaust was finished in black chrome and made a nice contrast to the Pearl Presto Blue paint. A six-speed gearbox provided plenty of ratios for spirited riding.

The GB500 Tourist Trophy was another new model that looked more like an antique than a modern Honda, but it was created to appeal to a classic rider. A single-cylinder, 499cc overhead-cam motor was the first sign of a better, simpler time. A multitude of British machines had been powered by "thumper" motors in their heyday and that GB embodied that emotion. A two-into-one exhaust handled the departing gases and the muffler was large

The GB500 Tourist Trophy looked much like a British bike of the 1960s, but featured plenty of modern hardware for the contemporary rider.
Owner: Dennis French

The single-cylinder engine of the 1989 GB500 was a reminder of how simple a motorcycle could be.

The rear cowling truncated the saddle to fit only one, and was a simple statement of style on the GB500.

Silver wire wheels were another throwback to the earlier days of motorcycling. Only the drilled disc brake is a hint of the GB's modern vintage.

and finished in chrome. Starting the GB was accomplished via electric or kick-start pedal. It had been many moons since Honda included the manual method of starting a street-going machine. The solo saddle was truncated by a small rear cowling that, along with the classic fuel tank, was draped in Black Green Metallic paint and offset with gold pinstripes.

Everything about the Tourist Trophy said "classic," right down to the spoke wheels at either end. Low-mounted handlebars and a 5-speed gearbox completed the laundry list of features.

CBR600F models were "CBR" models instead of "Hurricane." Graphics were the only

1989 MODELS

Model	Product Code	Engine Type/ Displacement	Transmission	Year(s) Available
CB400F CB-1	KAF	DOHC Inline Four/399cc	6-Speed	1989
GB500 Tourist Trophy	MK6	OHC Single/499cc	5-Speed	1989
CBR600F	MT6	DOHC Inline Four/598cc	6-Speed	1989
VT600C Shadow VLX	MR1	SOHC V-Twin/583cc	4-Speed	1989
XL600V Transalp	MM9	OHC V-Twin/583cc	5-Speed	1989
NT650 Hawk GT	MN8	SOHC V-Twin/647cc	5-Speed	1989
PC800 Pacific Coast	MR5	SOHC V-Twin/800cc	5-Speed	1989
VT1100C Shadow	MM8	SOHC V-Twin/1099cc	4-Speed	1989
GL1500 Gold Wing	MN5	SOHC Opposed Six/1520cc	5-Speed	1989

revision to the '89 models with Pearl Crystal White being paired with Winter Lake Blue Metallic or Terra Blue and Fighting Red. "CBR" decals replaced the previous "Hurricane" on the fuel tank.

The only change to the 1989 VT600C Shadow VLX was a script style logo on the tank.

First seen in 1989, the XL600V Transalp was kind of a gentleman's enduro bike. Loads of ground clearance and protective shrouds gave the impression that this bike was meant to get dirty, but the full-frontal fairing and comfortable saddle looked like open road features.

Powered by a 583cc, liquid-cooled V-Twin motor, the Transalp shifted through a five-speed gearbox and had an exhaust that exited high under the tail section.   Pearl Crystal White was trimmed with red and blue stripes.

The NT650 Hawk GT returned unchanged, except for the new Italian Red paint.

Three no-shows for 1989 were the VF750C V45 Magna, VT800C Shadow and CBR1000F Hurricane. Honda often pulled a model for a single year, only to have it return the following year as a revised and improved unit.

With Honda's GL1500 dominating the large touring bike market, there was no reason for the company to add a new model to that family. For those wanting a sizeable machine, but not quite as opulent or pricey as the GL1500, the PC800 Pacific Coast was unveiled for 1989. The 800cc, SOHC V-Twin mill and its shaft drive were all housed within a set of graceful, full-coverage bodywork. Beneath the saddle, a spacious storage compartment carried the things a medium-distance rider needed. Pearl Pacific White paint melded with sections of Ocean Gray Metallic.

The shrinking cruiser segment still claimed the VT1100C Shadow as one of its own, and the only change was the application of a script logo on the fuel tank. The previous year's Black paint was replaced by Indian Lake Blue Metallic in 1989.

With the GL1500 being an all-new model in 1988, only a few alterations were applied to the 1989 model. Perhaps the biggest was that the Gold Wing was built in the U.S. beginning this year. The "1500/6" emblem went missing from the saddlebags as of 1989, and color-keyed front brake housings were used when buying the Commodore Blue-Green Metallic and Triton Blue Metallic or Martini Beige with Haze Brown Metallic paint. A silver cover was still found on the Candy Wineberry Red and Burgundy Red Metallic version.

The Transalp offered a variety of features to the rider who was interested in heading down the driveway and off the beaten path.
Owner: Marion Robinson

Despite its rugged demeanor, the Transalp came complete with full instrumentation.

Helping to avoid brush fires, the dual exhaust canisters exited high and to the very back of the machine.

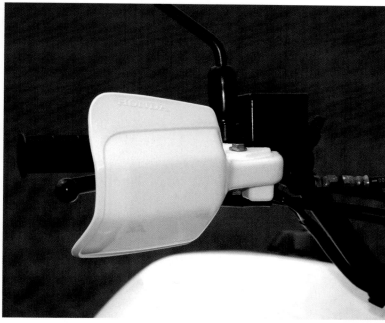

Part of the allure of the 1989 Transalp was its ability to handle some mildly rugged conditions. The plastic hand shields provided protection when the bike ventured off the pavement.

A set of engine guards wrapped around the sides of the fairing of the Transalp and the lower segment was protected by a molded plastic shield.

1990

While 1989 might have been uneventful when it came to new bikes for Honda, 1990 made amends with some exciting new models.

Although only a carry-over from 1989, the CB-1 sold for $400 less in 1990. There had been some talk of Honda motorcycles being overpriced, so the lower-priced CB-1 was one way to dispel the notion. The GB500 Tourist Trophy was another return model with no changes, but a $500 reduction was made to its sticker price.

An additional 10 horsepower was added to the output of the 1990 CBR600F, but it was physically unchanged from the 1989 unit. Two new duo-tone combos were offered in Pearl Crystal White with Blitz Gray Metallic or Black with Monza Red.

The loss of the VT600C Shadow VLX from the 1990 catalog left only the VT1100C in the cruiser lineup, but changes in that market segment would soon alter the balance of sport and custom offerings.

Different color choices were the only alterations made for the Transalp. Moonstone Beige Metallic with brown and black stripes or

Sold for only one year in the U.S., the 1990 RC30 was little more than a street-legal race bike. The RC30 bristled with race technology, but was street legal in the states.
Owner: Matt Jonas

Fighting Red with silver were the 1990 hues. This was the final appearance of the XL600V in Honda's catalogs.

Another returning model was the NT650 Hawk GT. Absolutely no changes were seen in either features or color for the 1990 version of the 1989 model.

Last applied to a Honda in 1986, the VFR750F moniker was back and affixed to a better-than-ever version of the V-four sport bike. Influenced by the RC30, the VFR chassis now featured a twin-spar design and single-sided swing arm. The latest iteration of the V-four motor was more compact than ever before, yet produced more than 100 horsepower.

Rigid 41mm front forks were joined by a single, gas-charged shock absorber on the cast aluminum swing arm. Seventeen-inch rims were mounted to both axles with radial tires keeping them off the pavement. A saddle height of 30.8 inches and wet weight of 540 lbs. was deftly managed by the bike's expertly designed chassis and geometry. The Italian Red machine was set off by the white wheels and retailed for $6,998.

As good as the latest VFR was, some buyers still wanted more. To satisfy their hunger, Honda sold the VFR750R RC30. For a mere $14,998, and for the first time in the U.S., you could ride home on one of Honda's most exotic machines.

More like a thinly disguised race bike, the RC30 was chock full of race-level technology and weight saving materials. The 748cc engine was similar in appearance to that used in the VFR, but within the alloy cases they bikes had little in common. A close-ratio gearbox, titanium connecting rods and an entirely different top-end set the RC30 apart. The light alloy chassis steered with a set of 43mm front forks and a single-sided swing arm. The combination of weight-saving materials gave the RC30 a full-tank weight of only 475.5 lbs., which was 65 lbs. fewer than the nimble VFR.

The cockpit of the RC30 was all business and hid behind a race-inspired fairing and windscreen. The tachometer showed a red line

The compact design of the RC30 showed a close connection to Honda's race-only machines, and the aerodynamic fairing only added to the similarities.

Devoid of any comfort or convenience features, the cockpit of the RC30 was strictly business and included a 12,500-rpm redline tach and 185-mph speedometer.

of 12500 rpm and the speedometer ran all the way up to 185 mph—both serious numbers for a street-legal, factory-built motorcycle. Clip-on handlebars continued the race-bike-in-street-clothing motif, as did the thinly padded pillion with no passenger allowance. A pair of round headlights were ensconced within the race-bred fairing, and all bodywork was clad in a combination of Ross White, Wistaria Blue, Seychell Blue and Red. 1990 was the only year the RC30 was sold stateside.

A historical footnote should be made reguarding the hyper-exotic NR 750 built by Honda in 1990. Built around a 748cc motor featuring oval pistons, the NR was like nothing seen before. Eight valves per cylinder and twin overhead cams only added to the mystique of the NR. Despite grand plans, the NR never saw production and spent very little time on the Gran Prix circuits it was designed to conquer.

Back in the real world, the PC800 Pacific Coast had been upgraded with 62 minor changes according to Honda. The most obvious were a taller windscreen and the new Candy Glory Red paint with Griffin Gray Metallic accents.

Last sold in the U.S. in 1988, the CBR1000F returned in 1990, but was stripped of the "Hurricane" moniker. Only incremental alterations were made to the latest model, including revised fairing contours and the installation of radial tires. Two exterior color palettes were

The 1990 RC30 was hauled to a stop with a set of huge front disc brakes.

1990 MODELS

Model	Product Code	Engine Type/ Displacement	Transmission	Year(s) Available
CB400F CB-1	KAF	DOHC Inline Four/399cc	6-Speed	1990
GB500 Tourist Trophy	MK6	OHC Single/499cc	5-Speed	1990
CBR600F	MT6	DOHC Inline Four/598cc	6-Speed	1990
XL600V Transalp	MM9	OHC V-Twin/583cc	5-Speed	1990
NT650 Hawk GT	MN8	SOHC V-Twin/647cc	5-Speed	1990
VFR750F VFR	MT4	DOHC V-Four/748cc	6-Speed	1990
VFR750R RC30	MR7	DOHC V-Four/748cc	6-Speed	1990
PC800 Pacific Coast	MR5	SOHC V-Twin/800cc	5-Speed	1990
CBR1000F	MS2	DOHC Inline Four/998cc	6-Speed	1990
ST1100	MT3	DOHC V-Four/1084cc	5-Speed	1990
VT1100C Shadow	MM8	SOHC V-Twin/1099cc	4-Speed	1990
GL1500 Gold Wing	MT8	SOHC Opposed Six/1520cc	5-Speed	1990
GL1500SE Gold Wing	MT8	SOHC Opposed Six/1520cc	5-Speed	1990

sold: two-tone Zeus Silver Metallic with Medium Gray Metallic, or Pearl Crystal White with Red, Blue, Gray and Gold.

First sold in the spring of 1990, the new ST1100 was actually classified as a 1991 model by Honda. Since it was available to the public in 1990, we have begun the listing here.

Assembled around a steel chassis, the ST1100 ran with a 1084cc V-four engine that was liquid cooled. A five-speed gearbox fed the power into a shaft drive to keep things neat and quiet. The camshafts were driven by rubber belts, also helping to limit engine noise. Aerodynamic bodywork included a pair of quick-release saddlebags, each capable of swallowing a full-face helmet. When the bags are removed from the bike, small panels flip into place, concealing the mounting hardware from view. An enormous 7.7-gallon fuel tank provided the rider and passenger with long runs between fill-ups, exposing the true nature of the svelte touring machine.

The VT1100C Shadow was the only remaining cruiser in the Honda catalog for 1990, and was delivered with no changes from the previous year's example. Only Indian Lake Blue Metallic was offered.

The standard GL1500 Gold Wing received a few alterations in the color department, but no mechanical upgrades were applied. Candy Wineberry Red was joined with Rime Gray

Metallic, or a buyer could opt for the Carmel Blue Metallic with Snow Shadow Gray Metallic. Either selection was fitted with color-keyed front disc brake covers.

For a handful of lucky buyers, a Special Edition GL1500 was offered in 1990. Carrying a retail price tag of $13,498, the Special Edition was host to several enhanced features not found on the standard model. Pearl White paint was subtly accented with Eagle Silver Metallic and Ocean Gray Metallic to set the SE apart. An aerodynamic rear trunk spoiler was joined by brake and running lights that were now integrated into the contours. Passengers now had control over the position of their footrests and the pilot could send waves of warm air over his boots on demand. An advanced audio system was installed complete with illuminated switches on both the handlebars and radio. An automatic volume control and intercom were both a part of the latest package.

The rear cowling was fixed in place, thus limiting the saddle space.

1991

The 1991 Honda catalog was an amalgam of returning models, replaced machines and fresh faces.

Honda's lineup had been lacking an entry-level unit for a few years, so the introduction of the CB250 Nighthawk was a welcome sight. A 234cc parallel twin engine resided beneath sleek bodywork that belied the simple nature of the CB250. Simple spoke wheels and silver "Nighthawk" graphics were complemented by the basic Passion Red paint. The comfortable two-person seat was paired with a set of handlebars that kept the rider in a mild crouch, but nothing approaching awkward.

The CB-1 and GB500 were both missing from the 1991 catalog, and were never to be seen again.

CBR600F fans applauded the new version of the popular sport bike, unless they'd purchased a 1990 model. The 1991 CBR600F2 was loaded with new power and performance, yet sold for the same price as last year's model. The 600 class was proving to be most popular and upgrades to the CBR pushed it to the head of the class.

The CBS's frame was all-new and held the improved motor further back and lower than before. The perimeter design was crafted in rectangular section steel and employed the motor as a stressed member for added rigidity with less weight. Overall, the new CBR600F2 weighed 8 lbs. less than the 1990 model. While retaining the same characteristics as the previous motor, the F2's mill was smaller, lighter and spun up to 13,000 rpm.

The combined efforts of the designers resulted in a compact engine that delivered 7 more horsepower than last year's model, all while saving space and weight. Achieving more than 100 ponies from a 599cc mill was quite a feat, even for Honda. The 32mm 1990 carbs were replaced by 34mm flat-sided models that drew breath through a larger 6.2-liter airbox. Spent gases flowed through a four-into-two-into-one exhaust that was tuned for maximum withdrawal. Lightweight, six-spoke alloy rims were used at both ends and 60 series radial tires added to the handling of the improved F2. All of this performance was available in one of two color combinations: Ross White with Fighting Red, or Black with Real Blue, Light Blue and Pink graphics. It only took $4,998 to bring a copy home.

Returning for another few rounds was the VT600C Shadow VLX. With the exception of the new Black paint, it was unchanged from the 1989 model. The NT650 Hawk GT also returned in 1991, but was unchanged, including the Italian Red hue seen on the 1990 version.

Another new naked bike for 1991 was the CB750 Nighthawk. Motivated by a 747cc, in-line four motor that was based on the European CBX750F model, it provided a stable and powerful mount for those wanting something simpler. A five-speed transmission sent power to the rear wheel via chain drive, and five-spoke alloy rims kept the rubber in place. Candy Bourgogne Red paint was trimmed with silver "Honda" wing and "Nighthawk" graphics.

The hugely popular VFR750F was given gold wheels for 1991, but everything else on the bike stayed the same. The PC800 Pacific Coast went on hiatus until the 1994 model year. The big CBR1000F was also unchanged, except for Passion Red with Checker Black Metallic paint.

The ST100, although sold in the Spring of 1990, was officially released for 1991. Only Black was sold in the spring, with Sparkling Silver Metallic being added in the Fall of 1990.

The VT600C returned in 1991, but the VT1100C would be a no-show until 1992.

1991 MODELS

Model	Product Code	Engine Type/ Displacement	Transmission	Year(s) Available
CB250 Nighthawk	KBG	OHC Parallel Twin/234cc	5-Speed	1991
CBR600F2 Super Sport	MV9	DOHC Inline Four/599cc	6-Speed	1991
VT600C Shadow VLX	MY0	SOHC V-Twin/583cc	4-Speed	1991
CB750 Nighthawk	MW3	DOHC Inline Four/747cc	5-Speed	1991
NT650 Hawk GT	MN8	SOHC V-Twin/647cc	5-Speed	1991
VFR750F VFR	MT4	DOHC V-Four/748cc	6-Speed	1991
CBR1000F	MW7	DOHC Inline Four/998cc	6-Speed	1991
ST1100	MT3	DOHC V-Four/1084cc	5-Speed	1991
GL1500A Gold Wing Aspencade	MW5	SOHC Opposed Six/1520cc	5-Speed	1991
GL1500I Gold Wing Interstate	MW5	SOHC Opposed Six/1520cc	5-Speed	1991
GL1500SE Gold Wing	MW5	SOHC Opposed Six/1520cc	5-Speed	1991

Gold Wing buyers with an eye on the GL1500 were once again faced with a decision. Three different variations were offered, each wearing an added quantity of goodies. The Aspencade was a 10th Anniversary model and wore gold emblems and a commemorative number plate and logo. Black was the only color sold, and a chrome front brake cover was also a part of the appearance package. The Interstate name was again seen, and was also a 10th Anniversary model. Stripped of the reverse gear and cruise control, the GL1500I did include the Hondaline AM/FM radio unit as standard equipment. Rear passenger floorboards were replaced with foot pegs. Cinnamon Beige Metallic with Valiant Brown Metallic was the only color listed. Another SE model was also part of the Gold Wing lineup and it remained as the fully equipped version sold in 1990. Sunflash Gold Metallic was complemented by Valiant Brown Metallic and 10th Anniversary badges and a number plate were a part of the plan.

1992

Almost every model in the 1992 lineup was a return from the previous year. Very few changes were made as Honda began to find balance in its offerings.

The neophyte CB250 Nighthawk was now sold in a choice of Passion Red or Myth Blue Metallic, but no other alterations were made.

New colors and their layout were the only changes made to the CBR600F2 as well. Black with Palette Purple or a solid Fighting Red finish were both 1992 options. The VT600C Shadow wore a new shade in its Candy Glory Red, and also sported new tank graphics. The NT650 Hawk GT was removed from the family after years of no changes and poor sales.

In the 750 line, the CB750 Nighthawk was available in Black or Candy Bourgogne Red with no other revisions listed. The 1992 VFR750F received a boost in horsepower and mildly revised suspension. A silver "VFR" decal with purple outline adorned the fuel tank, which, along with the rest of the bike, was delivered in Granite Blue Metallic. Metallic gray wheels replaced the gold rims seen in 1991.

The CBR1000F took another year off, but would be seen as a highly modified 1993 model.

The ST1100 was only sold in Candy Glory Red and the brake calipers and wheels were all finished in gray. A new version of the ST1100 had all of the same features of the standard model, but added the safety benefits of anti-lock brakes and traction control. The ST1100A was the official designation for this model, and gold wheels and brake calipers set it apart from the ST1100.

The on-again, off-again existence of the VT1100C Shadow was "on" for another year, but only changes in paint colors were made. In addition to four factory colors being offered, a new custom color program was installed, allowing the rider to create a personal color combination to fit his own desires. Twenty-four different combinations of colors and graphics were offered. The four factory colors for 1992 were Cascade Silver Metallic, Candy Spectra Red, South Pacific Blue Metallic and Black.

Color variations were the name of the game in 1992, and the GL1500's were no exception. The Aspencade was offered in Candy Spectra Red or Cambridge Blue Metallic. The Interstate was also available in those same hues, and was also fitted with an improved AM/FM sound system complete with a 25-watt amplifier and an output jack. The SE was sold in a two-tone paint scheme of Barbados Blue Metallic and Laguna Blue Metallic.

1992 MODELS

Model	Product Code	Engine Type/ Displacement	Transmission	Year(s) Available
CB250 Nighthawk	KBG	OHC Parallel Twin/234cc	5-Speed	1992
CBR600F2 Super Sport	MV9	DOHC Inline Four/599cc	6-Speed	1992
VT600C Shadow VLX	MY0	SOHC V-Twin/583cc	4-Speed	1992
CB750 Nighthawk	MW3	DOHC Inline Four/747cc	5-Speed	1992
VFR750F VFR	MT4	DOHC V-Four/748cc	6-Speed	1992
ST1100	MY3	DOHC V-Four/1084cc	5-Speed	1992
ST1100A ABS-TCS	MY3	DOHC V-Four/1084cc	5-Speed	1992
VT1100C Shadow	MM8	SOHC V-Twin/1099cc	4-Speed	1992
GL1500A Gold Wing Aspencade	MY4	SOHC Opposed Six/1520cc	5-Speed	1992
GL1500I Gold Wing Interstate	MY4	SOHC Opposed Six/1520cc	5-Speed	1992
GL1500SE Gold Wing	MY4	SOHC Opposed Six/1520cc	5-Speed	1992

Another year of minor revisions was in store for 1993, but a few new team members made their way onto the playing field.

With the exception of three new colors being offered, the CB250 Nighthawk was unchanged for 1993. Black, Candy Bourgogne Red or Candy Tahitian Blue were now on tap.

CBR600F2 models rolled on improved BT50 radial tires and featured fresh graphics and colors. Two different three-color themes were sold: Black with Seed Silver Metallic and NR Red, or Ross White, Real Blue and NR Red. The standard VT600C Shadow VLX was finished in Black, but wore carry-over graphics for the 1992 model.

Joining the VT600C was the VT600CD Shadow VLX Deluxe. While mirroring the mechanicals of the standard issue machine, the Deluxe was better dressed. A two-tone wardrobe featured Pearl Coral Reef Blue and Black paint and was accented by chrome on the engine cases and valve covers. Handlebars were wider with a new shape, and the saddle was now a two-piece affair with upholstery buttons adding some texture to the theme.

Only a third color was added to the game for the CB750 Nighthawk. Candy Tahitian Blue joined Black and Candy Bourgogne Red as buying options. The VFR750F also received nothing more than a few cosmetic tweaks for the new year. Pearl Crystal White paint and white wheels were the centerpieces of the latest arrangement. "Honda," "VFR750F," and the Honda "Wing" were all-new graphics applied to the existing bodywork.

Another new model, the CBR900RR, was based on an 893cc inline four motor. The 900RR weighed only 408 lbs. dry and was another Honda bike that raised the performance bar by several notches in its class. The curb weight was only a hair more than most 600cc machines being sold. The compact design was reminiscent of race-going GP bikes and delivered nearly comparable performance. Suddenly, liter-bike performance was available in a more concise package.

The 16-valve motor was wrapped in a twin-spar frame that was cast in aluminum. The four-into-two-into-one exhaust made efficient use of the exiting gases and the aluminum canister saved weight. Massive 45mm front forks and Honda's Pro-Link rear suspension kept both tires planted firmly on the asphalt. The race-inspired fairing included "fairing penetration technology," which translated into perforations in the front fascia that allowed air to flow through and around the slippery shape.

A matching set of headlights was also housed in this full-coverage bodywork. The two-level seating was capable of carrying a rider and passenger, but long days on the open road were not part of the 900RR's intentions. Two choices of three-color graphics were on the 1993 order sheets: Ross White with Real Blue and NR Red graphics, or Black with Seed Silver Metallic and NR Red.

After yet another year away, the CBR1000F was back, but was wearing new clothes. Sleek new bodywork was wrapped around the returning chassis and drive train. A linked braking system helped to keep things under control in panic situations. Although new, only one set of colors was sold for 1993. The lower cowl of gray was joined by Black, Red, Blitz Gray Metallic and Medium Gray Metallic surfaces on the rest of the panels.

Both versions of the ST1100 were in the 1993 lineup again, but neither the ST1100 or ST1100A sported any changes in appearance or running gear.

The VT1100C Shadow was entered into the Custom Color Program in 1992, and that was expanded in 1993 to include 26 combinations of colors and graphics. American Red, Pearl

1993 MODELS

Model	Product Code	Engine Type/ Displacement	Transmission	Year(s) Available
CB250 Nighthawk	KBG	OHC Parallel Twin/234cc	5-Speed	1993
CBR600F2 Super Sport	MV9	DOHC Inline Four/599cc	6-Speed	1993
VT600C Shadow VLX	MY0	SOHC V-Twin/583cc	4-Speed	1993
VT600CD Shadow VLX Deluxe	MY0	SOHC V-Twin/583cc	4-Speed	1993
CB750 Nighthawk	MW3	DOHC Inline Four/747cc	5-Speed	1993
VFR750F VFR	MY7	DOHC V-Four/748cc	6-Speed	1993
CBR900RR	MW0	DOHC Inline Four/893cc	6-Speed	1993
CBR1000F	MZ2	DOHC Inline Four/998cc	6-Speed	1993
ST1100	MY3	DOHC V-Four/1084cc	5-Speed	1993
ST1100A ABS-TCS	MY3	DOHC V-Four/1084cc	5-Speed	1993
VT1100C Shadow	MM8	SOHC V-Twin/1099cc	4-Speed	1993
GL1500A Gold Wing Aspencade	MZ3	SOHC Opposed Six/1520cc	5-Speed	1993
GL1500I Gold Wing Interstate	MZ3	SOHC Opposed Six/1520cc	5-Speed	1993
GL1500SE Gold Wing	MZ3	SOHC Opposed Six/1520cc	5-Speed	1993

Coronado Blue and Pearl Glacier White joined the four colors listed in 1992.

After a year or so of receiving no improvements, the GL1500A Aspencade received a few tweaks on the standard equipment list. Air caps on the front shocks were now standard, and needle bearing rocker arm pivots assisted in smooth and quiet operation of the opposed-six motor. The cruise control was also improved and now held a given speed with more accuracy. Black was also added to the color list for 1993, bringing the total array to three. The same Black option was added to the GL1500I Interstate list as well, but no other changes were seen.

Being at the top of its game, the SE Gold Wing needed little improvement, so Honda merely made the CB radio and rear speakers standard equipment for 1993. Three new colors were also added to the order sheets with Pearl Glacier White, Pearl Glacier White with Light Blue and Pearl Coronado Blue with Light Blue adding a new decision to the buyer's list.

With two returning models and a pair of fresh units rolling in for 1994, it would be another fairly tame year for Honda.

The CB250 Nighthawk soldiered on, and only two new colors were found in the revision listing. Candy Red replaced Candy Bourgogne Red and Candy Tahitian Blue gave way to Metallic Blue.

The CBR600F2 was also the recipient of new paint options for 1994 with no underlying modifications made to the hardware. A trio of three-color palettes were offered in Ross White with Black and Atomic Red, Black with Uranus Violet and Atomic Red, or Black, Uranus Violet and Chartreuse Yellow. Candy Glory Red was added to the list of available VT600C Shadow VLX hues, but no other alterations were seen. A choice of Red with Pearl White or Teal with Pearl White were sold on the returning VT600CD Shadow VLX Deluxe.

The CB750 Nighthawk took a year off and would return in 1995.

Although only 300 copies of the RC30 were

The CB1000 combined the brute power of a 998cc motor with the basics of a standard motorcycle, providing the rider with a flexible mount capable of tackling many styles of riding.
Owner: Dennis Wilda

With the four-into-one exhaust exiting on the right side of the chassis, the left side profile provides an uncluttered view of the CB1000's drive train.

Being liquid-cooled, the 998cc motor of the 1994 CB1000 was devoid of the cooling fins needed on an air-cooled power plant.

Rear suspension on the CB1000 was provided by a pair of remote reservoir shocks, instead of a Pro-Link arrangement.

sold in 1990, Honda upped the ante with a new RVF750R RC45 in 1994. An all-new, 749cc, 90-degree V-four motor featured titanium connecting rods, just as the RC30 had. Feeding this new mill was a computer-operated programmed fuel injection system that was more precise than previous versions. A single-sided swing arm was retained, as was the racing-style bodywork and fairing. Like the RC30, the RC45 was only fitted with a saddle made for one, keeping its racing intent clear. Ross White paint was mated with graphics of Sparkling Red and Purple.

Last seen as a 1988 model, the VF750C Magna was back in 1994. Although bearing the same name, it was an entirely new machine from the fuel tank down. Motor, wheels, exhaust and bodywork were all fresh on the machine, but a V-four motor still throbbed beneath the saddle. Magna Red, Black and Pearl Shining Yellow were the available colors.

The VFR750F VFR was Honda bearing the same name as the previous model, yet riding with all new hardware. Its intent was unchanged, but its chassis, bodywork and running gear all received modifications. The VFR was proving to be a great all-around machine, capa-

The big CB1000 featured a pair of drilled disc brakes up front and a third, smaller unit on the rear wheel.

A circular temperature gauge was flanked by an easy-to-read speedometer and tachometer. A small bank of warning lights provided the rest of the details.

1994 MODELS

Model	Product Code	Engine Type/ Displacement	Transmission	Year(s) Available
CB250 Nighthawk	KBG	OHC Parallel Twin/234cc	5-Speed	1994
CBR600F2 Super Sport	MV9	DOHC Inline Four/599cc	6-Speed	1994
VT600C Shadow VLX	MZ8	SOHC V-Twin/583cc	4-Speed	1994
VT600CD Shadow VLX	Deluxe MZ8	SOHC V-Twin/583cc	4-Speed	1994
RVF750R RC45	MW4	DOHC V-Four/749cc	6-Speed	1994
VF750C Magna	MZ5	DOHC V-Four/748cc	6-Speed	1994
VFR750F VFR	MZ7	DOHC V-Four/748cc	6-Speed	1994
PC800 Pacific Coast	MR5	SOHC V-Twin/800cc	5-Speed	1994
CBR900RR	MW0	DOHC Inline Four/893cc	6-Speed	1994
CB1000	MZ1	DOHC Inline Four/998cc	5-Speed	1994
CBR1000F	MZ2	DOHC Inline Four/998cc	6-Speed	1994
ST1100	MAJ	DOHC V-Four/1084cc	5-Speed	1994
ST1100A ABS-TCS	MAJ	DOHC V-Four/1084cc	5-Speed	1994
VT1100C Shadow	MM8	SOHC V-Twin/1099cc	4-Speed	1994
GL1500A Gold Wing Aspencade	MAF	SOHC Opposed Six/1520cc	5-Speed	1994
GL1500I Gold Wing Interstate	MAF	SOHC Opposed Six/1520cc	5-Speed	1994
GL1500SE Gold Wing	MAF	SOHC Opposed Six/1520cc	5-Speed	1994

ble of sporting runs as well as medium to long-distance touring. The Pure Red paint was offset by black wheels and a N.A.R.T.-style intake vent on the side of the full-coverage fairing. After slipping off the radar in 1991, the PC800 Pacific Coast was back in 1994. Except for the Black-Z color, no other revisions were listed.

The feather-weight CBR900RR rolled with a new front tire profile and some new paint, but was otherwise unchanged from its debut year. Ross White with Red and Black, or Black with Uranus Violet and Yellow were now your choices.

Bringing a new model into the standard, or naked bike, formula the CB1000 was a powerful example of what could be accomplished. A double-overhead cam, 998cc, liquid-cooled motor provided the motivation and a five-speed gearbox handled the distribution. Three-spoke mag wheels finished in the same Gloss Black as the machine itself were fitted with triple disc brakes. A four-into-one exhaust was plated in chrome and matched to an aluminum muffler. Each rear shock was of the remote reservoir variety, allowing for a high degree of comfort and adjustability.

Cloaked in the same all-new bodywork installed for 1993, the CBR1000F had only a few new details for 1994. The upper section of the cowl now featured bumpers to protect the bodywork in case of a drop. The latest Matt Black, Ross White and Red color scheme and pattern was also altered from the previous year.

Both the ST1100 and ST1100A were now finished in Gloss Black, but saw no additional revisions. For the VT1100C Shadow's Custom Color Program, few new shades replaced earlier variants. Solid color models were only seen with the standard logo while two-tone versions could opt for the standard or secondary badges. Cascade Silver Metallic and Pearl Glacier White were supplanted by Pearl Atlantis Blue and Pearl Bermuda Green.

1994 Aspencade and Interstate Gold Wings now featured a lower body cowling that was finished in the same color as the upper bodywork. Both versions were sold in Candy Spectra Red, Pearl Atlantis Blue or Black-Z. The SE retained the lower cowling in silver, while the upper segments were seen in Pearl Bermuda Green, Pearl Atlantis Blue, Candy Spectra Red or Pearl Glacier White.

Honda's focus for 1995 remained mostly on finding ways to improve returning models and adding a few upgraded model options to the mix.

Only two colors were offered for the CB250 Nighthawk with Metallic Blue being eliminated from the options chart. Black and Candy Red remained and no other changes were implemented.

1995 CBR600s now carried the F3 designation as minor modifications improved the breed. A dual-stage induction system aided in breathing and the headlight assembly was all plastic to shave a few ounces from the overall weight. Two fresh color combinations were used as well as revised graphics. Black with Uranus Violet and Chartreuse Yellow was the first option with Ross White, Uranus Violet and Chartreuse Yellow following close behind.

Both versions of the VT600 Shadow received new fuel tanks and handlebars as well as refreshed logo art. The VT600C Shadow was sold in the same hues as last year, while the Deluxe edition wore Candy Burgundy with Pearl White or Pearl Purple with Pearl White paint.

Having missed a year of sale, the CB750 Nighthawk returned for 1995 and featured a few new bits. Whether you bought a Magna Red or Black model, the lower fork legs were now polished aluminum and the headlight bucket and support brackets were chrome.

1995 VF750 Magnas came in a choice of Candy Glory Red or Pearl Shining Yellow, but no other revisions were made. Joining the Magna lineup was the VF750CD Deluxe. A small, bikini fairing surrounded the headlight and two-tone paint was applied. Pearl Paragon Purple with Pearl Fadeless White or Black with Pearl Salem Mint were your choices. No other distinctions were made between the two models.

Like its sibling before it, the RC45 would only be seen for a single model year and was missing from the 1995 catalog. The VFR750F was unchanged for 1995, including the Pure Red paint.

Another model returning with no changes was the PC800 Pacific Coast. Even the Black-Z paint was the only hue listed for the latest year of sale.

Changes to the ultra-light CBR900RR were minimal and included fresh graphics with altered paint and a revised fairing. Ross White joined with Uranus Violet and Yellow and the Black combination seen in 1994 remained.

Besides being sold in Pure Red Pearl, the CB1000 rolled on without alteration from the 1994 version. 1995 would prove to be the final year for the big naked bike as riders chose either sport or cruise machines more often. The fully faired CB1000F was only draped in new colors for 1995, and would only be sold for one more year beyond 1995. Gloss Black, Blitz Gray Metallic and Yellow were laid onto the bodywork in the same pattern seen in 1994.

ST1100s and ST1100As were both sold in Pure Red for 1995, and featured improved air intakes and windscreens that were stiffer and wider than those used in 1994.

VT1100 Shadows touted new model name artwork, and Pearl Royal Magenta replaced Pearl Bermuda Green in the paint department. Foregoing Japanese smoothness for more "Milwaukee" thump, the VT1100 motors were assembled with a single-pin crankshaft that added some of the familiar vibrations so well known in the U.S.-built offerings.

Taking the VT1100 a bit closer to the "Milwaukee" offerings, the VT1100C2 American Classic Edition, or ACE, sported bodywork and exhaust that closely mimicked that of some Harley-Davidson models. Wire wheels were installed in place of the cast spokes

1995 MODELS

Model	Product Code	Engine Type/ Displacement	Transmission	Year(s) Available
CB250 Nighthawk	KBG	OHC Parallel Twin/234cc	5-Speed	1995
CBR600F3 Super Sport	MAL	DOHC Inline Four/599cc	6-Speed	1995
VT600C Shadow VLX	MZ8	SOHC V-Twin/583cc	4-Speed	1995
VT600CD Shadow VLX Deluxe	MZ8	SOHC V-Twin/583cc	4-Speed	1995
CB750 Nighthawk	MW3	DOHC Inline four/747cc	5-Speed	1995
VF750C Magna	MZ5	DOHC V-Four/748cc	6-Speed	1995
VF750CD Magna Deluxe	MZ5	DOHC V-Four/748cc	6-Speed	1995
VFR750F VFR	MZ7	DOHC V-Four/748cc	6-Speed	1995
PC800 Pacific Coast	MR5	SOHC V-Twin/800cc	5-Speed	1995
CBR900RR	MAE	DOHC Inline Four/893cc	6-Speed	1995
CB1000	MZ1	DOHC Inline Four/998cc	5-Speed	1995
CBR1000F	MZ2	DOHC Inline Four/998cc	6-Speed	1995
ST1100	MAJ	DOHC V-Four/1084cc	5-Speed	1995
ST1100A ABS-TCS	MAJ	DOHC V-Four/1084cc	5-Speed	1995
VT1100C Shadow	MAA	SOHC V-Twin/1099cc	4-Speed	1995
VT1100C2 Shadow A.C.E.	MAH	SOHC V-Twin/1099cc	4-Speed	1995
GL1500A Gold Wing Aspencade	MAF	SOHC Opposed Six/1520cc	5-Speed	1995
GL1500I Gold Wing Interstate	MAF	SOHC Opposed Six/1520cc	5-Speed	1995
GL1500SE Gold Wing	MAF	SOHC Opposed Six/1520cc	5-Speed	1995

found on the Shadow, and front and rear fenders now provided more coverage. Two-tone paint was available in four different hues: Black, American Red, Pearl Atlantis Blue and Pearl Royal Magenta.

All three variations on the Gold Wing theme wore 20th anniversary badges for 1995. Other revisions included suspension calibration and improved saddlebag and trunk liners. As was typical, new colors were available for each model in the GL family—Candy Spectra Red, Pearl Royal Magenta, and Pearl Sierra Green for the Aspencade; Candy Spectra Red and Pearl Sierra Green for the Interstate. The SE offered three different two-tone choices with Pearl Royal Magenta/Purple, Pearl Sierra Green/Toscana Green and Candy Spectra Red/Italian Red. For those seeking a monotone effect, Pearl Glacier White was offered as a solid color.

1996

The revised 1996 GL1500 Interstate appeared in 1988, and the molded front-brake cover was still being used on the 1996 models.
Owner: Niehaus Cycle Sales

With the exception of Honda's ever-changing color palette, things were again quiet at the company as the 1995 model year wound down and 1996 arrived. One model returned to the fray, while another gained a special paint scheme.

The unchanged CB250 Nighthawk was rejoined by the returning CMX250C Rebel. Last seen in 1987, the Rebel brought a higher-level "cruiser" to the small bike market. With only Magna Red paint available, the Rebel was a mirror image of its previous edition.

The CBR600F3 Super Sport wore new graphics and colors, but was otherwise unchanged. Ross White with Magna Red and Black accents or Uranus Violet with Pearl Shining Yellow and Ross White trim were offered. To mark the success of their racing efforts, a limited edition Smokin' Joe Replica was also marketed for 1996. The Pearl Paragon Blue or Pearl Shining Yellow versions bore the "Smokin Joe's" name and camel logo, but were the same CBR600F3 beneath the boy-racer bodywork.

Color choices were the only things altered for the VT600C Shadow VLX and Deluxe models. The standard VLX was only sold in Black, while the Deluxe iteration had three different two-tone choices: Red with Black, Black with Pearl Mint or Pearl Purple with Pearl White.

The CB750 Nighthawk was unchanged in the chassis department, but the inline four motor was still finished in black with accents of polished heads and engine cooling fins. Black or Shining Yellow paint could be had on the bodywork. The VF750 models claimed new

Compared to the first editions of the Gold Wing, the 1996 models had grown in size and weight, but still provided the rider a well-equipped machine that could soak up miles like no other.

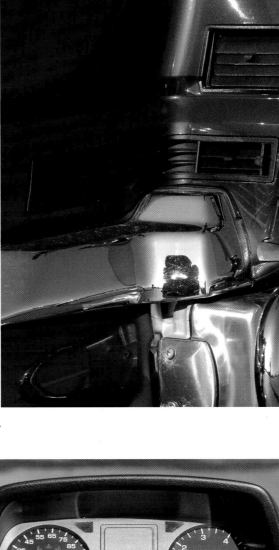

By adjusting the air vents found in the front fairing of the Interstate, the rider could control the flow of air to keep things comfortable behind the massive housing.

Seating for the GL1500 Intestate passenger was still considered the best in the business and included the padded armrests, audio speakers and storage compartments.

A full complement of gauges were installed in the full-coverage fairing and kept the Interstate rider fully informed.

1996 MODELS

Model	Product Code	Engine Type/ Displacement	Transmission	Year(s) Available
CB250 Nighthawk	KBG	OHC Parallel Twin/234cc	5-Speed	1996
CMX250C Rebel	KEN	OHC Parallel Twin/234cc	5-Speed	1996
CBR600F3 Super Sport	MAL	DOHC Inline Four/599cc	6-Speed	1996
CBR600SJR	MAL	DOHC Inline Four/599cc	6-Speed	1996
VT600C Shadow VLX	MZ8	SOHC V-Twin/583cc	4-Speed	1996
VT600CD Shadow VLX Deluxe	MZ8	SOHC V-Twin/583cc	4-Speed	1996
CB750 Nighthawk	MW3	DOHC Inline Four/747cc	5-Speed	1996
VF750C Magna	MZ5	DOHC V-Four/748cc	6-Speed	1996
VF750CD Magna Deluxe	MZ5	DOHC V-Four/748cc	6-Speed	1996
VFR750F VFR	MZ7	DOHC V-Four/748cc	6-Speed	1996
PC800 Pacific Coast	MR5	SOHC V-Twin/800cc	5-Speed	1996
CBR900RR	MAE	DOHC Inline Four/893cc	6-Speed	1996
CBR1000F	MZ2	DOHC Inline Four/998cc	6-Speed	1996
ST1100	MAJ	DOHC V-Four/1084cc	5-Speed	1996
ST1100A ABS-TCS	MAJ	DOHC V-Four/1084cc	5-Speed	1996
VT1100C Shadow	MAA	SOHC V-Twin/1099cc	4-Speed	1996
VT1100C2 Shadow A.C.E.	MAH	SOHC V-Twin/1099cc	4-Speed	1996
GL1500A Gold Wing Aspencade	MAF	SOHC Opposed Six/1520cc	5-Speed	1996
GL1500I Gold Wing Interstate	MAF	SOHC Opposed Six/1520cc	5-Speed	1996
GL1500SE Gold Wing	MAF	SOHC Opposed Six/1520cc	5-Speed	1996

tank logos on the Magna, which was now sold in Pure Red or Pearl Shining Yellow. The Deluxe edition bore a scalloped paint arrangement on the fuel tank and retained the bikini fairing of the 1995 model. The two-tone scallops were seen in Pearl Paragon Purple with Pearl Fadeless White or in Black and Pure Red. The VFR750F was again a carry-over model, including paint.

1996 Pacific Coast machines were now finished in Magna Red, but were otherwise the same as the 1995 models.

CBR900RRs were treated to a long list of upgrades to the motor and bodywork for 1996. The machines received better performance from the compact mill and enhanced aerodynamics. Only one color combination was sold— Glass Black with Pure Red and Atomic Red details.

1996 was the final year of sale for the CBR1000F and no changes were made to the fully faired model.

Both the ST1100 and ST1100A were now fitted with 40-amp alternators. Along with the more-powerful air-cooled alternator, the ST1100A was given a linked-brake system to enhance the ABS and traction control already in place.

VT1100C Shadows played with their color offerings and replaced Pearl Royal Magenta with two new hues of Pearl Majestic Purple and Pearl Hot Rod Yellow. Three additional colors were added to those carried over from 1995. Pearl Majestic Purple, Pearl Hot Rod Yellow and Pearl Glacier White added to the dizzying number of color combinations already offered.

Minor changes of a full-logic audio system and the availability of Pearl Sparkling Blue were added to the GL1500A Aspencade's listing. No changes were seen for the 1996 GL1500I Interstate and it would also be the final year of sale for the mid-level trim package. Four new two-tone color selections were offered for the GL1500SE; Candy Spectra Red with Italian Red, Pearl Royal Magenta with Purple, Pearl Sierra Green with Toscana Green and Pearl Glacier White with Summer Blond Metallic.

After Miguel Duhamel's victory at the Daytona 200 in 1995 aboard a race-prepped CBR, Honda offered a street-legal variant for fans and collectors.

The Smokin' Joe's Replica was a spitting image of its race-bred brethren, but lacked most of the high-performance gear used to win the 200-mile race at Daytona.

A copy of Miguel Duhamel's signature and a list of his achievements aboard his CBR600 graced the fuel tank.

A tidy cockpit was filled with just enough instrumentation to get the rider by—no clocks, fuel gauges or radios, much like the racing machine it was inspired by.

Coloration and graphics were easy to spot and did nothing to infringe on the sporting nature of the CBR600. A pair of massive, drilled rotors were mounted to the yellow front wheel and slowed both the bike and passers by.

The CBR600's colorful graphics made it clear the machine was from Honda.

Looking dapper in his checkered victory scarf, Smokin' Joe was found in several places on the CBR bodywork.

First sold as a 1990 model, the VFR750F trundled along receiving a variety of upgrades through its product cycle. By 1996, not much was changing, but why mess with a good thing?

A pair of drilled, floating rotors helped to slow the VFR down and the glossy black rims set off the red body panels nicely.

A pair of headlights were mounted behind the flowing red bodywork of the VFR750F.

A stout swing arm held things in place out back and the final chain drive made efficient use of the power coming its way.

Feel like riding solo? By attaching the VFR's rear cowling over the stock saddle you could look and feel like a Moto GP rider.

When the need arose to take along a rider, the VFR's saddle provided plenty of space and comfort.

The white-faced tach was all business, but the VFR also provided a nice display of gauges for the rider's use.

Three new models spiced up an otherwise quiet year for Honda, with subtle changes being applied to remaining machines.

Both the CB250 Nighthawk and CMX250C Rebel were done after the 1997 model year, and no changes were made to the CB. Black with Enamel Cream or Pearl Shining Yellow and White were the two-tone color schemes available for the CMX.

Engine enhancements on the CBR600F3 boosted horsepower ratings to 105 and a lightweight drive chain helped deliver the newfound power to the rear sprocket. An "SE" model was built wearing Purple and Yellow paint, while standard models were sold in a Black and White two-tone or a solid Sparkling Red ensemble.

Another 600cc model to perform its swan song in 1996 was the VT600C Shadow VLX. Black seemed to be a fitting color for its final appearance. The Deluxe model of the same cycle remained until the 1998 model year. 1997 Deluxe models wore Magna Red with Pearl Classical Cream or Black with Pearl Shining Yellow paint.

The penultimate year for the CB750 Nighthawk saw no changes. The VF750C Magna was now an all-black model, while the VF750C2 (previously the CD) wore two-tone scalloped paint on the tank. Pure Red with Black or Black with Pearl Shining Yellow were the '97 hues. The VFR750F VFR was in its final year of sale as a 750cc model, and no alterations were seen.

A two-tone finish of Magna Red and Ostrich Black was applied to the 1997 PC800 and the molded front disc brake cover was removed. The self-canceling turn signals were replaced by a push-to-cancel system.

After a big makeover for the CBR900RR in 1996, only graphics and paint would be revised for 1997. Black with Atomic Red and Matt Axis Gray Metallic, Black with Pearl Shining Yellow and Ross White or the Pure Red option were all sold on the '97 models.

With the loss of the CBR1000F still fresh on super sport enthusiasts' minds, the latest offering from Honda would set things right again. The 1997 CBR1100XX combined a terrific list of features and wrapped them in sleek bodywork that cheated the wind. The Black Bird, as it was also known, was motivated by a lightweight motor that displaced 1137cc, packaged in an inline four configuration. The upper crankcase and cylinder block were a single casting, providing simplicity and stiffness while saving weight. A linked braking system like that used on the ST1100 allowed the XX to be slowed as easily as it was brought to speed.

The pointed beak of the fairing lent itself to the given moniker of Black Bird, as did the Mute Black Metallic paint. The combination of power, handling, comfort and appearance catapulted the XX to the top of many sport riders' wish lists.

The ST1100 was unscathed, and even retained the same Pure Red paint used on the '96 models. The ST1100A was now tagged with the ABS II moniker. An improved anti-lock (ABS) system was tied to the linked braking introduced on the 1996 version. Pure Red was also applied to the ABS II.

Changes to the VT1100 family were largely in name only, but a few enhancements awaited buyers. The VT1100 Shadow became the Shadow Spirit and featured oil and coolant lines that had been repositioned to be invisible, or certainly harder to find. This styling effort was teamed with five new color variations. An all-Black model was joined by four two-tone combinations: Black with Pearl Ivory Cream, Pearl Hot Rod Yellow and Black, Ocean Gray Metallic with with Pearl Glacier White and American Red teamed with Glacier White.

The VT1100C2, American Classic Edition

was seen in a Black-only model, or a two-tone edition. All switches were now marked with international symbols for use on both sides of the pond. The two-tone ACE models provided the buyer with a choice of five different combinations: Pearl Sedona Red with Pearl Ivory Cream, Black with Pearl Hot Rod Yellow, American Red with Pearl Ivory Cream, Black with Pearl Ivory Cream and Ocean Gray Metallic with Pearl Glacier White.

The Gold Wing clan had lost its Interstate member and changes to the remaining models would include hardware found on the latest opposed-six powered machines. Both the Aspencade and SE now featured the same internationally approved handlebar switches and some new gearbox and clutch internals found on the new Valkyrie. The Aspencade was sold in Candy Spectra Red, Pearl Sonoma Green or Pearl Glacier White. The dressier SE offered Candy Spectra Red with Spectra Red, Pearl Sonoma Green with Dark Green, Pearl Glacier White with Silver or an all-Pearl Sapphire Black finish.

The all-new 1997 Valkyrie was powered by the same 1520cc, opposed-six motor from the Gold Wing. The motor was fed through a set of six carburetors in place of the fuel injection used on the GLs.

The GL1500C was stripped of all touring accessories, and featured simple trim commonly used on other cruisers. Of course, other cruisers weren't powered by the massive six-cylinder motor or were of the same enormous dimensions as the Valkyrie. Although mostly the same motor as the Gold Wing, the Valkyrie's mill was tuned for performance, and the six-into-six exhaust made noises like no other cruiser on the planet. A pair of full fenders were employed to cover the large tires found at both ends. Ergonomics of the Valkyrie were similar to the Gold Wings with the large saddle and handlebars that reached back to greet the rider's grip. Four color options were seen for the '97 GL1500C: Black, American Red with Pearl Glacier White, Pearl Majestic Purple with Pearl Glacier White or Black with Pearl Hot Rod Yellow.

For those seeking a bit more convenience, the GL1500CT Valkyrie Tourer provided all of the stripped model's goodies, along with a wide windshield and a set of hard-sided saddlebags. Three color options awaited the Valkyrie Tourer buyer: Black, American Red with Pearl Glacier White or Pearl Sonoma Green with Pearl Ivory Cream.

1997 MODELS

Model	Product Code	Engine Type/ Displacement	Transmission	Year(s) Available
CB250 Nighthawk	KBG	OHC Parallel Twin/234cc	5-Speed	1997
CMX250C Rebel	KEN	OHC Parallel Twin/234cc	5-Speed	1997
CBR600F3	MAL	DOHC Inline Four/599cc	6-Speed	1997
VT600C Shadow VLX	MZ8	SOHC V-Twin/583cc	4-Speed	1997
VT600CD Shadow VLX Deluxe	MZ8	SOHC V-Twin/583cc	4-Speed	1997
CB750 Nighthawk	MW3	DOHC Inline Four/747cc	5-Speed	1997
VF750C Magna	MZ5	DOHC V-Four/748cc	6-Speed	1997
VF750C2 Magna Deluxe	MZ5	DOHC V-Four/748cc	6-Speed	1997
VFR750F VFR	MZ7	DOHC V-Four/748cc	6-Speed	1997
PC800 Pacific Coast	MR5	SOHC V-Twin/800cc	5-Speed	1997
CBR900RR	MAS	DOHC Inline Four/893cc	6-Speed	1997
CBR1100XX Black Bird	MAT	DOHC Inline Four/1137cc	6-Speed	1997
ST1100	MAJ	DOHC V-Four/1084cc	5-Speed	1997
ST1100A ABS II-TCS	MAJ	DOHC V-Four/1084cc	5-Speed	1997
VT1100C Shadow Spirit	MAA	SOHC V-Twin/1099cc	4-Speed	1997
VT1100C2 Shadow A.C.E.	MAH	SOHC V-Twin/1099cc	4-Speed	1997
VT1100C2 Shadow A.C.E. 2-Tone	MAH	SOHC V-Twin/1099cc	4-Speed	1997
GL1500A Gold Wing Aspencade	MAM	SOHC Opposed Six/1520cc	5-Speed	1997
GL1500SE Gold Wing	MAM	SOHC Opposed Six/1520cc	5-Speed	1997
GL1500C Valkyrie	MZ0	SOHC Opposed-Six/1520cc	5-Speed	1997
GL1500CT Valkyrie Tourer	MZ0	SOHC Opposed-Six/1520cc	5-Speed	1997

With both 250cc offerings sacked, the smallest 1998 Honda displaced 600cc, but there were plenty of bigger machines higher up in the lineup.

With the exception of new colors, the CBR600F3 remained unaltered. Sparkling Red, Sparkling Red with Black or Black with Dark Crimson Red were the 1998 choices. For fans of Miguel Duhamel, a Smokin' Joe's Replica was also offered and it bore a copy of his signature on the fuel tank, along with the Pearl Paragon Purple and Pearl Shining Yellow paint that mirrored Miguel's race-winning Honda.

The VT600C was dropped, leaving only the Deluxe version behind. All-aluminum foot pegs were bound with wide rubber panels and Black with Jade Green or Ocean Gray Metallic with Black paint were seen for 1998.

The CB750 Nighthawk was the only one left in the family with the dismissal of the CB250. Only Black was sold for 1998 with no other alterations made. The VF750C Magna was another Black-only model with no additional changes. Only color differences were applied to

The base model Valkyrie returned for its second year in 1998 and remained an imposing machine, despite the lack of bodywork.

the VF740C2 Magna with Black being mated to your choice of Terra Silver Metallic or Pearl Sparkling Blue.

The VT750C Shadow was last seen in 1983, but returned as an American Classic Edition for 1998. A 745cc V-Twin motor powered the latest iteration, and it was also all-new in the cosmetics department. With a profile that closely mimicked a Harley-Davidson FLSTF, the latest ACE rolled on wire wheels, unlike the solid discs used on the Honda Fat Boy. Sold only in Black, it was joined by the VT750CD Shadow ACE Deluxe, which was available in Black or a choice of two, two-tone combinations: Black with Pearl Canyon Copper or Pearl Sedona Red with Pearl Ivory Cream paint. There was additional chrome on the Deluxe version.

The Pacific Coast model would ride into the sunset at the end of the 1998 model year, and was unchanged from the previous offering.

The all-new VFR800FI Interceptor replaced the VFR750F. Built using a pivotless frame and powered by a 781cc V-four motor, the new VFR quickly became a popular all-around machine. The electronic fuel injection delivered flawless performance, and the linked braking provided a safer level of stopping power. Wrapped in fresh Italian Red bodywork the new Interceptor made friends fast.

For riders wanting a more purpose-built sport bike, the CBR900RR was both lighter and more powerful in 1998. With a newly reduced dry weight of only 396 lbs. it was easily one the lightest in the open class. Power was boosted to 123 horsepower as well, creating a nearly unbeatable machine. A choice of three solid colors included Black, Pearl Shining Yellow and Pure Red.

A new entry into the Honda lineup was the VTR1000F Super Hawk. The alloy frame cradled a 996cc, 90-degree V-Twin power plant and was positioned as a sport model. A frame-mounted ¾ fairing provided rider protection, but still allowed a view of the motor's case.

1998 MODELS

Model	Product Code	Engine Type/ Displacement	Transmission	Year(s) Available
CBR600F3	MAL	DOHC Inline-Four/599cc	6-Speed	1998
CBR600SE Smokin' Joe	MAL	DOHC Inline-Four/599cc	6-Speed	1998
VT600CD Shadow VLX Deluxe	MZ8	SOHC V-Twin/583cc	4-Speed	1998
CB750 Nighthawk	MW3	DOHC Inline-Four/747cc	5-Speed	1998
VF750C Magna	MZ5	DOHC V-Four/748cc	6-Speed	1998
VF750C2 Magna	MZ5	DOHC V-Four/748cc	6-Speed	1998
VT750C Shadow A.C.E.	MBA	SOHC V-Twin/749cc	6-Speed	1998
VT750CD Shadow A.C.E. Deluxe	MBA	SOHC V-Twin/749cc	6-Speed	1998
PC800 Pacific Coast	MR5	SOHC V-Twin/800cc	5-Speed	1998
VFR800FI Interceptor	MBG	DOHC V-Four/781cc	6-Speed	1998
CBR900RR	MAS	DOHC Inline-Four/893cc	6-Speed	1998
VTR1000F Super Hawk	MBB	DOHC V-Twin/996cc	6-Speed	1998
CBR1100XX Black Bird	MAT	DOHC Inline-Four/1137cc	6-Speed	1998
ST1100	MAJ	DOHC V-Four/1084cc	5-Speed	1998
ST1100A ABS II	MAJ	DOHC V-Four/1084cc	5-Speed	1998
VT1100C Shadow Spirit	MAA	SOHC V-Twin/1099cc	4-Speed	1998
VT1100C2 Shadow A.C.E.	MAH	SOHC V-Twin/1099cc	4-Speed	1998
VT1100C2 Shadow A.C.E. 2-Tone	MAH	SOHC V-Twin/1099cc	4-Speed	1998
VT1100C3 Shadow Aero	MBH	SOHC V-Twin/1099cc	4-Speed	1998
VT1100T Shadow A.C.E. Tourer	MBC	SOHC V-Twin/1099cc	4-Speed	1998
GL1500A Gold Wing Aspencade	MAM	SOHC Opposed-Six/1520cc	5-Speed	1998
GL1500SE Gold Wing	MAM	SOHC Opposed-Six/1520cc	5-Speed	1998
GL1500C Valkyrie	MZO	SOHC Opposed-Six/1520cc	5-Speed	1998
GL1500CT Valkyrie Tourer	MZO	SOHC Opposed-Six/1520cc	5-Speed	1998

Italian Red paint completed the package.

Climbing to the next rung of the performance ladder, the CBR1100XX was back with no changes for 1998.

Both versions of the ST1100 were now sold in Black-Z only, but everything else about the bikes remained the same.

New two-tone paint options were available for the VT1100C Shadow Spirit, but nothing mechanical was touched. Pearl Phoenix Orange with Black or Blaze Yellow with Pearl Glacier White joined carry-over hues of Black and Black with Pearl Ivory Cream. The VT1100C2 Shadow ACE was unchanged in its all-Black finish and blackwall tires. Four new two-tone color combinations graced the VT1100C2 Shadow ACE: Black/Pearl Jade Green, Pearl Canyon Copper/Pearl Ivory Cream, Blaze Yellow/Pearl Ivory Cream and Pearl Sonoma Green/Pearl Ivory Cream.

Two new models joined the VT1100 family. The C3 Shadow Aero provided a more "classic" look. The Aero was also the recipient of many chrome doo-dads, a two-into-one exhaust and a rubber-mounted V-Twin motor. The speedometer was housed in the oversized headlight housing and a two-piece saddle finished off the list of features. Five different color options were listed: Black, Somerset Orange with Pearl Antique White, Pearl Sonoma Green with Pearl Antique White, or Black with Pearl Twilight Silver or Pearl Sedona Red. All the paint schemes were joined by wire wheels and whitewall tires.

The final entry in the VT1100 clan was the T ACE Tourer. With cast-spoke rims, a windshield and a set of matching hard-sided saddlebags, the Tourer was ready for the open road. A different front fender was trimmed with a chrome splash guard and four different hues were offered. All-Black was seen alongside Pearl Jade Green with Pearl Ivory Cream, or Black was paired with your choice of Pearl Ivory Cream or Pearl Sedona Red.

Both the Aspencade and SE versions of the Gold Wing were fitted with revised cylinder head covers that featured fresh emblems. Tachometer and speedometer faces were now delivered with white faces. The GL1500A was sold in Candy Spectra Red or Black, while the SE had five selections on the menu: Black-Z, Candy Spectra Red with Garnet Red, Pearl Chaparral Beige with Dark Chaparral Beige, Pearl Twilight Silver with Dark Twilight Silver or Pearl Glacier White with Ocean Gray Metallic.

Both versions of the Valkyrie were treated to new paint for 1998, but no other modifications were seen. The GL1500C offered the buyer Black, Pearl Coronado Blue with Pearl Ivory Cream, Blaze Yellow with Pearl Ivory Cream or Pearl Sedona Red with Pearl Ivory Cream. The GL1500CT Tourer sported Black, Black with Pearl Jade Green, or Pearl Sedona Red with Pearl Ivory Cream.

1999

After only a year-long hiatus, the CB250 and CMX250C returned for 1999. No changes were found on the Nighthawk, and the Rebel was now only sold in Black. A third option in the 250cc segment was the CMX250C2 Rebel 2-Tone. Candy Glory Red with Black paint on the C2 was the only real difference between the two bikes.

1999 CBR600 models were revised to F4 status, and the transformation was fairly dramatic. Nestled into a fresh chassis was a revamped 599cc motor that was smoother and more powerful than the last. Enhanced bodywork improved aerodynamics, and a raft of other changes, including three-spoke cast wheels, saved weight. Black graphics accented a choice of Sunrise Yellow or Italian Red.

The standard VT600C Shadow VLX was gone in 1998, but back in 1999. A few revisions marked the latest version of the C, the most obvious of which was the new saddle that now put the rider only 25.6 inches from the ground. The contours of the seat were now narrower in the front, but wider and lower at the rear. The V-Twin motor was fed through a single carburetor, which was warmed by engine coolant. Both VT600C and VT600CD models were available in Black only. The VT600CD2 was offered in two-tone paint of Black with either Pearl Halcyon Silver or Pearl Sedona Red.

The CB750 Nighthawk returned for another year, but was unchanged from 1998. The VF750C Magna was also a repeat of 1998, but had Italian Red added to the palette. A single two-tone Orange and Black combination was sold for the VF750C2. The VT750C Shadow ACE and VT750CD ACE Deluxe were sold in the same configurations and colors as the year before. The VT750CD2 was sold in two-tone combinations of Black with Pearl Dark Red or Pearl Olive Green with Pearl Ivory.

With a complete revamp under its belt in 1998, the VFR800FI returned in 1999 with no modifications. Having lost weight and gained power for 1998, the CBR900RR also returned with no mechanical alterations. White was teamed with either Black or Pearl Shining Yellow for the 1999 editions.

VTR1000F Super Hawks were now finished in Mute Black Metallic or Pearl Shining Yellow in place of the 1998 Italian Red.

A few minor tweaks were made to the CBR1100XX, including an improved ram-air system that boosted power, and a stacked, dual-taillight design.

Mute Black Metallic was still the only hue offered for the Black Bird. ST1100 and ST1100 ABS II models returned with no changes from the previous year.

There were now five different flavors on the VT1100 menu to cater to a wide variety of riders. The VT1100C Shadow Spirit saw no revisions except in the colors offered. An all-Black exterior was sold alongside Black with either Twilight Silver or Blaze yellow. The C2 Shadow ACE was seen wearing only Black, while the C3 Shadow Aero had five options listed: Solid Black or Black mated to Pearl Vermont Green or Pearl Gray Blue, Somerset Orange with Pearl White, and Pearl Sedona Red with Pearl Silver. The D2 designation pertained to the two-tone version of the Shadow, and Black with Orange or Pearl Dark Red were the choices available. The VT1100T Shadow ACE Tourer was also back and sold in one of four different themes: solid Black, Pearl Silver and Black, Pearl Vermont Green and Pearl White, or Pearl Sedona Red and Black.

Gold Wing models for 1999 commemorated Honda's 50th anniversary by bearing special badges and ignition keys. The Aspencade was sold in the same hues as in 1998. The SE was available in Black-Z, Candy Spectra Red with Candy Dark Red, Pearl Merced Green with

1999 MODELS

Model	Product Code	Engine Type/ Displacement	Transmission	Year(s) Available
CB250 Nighthawk	KBG	OHC Parallel Twin/234cc	5-Speed	1999
CMX250C Rebel	KEN	OHC Parallel Twin/234cc	5-Speed	1999
CMX250C2 Rebel 2-Tone	KEN	OHC Parallel Twin/234cc	5-Speed	1999
CBR600F4	MBW	DOHC Inline Four/599cc	6-Speed	1999
VT600C Shadow VLX	MZ8	SOHC V-Twin/583cc	4-Speed	1999
VT600CD Shadow VLX Deluxe	MZ8	SOHC V-Twin/583cc	4-Speed	1999
CB750 Nighthawk	MW3	DOHC Inline Four/747cc	5-Speed	1999
VF750C Magna	MZ5	DOHC V-Four/748cc	6-Speed	1999
VF750C2 Magna	MZ5	DOHC V-Four/748cc	6-Speed	1999
VT750C Shadow A.C.E.	MBA	SOHC V-Twin/749cc	6-Speed	1999
VT750CD Shadow A.C.E. Deluxe	MBA	SOHC V-Twin/749cc	6-Speed	1999
VT750CD2 Shadow ACE Dlx 2-Tone	MBA	SOHC V-Twin/749cc	6-Speed	1999
VFR800FI Interceptor	MBG	DOHC V-Four/781cc	6-Speed	1999
CBR900RR	MAS	DOHC Inline Four/893cc	6-Speed	1999
VTR1000F Super Hawk	MBB	DOHC V-Twin/996cc	6-Speed	1999
CBR1100XX Black Bird	MAT	DOHC Inline Four/1137cc	6-Speed	1999
ST1100	MAJ	DOHC V-Four/1084cc	5-Speed	1999
ST1100A ABS II	MAJ	DOHC V-Four/1084cc	5-Speed	1999
VT1100C Shadow Spirit	MAA	SOHC V-Twin/1099cc	4-Speed	1999
VT1100C2 Shadow A.C.E.	MAH	SOHC V-Twin/1099cc	4-Speed	1999
VT1100C3 Shadow Aero	MBH	SOHC V-Twin/1099cc	4-Speed	1999
VT1100D2 Shadow A.C.E.	MAH	SOHC V-Twin/1099cc	4-Speed	1999
VT1100T Shadow A.C.E. Tourer	MBC	SOHC V-Twin/1099cc	4-Speed	1999
GL1500A Gold Wing Aspencade	MAM	SOHC Opposed Six/1520cc	5-Speed	1999
GL1500SE Gold Wing	MAM	SOHC Opposed Six/1520cc	5-Speed	1999
GL1500C Valkyrie	MZ0	SOHC Opposed-Six/1520cc	5-Speed	1999
GL1500CF Valkyrie Interstate	MBY	SOHC Opposed-Six/1520cc	5-Speed	1999
GL1500CT Valkyrie Tourer	MZ0	SOHC Opposed-Six/1520cc	5-Speed	1999

Dark Gray Green, Twilight Silver with Dark Silver, or Glacier White with Metallic Gray.

A third trim level was made available in the Valkyrie lineup, but only color changes affected the original models. The new GL1500CF Valkyrie Interstate had a fork-mounted fairing and rear trunk with hard-sided saddlebags, making the big opposed-six monster ready for the highways and byways. It shared the same specially tuned motor found in the other Valkyrie models, as well as the six individual carbs. Black, Black and Red or Pearl Sonoma Green with Metallic Gray were listed the color choices.

2000

While the majority of the world was celebrating the new millennium with raucous parties and wild parties, Honda rolled in with only minor changes to the 1999 machines.

Neither the CB250 or CMX250C saw any alterations, but the two-tone CMX250C2 sported Pearl Halcyon Silver and Black paint for the 2000 model year.

The CBR600F4 wore fresh colors for 2000, but no additional mods were made. Sunrise Yellow and Black were joined by Dark Mandarin Orange and Black, or Accurate Silver Metallic and Red. Of the three VT600 variations, only the CD2 wore new colors. Pearl Halcyon Silver or Pearl Sedona Red were teamed up with Black.

For the third consecutive year the CB750 Nighthawk was unchanged. The VF750C Magna only offered Black, and the C2 now wore Pearl Light Orange with Black. Two of the VT750 Shadows were also unaltered for 2000, while the two-tone CD2 offered Pearl Silver or Red with Black.

Efforts to curb emissions on the VFR800FI included adding an air injection system and three-way exhaust catalyzer. Rear view mirrors were also revised to fold for ease of use in confined spaces. Pearl Shining Yellow replaced the Italian Red that was applied to the '98 and '99 models.

Previous iterations of the CBR900RR were some of the lightest machines in the open class and their power was second to none. Not able to leave well enough alone, Honda took the RR formula to the next level for 2000 with the CBR929RR. A six-speed gearbox was mated to the 929cc motor and the entire machine weighed a scant 375 lbs.—an amazing 21 lbs. fewer than the 900RR it replaced. A new fuel-injection system was pressurized and electronically programmed. Saving weight was part of the plan, and the titanium exhaust header led into a titanium muffler in an aluminum sleeve. A redesigned chassis and fresh bodywork kept the 929RR stiff and aerodynamically friendly. Cast, three-spoke rims spared a few more ounces over the six-spoke variants used on the '99 editions. Two new color combinations also set the '00 RR apart from its older siblings. Pearl Crystal White with Red or Pearl Shining Yellow teamed with Black were on the menu.

Fresh off the racetracks, the RVT1000R RC51 pulled into the Honda showroom for 2000. Positioned as a production super bike, the RC51 was packed with race-age technology. A 90-degree V-Twin motor displaced 999cc and each cylinder was fed by a pair of fuel injectors. Four valves per cylinder provided adequate breathing for the well-fed jugs. A close-ratio, six-speed gearbox was on board and a twin-spar aluminum chassis held the whole package together. Winning Red and Metallic Silver were the chosen hues to reflect Honda's track success.

Only Pearl Shining Yellow was sold on the VTR1000F Super Hawk with no other revisions being made.

The CBR1100XX Black Bird wore a set of Titanium Metallic feathers, but nothing else was changed from the 1999 edition. Candy Wineberry Red paint covered the bodywork of the ST1100 and ST1100A ABS II in 2000 and was the only notable modification.

The VT1100 family dwindled by one for 2000, but a new face was among the remaining four models. Joining the team for the new millennium was the VT1100C2 Shadow Sabre. Powered by the same 1099cc V-Twin mill used in the other VT1100s, the Sabre claimed numerous styling tweaks that separated it from the others. More fully valanced fenders rode above wheels that were machined from aluminum in a three-spoke pattern. The bulk of the motor was now finished in black and was contrasted by a set of chrome, two-into-two pipes. Solid Black was sold, as well as two-tone pairings of Black with Metallic Gray or Pearl Dark Red with Candy Dark Red.

The VT1100C Shadow Spirit listed American Red with Black as a new combination, but was otherwise unchanged. Changes to the VT1100C3 Shadow Aero were limited to new hues, and the VT1100T ACE Tourer was now sold only in Black.

2000 marked the 25th year of sale for the GL models, and birthday badges and keys were introduced to celebrate the occasion. The Aspencade was sold in the same colors as the '99 models, while the SE was available with a pair of new two-tone options along with two carry-overs. Coronado Blue with Candy Dark Blue or Glacier White with Pearl Gray Green were the two fresh mixes.

A lower saddle height of 28.9 inches graced the 2000 GL1500C Valkyrie, and only three color choices were shown. All-Black, or Black with Red or Yellow were the latest wardrobe options for the otherwise naked Valkyrie. One new two-tone duo of Coronado Blue and Pearl Silver was added to the Interstate's closet. Black and Black with Red were both returning options.

Black or Black with Red were the color options for the Tourer. The lower seat height also applied to the Tourer model.

2000 MODELS

Model	Product Code	Engine Type/ Displacement	Transmission	Year(s) Available
CB250 Nighthawk	KBG	OHC Parallel Twin/234cc	5-Speed	2000
CMX250C Rebel	KEN	OHC Parallel Twin/234cc	5-Speed	2000
CMX250C2 Rebel 2-Tone	KEN	OHC Parallel Twin/234cc	5-Speed	2000
CBR600F4	MBW	DOHC Inline Four/599cc	6-Speed	2000
VT600C Shadow VLX	MZ8	SOHC V-Twin/583cc	4-Speed	2000
VT600CD Shadow VLX Deluxe	MZ8	SOHC V-Twin/583cc	4-Speed	2000
VT600CD2 Shadow VLX Dlx 2-Tone	MZ8	SOHC V-Twin/583cc	4-Speed	2000
CB750 Nighthawk	MW3	DOHC Inline-Four/747cc	5-Speed	2000
VF750C Magna	MZ5	DOHC V-Four/748cc	6-Speed	2000
VF750C2 Magna	MZ5	DOHC V-Four/748cc	6-Speed	2000
VT750C Shadow A.C.E.	MBA	SOHC V-Twin/749cc	6-Speed	2000
VT750CD Shadow A.C.E. Deluxe	MBA	SOHC V-Twin/749cc	6-Speed	2000
VT750CD2 Shadow ACE Dlx 2-Tone	MBA	SOHC V-Twin/749cc	6-Speed	2000
VFR800FI Interceptor	MBG	DOHC V-Four/781cc	6-Speed	2000
CBR929RR	MCJ	DOHC Inline-Four/929cc	6-Speed	2000
RVT1000R RC51	MCF	DOHC V-Twin/999cc	6-Speed	2000
VTR1000F Super Hawk	MBB	DOHC V-Twin/996cc	6-Speed	2000
CBR1100XX Black Bird	MAT	DOHC Inline-Four/1137cc	6-Speed	2000
ST1100	MAJ	DOHC V-Four/1084cc	5-Speed	2000
ST1100A ABS II	MAJ	DOHC V-Four/1084cc	5-Speed	2000
VT1100C Shadow Spirit	MAA	SOHC V-Twin/1099cc	4-Speed	2000
VT1100C2 Shadow Sabre	MCK	SOHC V-Twin/1099cc	4-Speed	2000
VT1100C3 Shadow Aero	MBH	SOHC V-Twin/1099cc	4-Speed	2000
VT1100D2 Shadow A.C.E.	MAH	SOHC V-Twin/1099cc	4-Speed	2000
VT1100T Shadow A.C.E. Tourer	MBC	SOHC V-Twin/1099cc	4-Speed	2000
GL1500A Gold Wing Aspencade	MAM	SOHC Opposed Six/1520cc	5-Speed	2000
GL1500SE Gold Wing	MAM	SOHC Opposed-Six/1520cc	5-Speed	2000
GL1500C Valkyrie	MZO	SOHC Opposed-Six/1520cc	5-Speed	2000
GL1500CF Valkyrie Interstate	MBY	SOHC Opposed-Six/1520cc	5-Speed	2000
GL1500CT Valkyrie Tourer	MZO	SOHC Opposed-Six/1520cc	5-Speed	2000

2001

A thinning of the herd would occur for 2001 as Honda eliminated several models in the redundant cruiser segment. A revitalized Gold Wing brought new luster to the king of the big touring models.

The 250cc Nighthawk and Rebel remained on the roster, but the two-tone Rebel was eliminated.

The CBR400F4 of 2000 was a great bike that didn't need much for updates the following year, but Honda managed to improve the successful blend of power, comfort and handling. The 2001 version was now fed with electronic fuel injection, and a 15-percent larger air box assisted in the breathing. Even the exhaust was tuned for enhanced performance. A more rigid chassis delivered better handling to a machine that needed little help.

600cc Shadows lost a third of their line-up with the two-tone option removed from the catalog. The VT600C Shadow VLX and Deluxe remained with no changes from 2000.

Not even the price changed on the CB750 Nighthawk as it was sold again for 2001.

Based on the Valkyrie, the 2001 Interstate model provided a raft of creature comforts and storage options.
Owner: Niehaus Cycle Sales

Only one variant of the VF750C Magna was built for 2001, but it was given a few mechanical variations. Gear-driven cams were now driven by chain, and an automatic cam-chain tension device kept things adjusted properly. A final chain drive saved some weight and complexity and shaved a few dollars from the price tag.

The Shadow Spirit 750 was new for 2001. Unlike the VT1100 version, the 745cc Spirit was styled more closely to the pending VTX1800 that was to be released in March 2001 as an early 2002 model. The VT750CD Shadow ACE Deluxe was sold for another year, but with only minor changes. The speedometer was mounted atop the fuel tank ala many Harley-Davidson models. That move was appropriate since appealing to the H-D crowd was the goal of the ACE line in the first place.

VFR800FI Interceptors claimed no improvements for the 2001 model year but, according to most enthusiasts that rode one, nothing much was required.

With the exception of a larger 17-inch front wheel and tire, the CBR929RR was the same machine as in 2000.

Bringing the street machines one step closer to the track, an Erion Racing edition was sold alongside the standard graphics model.

Having conquered the 2000 AMA Superbike series in 2000, the RC51 needed nothing and received exactly that in 2001. It did cost an extra $1,000 to ride home a copy for yourself.

Another Honda returning with no alterations was the VTR1000F Super Hawk. Only the return to red paint separated the '01 models from the 2000s.

The CBR1100XX Black Bird was sold in Candy Red for 2001 and also had electronic fuel injection transplanted onto the motor. The linked braking system remained in place.

Introduced over a decade earlier, the ST1100 was still on the team and was joined by the ABS-enabled ST1100A for another round in 2001.

Shadow Spirits now rowed through a five-speed gearbox and combined many features found on previous iterations to make the best

The horizontally opposed, six-cylinder mill was still the chosen power plant for the Interstate, and the decorative cowlings helped with air flow and style.

The Interstate carried a graceful front fairing, complete with a twin set of headlights wrapped in a chrome sheath.

example yet. VT1100C2 Shadow Sabres were unchanged for 2001. Returning to its roots, the Shadow Aero was once again built using a staggered-crank motor in 2001, thus eliminating the vibrations installed in the '95 edition single-pin motors. The final model in the 2001 1100 Shadow family was the ACE Tourer. Although the ACE Tourer was unchanged

from the previous year, a price that was $700 less than in 2000 made it a better buy than ever before.

The Valkyrie crew was reduced to two models for 2001 with the Tourer edition eliminated at the end of 2000. While a brand new Gold Wing was being introduced for 2001, the Valkyries were still powered by the flat-six, 1520cc mill. Changes to the returning members were limited to colors.

Having ruled the roost in the big touring bike class for many years, the Gold Wing was starting to be upstaged by rival gear. Honda decided to push the bar higher in 2001 with an all-new Gold Wing.

While still embodying all the same traits as the previous versions, the latest 'Wing was built using a stiffer chassis and was powered by a larger motor. With the bump to 1832cc, the opposed-six motor was still smoother than anything else on the market, but now packed even more punch with eerie silence. The new engine was fed with a closed-loop fuel injection system that delivered fuel precisely while providing more power and efficiency. Increased capacity of the fuel tank provided hours of painless riding on the open roads. Push-button reverse made moving the 771-lb. beast easier when not at speed, but this weight was 24 lbs. fewer than in 2000.

Radial rubber and ABS brakes also added to the comfort and safety of the latest GL. Heated hand grips, a CD changer and improved sound system brought the improved Gold Wing right back to the top of the heap.

Hard-sided saddlebags were two-thirds of the Interstate's luggage capacity.

There was nothing subtle about the Valkyrie and the large chrome badge mounted to the fuel tank was part of the bold theme.

The rider could easily access all of the audio, CB and electronic features of the Interstate.

The 2001 Interstate's cavernous rear trunk carried a hefty load of goods, as well as the bank of four indicator lights.

2001 MODELS

Model	Product Code	Engine Type/ Displacement	Transmission	Year(s) Available
CB250 Nighthawk	—	OHC Parallel Twin/234cc	5-Speed	2001
CMX250C Rebel	—	OHC Parallel Twin/234cc	5-Speed	2001
CBR600F4i	—	DOHC Inline-Four/599cc	6-Speed	2001
VT600C Shadow VLX	—	SOHC V-Twin/583cc	5-Speed	2001
VT600CD Shadow VLX Deluxe	—	SOHC V-Twin/583cc	5-Speed	2001
CB750 Nighthawk	—	DOHC Inline-Four/747cc	5-Speed	2001
VF750C Magna	—	DOHC V-Four/748cc	6-Speed	2001
VT750CD Shadow A.C.E. Deluxe	—	SOHC V-Twin/749cc	6-Speed	2001
VT750 Shadow Spirit	—	SOHC V-Twin/745cc	5-Speed	2001
VFR800FI Interceptor	—	DOHC V-Four/781cc	6-Speed	2001
CBR929RR	—	DOHC Inline-Four/929cc	6-Speed	2001
RVT1000R RC51	—	DOHC V-Twin/999cc	6-Speed	2001
VTR1000F Super Hawk	—	DOHC V-Twin/996cc	6-Speed	2001
CBR1100XX Black Bird	—	DOHC Inline-Four/1137cc	6-Speed	2001
ST1100	—	DOHC V-Four/1084cc	5-Speed	2001
ST1100A ABS II	—	DOHC V-Four/1084cc	5-Speed	2001
VT1100C Shadow Spirit	—	SOHC V-Twin/1099cc	5-Speed	2001
VT1100C2 Shadow Sabre	—	SOHC V-Twin/1099cc	5-Speed	2001
VT1100C3 Shadow Aero	—	SOHC V-Twin/1099cc	5-Speed	2001
VT1100T Shadow A.C.E. Tourer	—	SOHC V-Twin/1099cc	5-Speed	2001
GL1500C Valkyrie	—	SOHC Opposed-Six/1520cc	5-Speed	2001
GL1500CF Valkyrie Interstate	—	SOHC Opposed-Six/1520cc	5-Speed	2001
GL1800 Gold Wing	—	SOHC Opposed-Six/1832cc	5-Speed	2001

2002

On the heels of the all-new GL1800 released for 2001, Honda rolled out a number of fresh and highly revised models for 2002, proving once again why they were number one in the motorcycle market.

CB250 Nighthawks were sold in Black and the CMX250C Rebel was available in Black or Red with no additional changes to either model.

CBR600F4i received no fresh mechanicals, but was dipped in your choice of Yellow or Red with Black, or Metallic Silver joined by Red. Both the standard and Deluxe versions of the VT600 Shadow were sold for another year without alterations.

The CB750 Nighthawk and VF750C Magna wore Black for 2002, but were otherwise unchanged. The VT750CD Shadow ACE Deluxe and Spirit models returned for an encore in the 750cc class.

The VFR800Fi Interceptor was greeted by a sister model complete with ABS braking. The additional hardware of the ABS version added 11 lbs. to the all-around machine, but was a welcome option for many riders. Fresh bodywork enclosed a revised 781cc motor that now claimed Honda's VTEC valve train. Many complaints had been aired about the lack of

By taking the already potent CBR929RR and boosting displacement, chassis and suspension, the CBR954RR was born.
Owner: DGY Motorsports

availability of matched luggage for the VFR in the past, but the 2002 models rectified the situation. The color-matched, hard-sided bags fit only the VFR and added a new level of usefulness to the capable Interceptor.

The nine-one-nine naked bike was unveiled for the 2002 model year. Powered by a motor based on the CBR900RR, the 919 carried the inline four in a minimalist chassis that utilized the engine as a stressed-member. Programmed fuel injection fed the four pots while a four-into-two exhaust traveled under the motor and exited high beneath the saddle. Unadorned with fairings, windscreens or saddlebags, the 919 weighed only 427 lbs. dry, providing an ample horsepower-to-weight ratio. The six-speed transmission allowed plenty of gears for the rider's needs. A pair of fully floating rotors with four-piston calipers slowed the 919 up front while another single-piston caliper was

on duty out back.

The semi-matte Asphalt paint was a new trend, and was pressed into action on other Honda models to come.

Taking the CBR929RR, bumping displacement and shaving weight resulted in the new CBR954RR. An extra 25cc of motor, along with a long list of minor tweaks, provided a horsepower rating of 154, which is four more than the 929 touted. Five pounds of weight were also trimmed from the 929 and a recontoured fuel tank carried its load lower in the frame for improved distribution. The capacity of the tank was unchanged at 4.8 gallons. A titanium muffler was installed to save a few more precious ounces with the total weight now at 370 lbs. dry.

The RC51 was introduced in 2000, and instantly set the pace for open class machines. The 2002 edition weighed 8 lbs. less and car-

2002 MODELS

Model	Product Code	Engine Type/ Displacement	Transmission	Year(s) Available
CB250 Nighthawk	—	OHC Parallel Twin/234cc	5-Speed	2002
CMX250C Rebel	—	OHC Parallel Twin/234cc	5-Speed	2002
CBR600F4i	—	DOHC Inline-Four/599cc	6-Speed	2002
VT600C Shadow VLX	—	SOHC V-Twin/583cc	5-Speed	2002
VT600CD Shadow VLX Deluxe	—	SOHC V-Twin/583cc	5-Speed	2002
CB750 Nighthawk	—	DOHC Inline-Four/747cc	5-Speed	2002
VF750C Magna	—	DOHC V-Four/748cc	6-Speed	2002
VT750CD Shadow A.C.E. Deluxe	—	SOHC V-Twin/749cc	6-Speed	2002
VT750 Shadow Spirit	—	SOHC V-Twin/745cc	5-Speed	2002
VFR800Fi Interceptor	—	DOHC V-Four/781cc	6-Speed	2002
VFR800Fi ABS Interceptor	—	DOHC V-Four/781cc	6-Speed	2002
CB900F 919	—	DOHC Inline-Four/919cc	6-Speed	2002
CBR954RR	—	DOHC Inline-Four/954cc	6-Speed	2002
RVT1000R RC51	—	DOHC V-Twin/999cc	6-Speed	2002
VTR1000F Super Hawk	—	DOHC V-Twin/996cc	6-Speed	2002
CBR1100XX Black Bird	—	DOHC Inline-Four/1137cc	6-Speed	2002
ST1100	—	DOHC V-Four/1084cc	5-Speed	2002
ST1100A ABS II	—	DOHC V-Four/1084cc	5-Speed	2002
VT1100C Shadow Spirit	—	SOHC V-Twin/1099cc	5-Speed	2002
VT1100C2 Shadow Sabre	—	SOHC V-Twin/1099cc	5-Speed	2002
VT1100C3 Shadow Aero	—	SOHC V-Twin/1099cc	5-Speed	2002
GL1500CD Valkyrie	—	SOHC Opposed-Six/1520cc	5-Speed	2002
GL1800 Gold Wing	—	SOHC Opposed Six/1832cc	5-Speed	2002
GL1800A ABS Gold Wing	—	SOHC Opposed-Six/1832cc	5-Speed	2002
VTX1800C	—	SOHC V-Twin/1795cc	5-Speed	2002
VTX1800R	—	SOHC V-Twin/1795cc	5-Speed	2002
VTX1800S	—	SOHC V-Twin/1795cc	5-Speed	2002

HONDA MOTORCYCLES: THE ULTIMATE GUIDE

ried three extra ponies under the hood. A record-setting 120 horsepower at the rear wheel was proof of Honda's ongoing efforts. All of the weight savings and power boost came at the same price as last year's model, another of Honda's specialties.

VTR1000F Super Hawks returned, but were unchanged from the 2001s. CBR1100XX models now wore a cloak of Metallic Silver, but were otherwise unchanged. ST1100s and ST1100As were also unaltered except for the Candy Dark Red paint. VT1100 Shadows in the Spirit, Sabre and Aero trim levels all returned with new colors. The Sabre was seen with new Pearl Flame paint in several colors, adding another "hot rod" flair to the popular cruiser.

The big Valkyrie cruiser was the only model left in the lineup and was delivered sans any bags or windscreens. The Hondaline catalog offered a wide variety of options to personalize the GL1500CD, but basic Black was the only color sold for 2002.

The Gold Wing flock faction grew by one with the introduction of the ABS-equipped version.

For cruiser buyers that believed there's no replacement for displacement, the series of VTX 1800 models rolled out in 2002. Driven by an 1800cc V-Twin mill, the VTX was the largest twin on the market. The C, R and S editions varied slightly from each other with two rolling on cast wheels and the third on spoked rims. Combining traditional cruiser styling with exaggerated dimensions and contemporary cues, the VTX family set yet another standard for the rest of the industry.

The majority of the 2003 lineup was returning faces, but a few new players hit the field to keep things interesting.

CB250 Nighthawks were sold in Red only, while the CMX250C Rebel offered a choice of Black or Pearl Blue. Nothing else on these bikes changed much from 2002.

Metallic Silver was teamed with Black or Red on the 2003 CBR6004i models but, again, nothing else was different from the previous year's models.

The CBR600RR was an innovative twist in the expanding 600cc class. Much like the 954RR, the 600 combined the best features available and delivered them in a tidy, lightweight machine. Borrowing heavily from Honda's own RC211V MotoGP-winning machine, it presented the street rider with a bevy of high-tech components and trickery. The in-line-four motor displaced the same 599cc as the CBR6004i, but spun 800rpm faster due to lighter pistons and a cylinder head with enhanced breathing. Dual Stage Fuel Injection fed the beast and allowed for a 15,000 rpm redline. The aluminum chassis was more rigid than the 4i's, but was similar in geometry. The 370-lb.

2003 MODELS

Model	Product Code	Engine Type/ Displacement	Transmission	Year(s) Available
CA100 Honda 50	005	OHV Single/49cc	3-Speed, Auto	1962-70
CB250 Nighthawk	—	OHC Parallel-Twin/234cc	5-Speed	2003
CMX250C Rebel	—	OHC Parallel-Twin/234cc	5-Speed	2003
CBR600F4i	—	DOHC Inline-Four/599cc	6-Speed	2003
CBR600RR	—	DOHC Inline-Four/599cc	6-Speed	2003
VT600C Shadow VLX	—	SOHC V-Twin/583cc	5-Speed	2003
VT600CD Shadow VLX Deluxe	—	SOHC V-Twin/583cc	5-Speed	2003
CB750 Nighthawk	—	DOHC Inline-Four/747cc	5-Speed	2003
VF750C Magna	—	DOHC V-Four/748cc	6-Speed	2003
VT750 Shadow Spirit	—	SOHC V-Twin/745cc	5-Speed	2003
VFR800Fi Interceptor	—	DOHC V-Four/781cc	6-Speed	2003
VFR800Fi ABS Interceptor	—	DOHC V-Four/781cc	6-Speed	2003
CB900F 919	—	DOHC Inline-Four/919cc	6-Speed	2003
CBR954RR	—	DOHC Inline-Four/954cc	6-Speed	2003
RVT1000R RC51	—	DOHC V-Twin/999cc	6-Speed	2003
VTR1000F Super Hawk	—	DOHC V-Twin/996cc	6-Speed	2003
CBR1100XX Black Bird	—	DOHC Inline four/1137cc	6-Speed	2003
VT1100C Shadow Spirit	—	SOHC V-Twin/1099cc	5-Speed	2003
VT1100C2 Shadow Sabre	—	SOHC V-Twin/1099cc	5-Speed	2003
ST1300	—	DOHC V-Four/1261cc	5-Speed	2003
ST1300 ABS	—	DOHC V-Four/1261cc	5-Speed	2003
VTX1300C	—	SOHC V-Twin/1312cc	5-Speed	2003
VTX1300S	—	SOHC V-Twin/1312cc	5-Speed	2003
GL1500CD Valkyrie	—	SOHC Opposed-Six/1520cc	5-Speed	2003
GL1800 Gold Wing	—	SOHC Opposed Six/1832cc	5-Speed	2003
GL1800A ABS Gold Wing	—	SOHC Opposed-Six/1832cc	5-Speed	2003
VTX1800C	—	SOHC V-Twin/1795cc	5-Speed	2003
VTX1800R	—	SOHC V-Twin/1795cc	5-Speed	2003
VTX1800S	—	SOHC V-Twin/1795cc	5-Speed	2003

dry weight was matched with a lower mounting point for the fuel tank, which sharpened the already crisp handling of Honda's other 600cc machine. A pair of 310mm front brake rotors were grabbed by four-piston calipers, providing ample slowing power at a squeeze of the lever. Black, Black and Red or Pearl Yellow were the latest colors of speed.

VT600C Shadow VLX and VT600CD Shadow VLX Deluxe were back but sported no amendments.

750 Nighthawks wore Red for the new year, while the Magna received Candy Blue. VT750C Shadow Spirits were unchanged.

VFR800Fi and ABS models offered Metallic Silver or Red paint for 2003.

New Smoke and returning Asphalt were the color choices for the 919. 2003 954RRs rewarded riders with their choice of Black with Metallic Titanium or Black with Red paint. The race-ready RC51 was as potent as ever and saw no modifications for the new year. The antediluvian VTR1000F Super Hawk was again seen in the catalog but now wore a coat of Candy Blue. Even the mighty CBR1100XX received no changes, except for the Metallic Black paint.

Promises of a bigger, stronger Black Bird were dispelled when it was pulled from the lineup for 2004.

The family of VT1100's shrank by one with the elimination of the Aero model. The remaining Spirit and Sabre were again unaltered.

Replacing the tried-and-true ST1100 was the completely new ST1300. Filling the same sport touring shoes as the departing 1100, the 1300 version was a thing of beauty. Enhanced features included the chassis, swing arm and 1261cc V-four motor. The five-speed gearbox was filled with lower-ratio gearing, and the previous carbs were supplanted by programmed fuel injection. All the engine refinements led to a new claim of 116 horsepower for the ST1300. The fairing and bodywork were also fresh for 2003 and provided the rider with a three-position saddle. For those who thought they'd miss the ABS system used on the ST1100A, the ST1300 was also sold with ABS as an option. Linked braking was found on both versions of the bigger ST. Metallic Dark Silver was the only hue listed for the revamped model.

For the cruiser fan who found the VTX1800 a bit too daunting, the VTX1300 was a great choice. Using the same design formula, the VTX 1300 featured all the key styling features of the 1800, but tied them together in a milder package. The 1312cc V-Twin motor drew breath through a single 38mm carburetor and exhaled through a two-into-two exhaust. The VTX1300S featured wire wheels while the VTX1300C rolled on a set of cast rims. The S model was actually sold in 2002 as an early-release 2003, but was still listed as an '03 model.

The Valkyrie returned in 2003, but was a carry-over in features and color. Additional returning, yet unchanged, models were the GL1800 with or without ABS, and the three flavors of the VTX1800.

As was becoming almost routine, the 2004 Honda team was largely a carry-over from 2003, but a few new flavors were added to the mix.

The 250 group retained both the Nighthawk and Rebel with no alterations outside of color. The CB250 Nighthawk was sold in Red and the CMX250C Rebel had Black or Red shown on the option sheet.

The new 599 filled the vacant slot in the UJM segment for 2004. It was powered by an inline-four motor based on the earlier CBR600F3, and the chassis provided an improved home for the somewhat dated motor design. In a world dominated by fuel injection, the 599 still sipped through a set of four carbs. A dry curb weight of 420 lbs. allowed for nimble handling when combined with the rigid chassis and modern suspension bits. Devoid of bodywork, the 599 did feature a comfortable pillion, mid-rise handlebars and exhaust that exited high on the frame. The stiff retail price of $7,099 may have sent some buyers packing, but the Asphalt Yellow paint was a terrific selling point for those that signed up. The 599 would be a one-year only machine.

Neither the CBR600F4i or the CBR600RR

The 750 Shadow remained a popular choice for riders wanting a healthy dose of power and style.
Owner: Niehaus Cycle Sales

The 750 Shadow's V-twin power plant delivered plenty of torque while looking terrific at the same time. The teardrop-shaped air cleaner added to the style of the Shadow.

received any upgrades, but colors differed from the 2003s. The F4i sported Black with Yellow or Red, while the RR offered Black with Red or Silver or the Candy Blue selection. The other machines in the 600 class, the Shadow VLX and VLX Deluxe, were also repeat versions of the 2003 editions.

A new twist on an old theme was the Shadow Aero, powered by a 745cc V-Twin mill. Honda's cruiser lineup was heavy in the top-end models, but the latest Aero helped those more timid riders to join in on the fun.

Metallic Silver was removed from the VFR800Fi and ABS order sheets, leaving only Red behind. The 919 lost its previous hues and gained Light Silver Metallic and Matte Uranium.

The 2004 CBR1000RR actually began its journey as the flyweight CBR900RR, then grew into the 929, then the 954. Borrowing

2004 MODELS

Model	Product Code	Engine Type/ Displacement	Transmission	Year(s) Available
CB250 Nighthawk	—	OHC Parallel-Twin/234cc	5-Speed	2004
CMX250C Rebel	—	OHC Parallel-Twin/234cc	5-Speed	2004
599	—	DOHC Inline-Four/599cc	6-Speed	2004
CBR600F4i	—	DOHC Inline-Four/599cc	6-Speed	2004
CBR600RR	—	DOHC Inline-Four/599cc	6-Speed	2004
VT600C Shadow VLX	—	SOHC V-Twin/583cc	5-Speed	2004
VT600CD Shadow VLX Deluxe	—	SOHC V-Twin/583cc	5-Speed	2004
VT750 Shadow Aero	—	SOHC V-Twin/745cc	5-Speed	2004
VFR800Fi Interceptor	—	DOHC V-Four/781cc	6-Speed	2004
VFR800Fi ABS Interceptor	—	DOHC V-Four/781cc	6-Speed	2004
CB900F 919	—	DOHC Inline-Four/919cc	6-Speed	2004
CBR1000RR	—	DOHC Inline-Four/998cc	6-Speed	2004
RVT1000R RC51	—	DOHC V-Twin/999cc	6-Speed	2004
VTR1000F Super Hawk	—	DOHC V-Twin/996cc	6-Speed	2004
VT1100C Shadow Spirit	—	SOHC V-Twin/1099cc	5-Speed	2004
VT1100C2 Shadow Sabre	—	SOHC V-Twin/1099cc	5-Speed	2004
ST1300	—	DOHC V-Four/1261cc	5-Speed	2004
ST1300 ABS	—	DOHC V-Four/1261cc	5-Speed	2004
VTX1300C	—	SOHC V-Twin/1312cc	5-Speed	2004
VTX1300S	—	SOHC V-Twin/1312cc	5-Speed	2004
GL1800 Valkyrie Rune	—	SOHC Opposed-Six/1832cc	5-Speed	2004
GL1800 Gold Wing	—	SOHC Opposed-Six/1832cc	5-Speed	2004
GL1800A ABS Gold Wing	—	SOHC Opposed-Six/1832cc	5-Speed	2004
VTX1800C	—	SOHC V-Twin/1795cc	5-Speed	2004
VTX1800N	—	SOHC V-Twin/1795cc	5-Speed	2004
VTX1800R	—	SOHC V-Twin/1795cc	5-Speed	2004
VTX1800S	—	SOHC V-Twin/1795cc	5-Speed	2004

The Shadow's exhaust system was truncated by a massive outlet that melded with the design and also kept things quiet.

A multitude of contours were used when creating the tail light for the Shadow and carried the design theme to the last edge of the bike.

Although liquid cooled, the Shadow carried its radiator discreetly on the front down tubes of the chassis.

heavily again from the MotoGP machine, the new RR was a pure sport machine that bristled with lightweight, high-tech components. The compact configuration of the departed 954 was even more pronounced on the 1000RR, stepping even closer to MotoGP specs. The 998cc's of displacement were divided equally into four inline cylinders and 16 valves allowed for performance-level breathing. Six speeds topped off the package that provided a whole lot of bang for the buck.

A dry weight of 396 lbs. was a clear indicator of the intentions of the sporting machine. All Black, or Black mated to either Red or Metallic Silver rounded out the options available for the latest rocket from Honda.

Returning with only Nicky Hayden paint in 2004, the RC51 was back with no other alterations. The 2003 revisions served the race-bred machine well and left little to the imagination.

The tried-and-true VTR1000F Super Hawk was back for another round and was fitted with a pair of gold rims to accent the Black paint. Both 1100 Shadow Spirit and Sabre rolled on with no marked revisions.

ST1300 and ST1300 ABS models now featured a power-operated windshield that could be raised or lowered and adjusted for angle at a touch of a button. The saddle was still delivered with its own level of fine-tuning, making the ST1300s highly amenable to almost any sport-touring rider. Pearl Dark Blue covered the flowing surfaces of the unaltered bodywork for 2004.

Both versions of the VTX1300 returned for another year and wore either spoke or cast rims, depending on your preference.

As popular as the early Valkyries had been, fans turned to V-Twin cruisers more often than not, leaving the opposed-six machine idling on the sideline. To spice up the game, Honda showed a radically designed machine in 2003. The Rune looked like nothing "production," but turned out to be just that. The enormous machine was powered by the gold Wing's 1832cc flat-six mill, but was sheathed in exotic bodywork and alloy components. The six-into-two exhaust exited via triangular canisters with triangular openings. A trailing-link front fork was slathered in chrome and the bulk of the exposed chassis was polished to a similar glow. A wheelbase of 68.9 inches was mated to a low saddle height of only 27.2 inches and helped to make the 794-lb. dry weight a bit more manageable.

Tail-dragger fenders were installed over both tires and accented the elongated fuel tank and space-age headlight. Every inch of the bizarre bodywork was covered in one of three hues; Candy Black Cherry, Illusion Blue or Double Clear Coat Black. Carrying an equally large sticker price in the neighborhood of $25,000, the Rune would have a limited buying audience, but drew a crowd wherever it was ridden.

GL1800 Gold Wings saw no revisions and were sold in a wide array of colors for the 2004 model year.

The 1800N was the newest face in the VTX1800 clan. The N was clad in bodywork that borrowed from the Rune, but was not quite as radical. The C, R and S versions remained on the roster, each bringing a different twist to the same basic recipe.

Gone for 2004 were the 750 Nighthawk, Magna and CBR1100XX models.

Along with many models that have been in the catalog for many years, a few recently introduced machines would disappear after a single year of being sold. The only fresh items were additional variations on a theme for 2005.

Extending their longevity for another year, the 250 Nighthawk and Rebel returned. Both were sold in Black, and the Rebel also had Candy Orange paint as an option.

The 599 was a one-year-only model, having been introduced and available in 2004 before being pulled from the ranks.

Both of Honda's successful 600cc sport bikes were again in showrooms. The RR version sported several enhancements, while the F4i remained unchanged. The CBR600RR lost 16 lbs. to put it on par with the competition. Other revisions include upside-down front forks, improved fuel injectors and ignition mapping. The frame was modified and lost 4 lbs. in the process. Although the exhaust was now fitted with a catalytic converter, the overall system weight was down by a pound. Radial-mount front brake calipers and fresh bodywork were included on the laundry list of refinements for the 2005 RR. A new black on black, tribal flame paint scheme was also offered.

A fully revised CBR1000RR was sold in 2005, and while the 2004 was no slouch, the latest iteration added a raft of new features and technology to the blend.
Owner: DGY Motorsports

An aerodynamically efficient front profile assisted the big CBR in slicing through the wind and looked terrific doing so.

The Shadow VLX was still offered in base or Deluxe trim, and the Deluxe carried chrome engine trim and two-tone paint while the standard was black-only and devoid of the engine glitter. The Shadow Spirit 750, fitted with bobbed fenders, shorty pipes and flame paint fit into almost any cruiser buyer's budget and delivered a lot for the money. The Shadow Aero was another cost-conscious choice in the cruiser segment and delivered full fenders and a lower saddle height along with the 745cc V-Twin motor.

VFR800Fi Interceptors returned unchanged and could still be had with ABS braking as an option. Red and Light Metallic Silver were listed as 2005 hues. The 919 was also back for another round and was sold in only Metallic Black.

CBR1000RRs for 2005 benefited from several important changes. With a new chassis using technology from the race-winning RC211V, the RR was stiffer, lighter and more nimble than before. A Honda Electronic Steering Damper kept handling safe and secure and was joined by Honda's Unit Pro-Link rear suspension. Fuel injection was dual-stage and the exhaust now exited through a center-mounted high pipe that lived in the tail section.

To highlight Honda's racing success, a Repsol replica paint ensemble was sold along with the three standard paint options. The Repsol edition sold for an extra $500 over the standard colors.

RVT1000R RC51s were treated to Black and Metallic Gray paint, but no other changes were seen. Another time-tested model, the VTR1000F Super Hawk, was back and the Black body with gold wheels was replaced by Titanium sheet metal and matching rims.

The VT1100 Shadow Spirit and Sabre were still among the living and wore fresh suits of color on unchanged mechanicals.

Candy Dark Red was the only color listed for the ST1300. The bikes came with or without ABS braking.

The VTX1300R was a new version of the recently introduced VTX1300 series. Joining the C and S styles, the R featured a longer set of handlebars, custom rims and a more shapely saddle. As with the rest of the cruiser line, a multitude of custom accessories could be bolted on to personalize your scooter.

Having been introduced in 2003 as a 2004 model, the Valkyrie Rune was missing from the 2005 lineup. Whether it was the $25,000 price tag or the avant-garde styling, the Rune found only a handful of buyers, but then again it wasn't targeted at the general riding public.

2005 marked 30 years of production for the Gold Wing and the GL1800 was decorated with several birthday badges and light-up panel to celebrate the occasion.

The VTX1800 team also expanded by one with the F model making its debut. Designated

2005 MODELS

Model	Product Code	Engine Type/ Displacement	Transmission	Year(s) Available
CB250 Nighthawk	—	OHC Parallel-Twin/234cc	5-Speed	2005
CMX250C Rebel	—	OHC Parallel-Twin/234cc	5-Speed	2005
CBR600F4i	—	DOHC Inline-Four/599cc	6-Speed i	2005
CBR600RR	—	DOHC Inline-Four/599cc	6-Speed	2005
VT600C Shadow VLX	—	SOHC V-Twin/583cc	5-Speed	2005
VT600CD Shadow VLX Deluxe	—	SOHC V-Twin/583cc	5-Speed	2005
VT750 Shadow Aero	—	SOHC V-Twin/745cc	5-Speed	2005
VFR800Fi Interceptor	—	DOHC V-Four/781cc	6-Speed	2005
VFR800Fi ABS Interceptor	—	DOHC V-Four/781cc	6-Speed	2005
CB900F 919	—	DOHC Inline-Four/919cc	6-Speed	2005
CBR1000RR	—	DOHC Inline-Four/998cc	6-Speed	2005
RVT1000R RC51	—	DOHC V-Twin/999cc	6-Speed	2005
VTR1000F Super Hawk	—	DOHC V-Twin/996cc	6-Speed	2005
VT1100C Shadow Spirit	—	SOHC V-Twin/1099cc	5-Speed	2005
VT1100C2 Shadow Sabre	—	SOHC V-Twin/1099cc	5-Speed	2005
ST1300	—	DOHC V-Four/1261cc	5-Speed	2005
ST1300 ABS	—	DOHC V-Four/1261cc	5-Speed	2005
VTX1300C	—	SOHC V-Twin/1312cc	5-Speed	2005
VTX1300R	—	SOHC V-Twin/1312cc	5-Speed	2005
VTX1300S	—	SOHC V-Twin/1312cc	5-Speed	2005
GL1800 Gold Wing	—	SOHC Opposed-Six/1832cc	5-Speed	2005
GL1800A ABS Gold Wing	—	SOHC Opposed-Six/1832cc	5-Speed	2005
VTX1800C	—	SOHC V-Twin/1795cc	5-Speed	2005
VTX1800F	—	SOHC V-Twin/1795cc	5-Speed	2005
VTX1800N	—	SOHC V-Twin/1795cc	5-Speed	2005
VTX1800R	—	SOHC V-Twin/1795cc	5-Speed	2005
VTX1800S	—	SOHC V-Twin/1795cc	5-Speed	2005

The revised 1000RR exhaust made its exit high in the rear tail section and was seen with a clear-lens brake light.

as a sport cruiser, the F rolled on an 18-inch-diameter rear wheel and was steered with a set of low drag bars. The slimmed-down pillion was another styling cue on the latest of five VTX1800s being sold. As with the rest of the VTX models, the new F was seen in three different build specifications, each delivering an altered level of trim and power.

The Gold Wing wore birthday trim for 2005 to mark its 30th year in production.
Owner: John Doe

Commemorative badges helped to celebrate the 'Wing's milestone year.

At right, creature comforts rose to new levels on the 20005 Gold Wing.

The 2005 Gold Wing provided the rider with a tastefully appointed cockpit.